MODERNISM, DAILY T
EVERYDAY LIF.

Bryony Randall explores the twin concepts of daily time and everyday life through the writing of several major modernist authors. The book begins with a contextualising chapter on the psychologists William James and Henri Bergson. It goes on to devote chapters to Dorothy Richardson, Gertrude Stein, H.D. and Virginia Woolf. These experimental writers, Randall argues, reveal everyday life and daily time as rich and strange, not simply a banal backdrop to more important events. Moreover, she shows how paying attention to the daily can be politically empowering and subversive. The specific social and cultural context of the early twentieth century is one in which the concepts of daily time and everyday life are particularly strongly challenged. By examining Modernism's engagement with or manifestation of these notions, she reveals a totally new perspective on its concerns and complexities.

BRYONY RANDALL is Lecturer in English Literature at the University of Glasgow.

MODERNISM, DAILY TIME
AND
EVERYDAY LIFE

BRYONY RANDALL

CAMBRIDGE
UNIVERSITY PRESS

CAMBRIDGE UNIVERSITY PRESS
Cambridge, New York, Melbourne, Madrid, Cape Town,
Singapore, São Paulo, Delhi, Tokyo, Mexico City

Cambridge University Press
The Edinburgh Building, Cambridge CB2 8RU, UK

Published in the United States of America by Cambridge University Press, New York

www.cambridge.org
Information on this title: www.cambridge.org/9780521174411

© Bryony Randall 2007

First published 2007
First paperback edition 2011

A catalogue record for this publication is available from the British Library

ISBN 978-0-521-87984-2 Hardback
ISBN 978-0-521-17441-1 Paperback

For David and Jennie Randall

Contents

Acknowledgements

My first thanks go to Laura Marcus, who supervised this project in its incarnation as my doctorate, for her unfailingly stimulating input, brilliant and enjoyable supervision, and her interest not only in this study but in my academic career in general. Her support and encouragement were the bedrock on which the gestation of thesis into book was founded. I am also grateful to Peter Nicholls for his ongoing help and advice as the project has developed, beyond the normal call of examiner's duty. Geoff Gilbert was there at the beginning, and is partly responsible for me being where I am, doing what I'm doing; for this, I am deeply grateful. He also gave generously of his time to read some of this in draft form, as did Gordon McMullan and Esther Saxey. Thanks also to Mac for answering all the questions that I couldn't ask anyone else, with patience and humour, and to the anonymous readers for Cambridge University Press for their helpful observations.

Among others whose advice on this project has been sought and gratefully received, I would particularly like to thank Catherine Silverstone, Lindsey Moore and Vicky Margree. Esther Saxey and Meredith Miller were the ideal office-mates, and a very great deal more, making the day to day experience of research bearable when appearing unbearable, sharing the pleasures to be found in the minutiae of everyday language and life. Thanks in particular to Meredith and Lindsey for their invaluable help and suggestions during the revision process, and to Vicky for reading things for me and thinking things through with me. Latterly, colleagues at the University of Glamorgan have been sympathetic and supportive as deadlines drew nearer.

There are very many others whose interest has inspired me, and whose love has sustained me, throughout the years I've spent with this project, and who have made my daily life inexpressibly happier and richer than anyone has the right to expect. In particular I would like to thank John and Rosemary Heuston, Salon and George (Kirstin Bourne, Catherine Brereton, George Clayton and Juliette Cox), Adam Dinham and Tom

Randall. My greatest debt, however, is to my parents, David and Jennie Randall, for their boundless support and enthusiasm for ideas, education and the life of the mind. This book is dedicated to them, with many thanks and much love.

I would like to acknowledge the financial support of the Arts and Humanities Research Council, who funded the doctoral research on which this book is based. A version of Chapter 3 appeared in *Critical Sense* (University of California-Berkeley, Spring 2002).

Abbreviations

A	H.D., *Asphodel*
BA	Virginia Woolf, *Between the Acts*
BMTL	H.D., *Bid Me To Live*
CE	Henri Bergson, *Creative Evolution*
CEL	Henri Lefebvre, *Critique of Everyday Life*
D	Virginia Woolf, *Mrs Dalloway*
ELMW	Henri Lefebvre, *Everyday Life in the Modern World*
H	H.D., *Her*
MM	Henri Bergson, *Matter and Memory*
O	Virginia Woolf, *Orlando*
P	Dorothy Richardson, *Pilgrimage*
PIT	H.D., *Paint It Today*
Psy	William James, *Psychology: Briefer Course*
TB	Gertrude Stein, *Tender Buttons*
TFW	Henri Bergson, *Time and Free Will*
TL	Gertrude Stein, *Three Lives*
TTF	H.D., *Tribute to Freud*
TTL	Virginia Woolf, *To the Lighthouse*
W	Virginia Woolf, *The Waves*

Introduction: dailiness

> I can say it enough but can I say it more than enough that the daily
> life is a daily life if at any moment of the daily life that daily life is all
> there is of life.[1]

The day is a unique temporal category in being, most of the time and in most
parts of the world, clearly bounded at beginning and end – by night – and
always recurring in a regular rhythm. Close to the poles days can become
exceptionally long or exceptionally short, but they will still wax and wane in
a predictable annual pattern. Thus, unlike the relatively artificial divisions
of the hour or the week, the day presents a naturally occurring, observable
temporal unit, one that technology and human innovation cannot change;
as Heidegger would concede, it is 'the "most natural" measure of time'.[2]
Even now, at the beginning of the twenty-first century, the fact of there
being a pattern of darkness and light that gives rise to something called
'a day' cannot ultimately be questioned, undermined, deconstructed we
might say; along with death, it is the only thing in life of which we can be
sure.

A century ago, during the period when the artistic movement we call
modernism was gathering pace, technology was becoming increasingly able
to modify and regulate the rhythms of life. Increased street lighting, for
example, and in particular the growing use of electric light in the home and
place of work, would serve artificially to extend the day. As Stephen Kern
emphasises in his major study on time and space in the years 1880 to 1918,
'one of the many consequences of this versatile, cheap, and reliable form of
illumination was a blurring of the division of day and night'.[3] Yet despite
such ongoing technological innovations, the day continues to present an
unchallengeable, unquestionable, temporal unit. What follows from this
opening assertion of the irreducibility of the day is that the ways in which
the day is represented, and the connotations of related terms such as 'everyday', invite attention. It is when something appears to be universal, essential,

or obvious, that it is particularly in need of exploration, and where such exploration takes place, it will reveal the range of interconnected assumptions (social, cultural, political, and so on) upon which the construction of this particular taken-for-granted category rests. In this study I explore both why and how the day and the everyday appear as particularly contested and revelatory concepts in a range of modernist texts, and I will use the term 'dailiness' to bring together these two distinct, though related, concepts: daily time, and everyday life.

In her discussion of Gertrude Stein's short text 'To Call It a Day', Barbara Will indicates the complexity of this apparently simple word – 'day' – as deployed by a quintessentially modernist writer. She explores Stein's incorporation of the everyday language of domesticity and consumption into her texts, in particular through cliché, interwoven with a variety of other discourses (geographical, historical, and so forth), and argues that from this perspective 'the effort to "call it a day" becomes highly complex. What is a "day", and what multitudes does "it" contain?'[4] This is precisely the question that this book sets out to explore. If, as Stein asserts, 'the daily life is a daily life if at any moment of the daily life that daily life is all there is of life', then what is that life like? How would one describe the 'dailiness' of that daily life? In this book, I use the question of what the dailiness of daily life consists in as the focus for my exploration of texts by William James and Henri Bergson (whose work also provides historical and conceptual ground for what follows), and then by the modernist writers Dorothy Richardson, Gertrude Stein, H.D. and Virginia Woolf. Exploring discourses around dailiness in the modernist literature of the early twentieth century not only adds another dimension to our understanding of the aesthetic context of modernism, but is also particularly revelatory of socio-cultural change and anxiety in this period.

The second and third sections of this Introduction will discuss the two strands of dailiness, everyday life, and daily time, respectively, laying out the ways in which the terms are used in my discussion. Broadly speaking, the everyday will describe content, or more specifically mode of attention to content, and daily time will of course describe temporality, or temporal structure. It goes without saying, therefore, that there will be constant dialogue between these aspects, as there always is between 'form' and 'content'. I want to begin, however, in the first section, by setting out key aspects of the socio-cultural and aesthetic context of the texts I will be addressing to explain why dailiness might be a particularly important focaliser, or 'chronotope' (a term taken from Mikhail Bakhtin which I discuss in more detail below, describing the confluence of temporal and spatial relations in a representative image or trope within a literary text), through which to examine some of the complexities of the early twentieth-century modernist text. In other words, I want to start by addressing the question 'why dailiness?', before going on to discuss 'how?'.

MODERNISM AND DAILINESS

There will be three strands to this first section, which will set the scene for my discussion in later chapters of how dailiness appears in modernist texts. Firstly, the socio-cultural context is laid out; the experience of time, and life, in the early decades of the twentieth century. Secondly, I discuss the aesthetic context, in particular the valuing and privileging of exceptional moments or kinds of experience associated with modernist aesthetics. Finally, *Ulysses*, a paradigmatically modernist, and daily, text, is used as a model for the ways in which dailiness has tended to be treated thus far in critical work on modernist literature.

'The catastrophe of the First World War, and before that, the labor struggles, the emergence of feminism, the race for empire, these inescapable forces of turbulent social modernisation were not simply looming on the outside as the destabilizing context of cultural Modernism; they penetrated the interior of artistic invention.'[5] Michael Levenson's summary of the socio-cultural context of the modernist period alerts us to the profundity of the impact of social change on aesthetic innovation, and many of these changes have particular relevance to the exploration of dailiness. For the purposes of this study, the key 'forces of social modernisation' (and aesthetic innovation) are technological change (as sketched out above), the First World War, the rise of the women's movement, and the development of psychology. It is these phenomena or events that are central to answering the question 'why dailiness?'.

The First World War radically disrupted the ways in which human temporality was or could be conceived. Paul Fussell's now classic text *The Great War and Modern Memory* describes in detail some of the most important structures to feature in representations of the First World War. Not only was the war an event without precedent, in brutality and scale, radically challenging attempts to create an historical narrative that would be able to incorporate it, but, as Fussell emphasises, there was a widespread belief in circulation at the time that 'the war would literally never end and would become the permanent condition of mankind'.[6] Fussell describes how the experience of fighting at the front, characterised by often apparently meaningless routine, the carrying out of illogical or downright contradictory orders, and absolute ignorance of what was going on even a few hundred yards down the line, let alone miles away, conspired to deprive temporality of its familiar characteristics of causality, logical succession and change. During battle in particular, chronological and even natural time is eclipsed, as day and night become indistinguishable. H.D.'s husband Richard Aldington describes his experiences as a combatant in the trenches in his autobiographical novel *Death of a Hero*: 'For Winterbourne, the battle was a timeless confusion, a chaos of noise, fatigue, anxiety, and horror. He did not know how many days and nights it lasted, lost completely the sequence of events, found great gaps in his conscious memory.'[7]

War literature also draws attention to the radically disrupted experience of time for non-combatants. Ford Madox Ford's *Parade's End*, for example, not only describes the drawn-out tedium of life in the trenches, 'the eternal waiting that is War', but also the 'suspended animation' of the lover left at home.[8] The traumatic effects of the disruption of daily life on the civilian is the central theme of my chapter on H.D. However, clearly the effects of the war reverberate through the work of all the writers addressed (with the possible exception of Dorothy Richardson). Virginia Woolf's work, for example, is increasingly being read in terms of its relationship to the First World War. The 'chasm of time' constituting the 'Time Passes' section of *To the Lighthouse* has long been seen as an attempt to negotiate the traumatic and inexpressible nature of the war, and explicitly represents it as both a disruption of human time and a kind of return to primordial time. *Jacob's Room* revolves around a character made absent by the war, as if Jacob's early death retrospectively renders his life simply a phantasm, void, intangible. *Mrs Dalloway* is often read as a book in which Woolf does not address the war except through the dramatic person of Septimus; however, it is also possible to detect war trauma resonating throughout the book – the burst tyre that sounds like a gunshot, boys in uniform laying a wreath on the Cenotaph. Finally, *Between the Acts* is shot through with the oncoming menace of the next war, and the attempt to encompass all of history within the pageant presented on a single day speaks of the desperate, almost manic, anxiety to make sense, to imagine continuity in the face of an unimaginable future.

By contrast, Gertrude Stein's writing on war, and the First World War in particular, expresses remarkable equanimity. Indeed, Stein and Alice B. Toklas actually appeared to enjoy World War One, meeting GIs and driving them around France, their adopted homeland, in their beloved car; this relatively carefree attitude is most in evidence in *The Autobiography of Alice B Toklas*, as perhaps befits such a playful text. However, Stein's style, particularly in *Wars I have Seen*, also draws attention to the experience of daily life during war, as the text metamorphoses into a diary of Stein's life during the Second World War. The negotiation of the everyday in the recreational strategies of 'Melanctha' and *Tender Buttons*, the texts I address in my chapter on Stein, forms a key part of Stein's pre-war everyday aesthetic, which might be viewed as a background against which to read Stein's daily war narratives. Through the everyday means of gossip and anecdote, and her characteristic repetition of stories or phrases, Stein's war narratives evoke the permeation of the ongoing patterns of everyday life with the effects of the war, while maintaining the awareness that day still follows day, that life still goes on and a way must be found to live it.

One of the many profound effects of the First World War on Western society was the part it played in the acceleration of the women's movement, as women were seen to be able to work and contribute to society in areas previously reserved for men. The prominence of issues around gender at this time needs no underlining; Woolf's *A Room of One's Own* is only the most well-known of the many literary documents of interwar feminism, and of course remains foundational to feminist thought. What Woolf drew attention to in this text, along with many other activists and writers, was the specific material conditions under which women had to live in Western societies – the conditions of their everyday lives. I will outline in more detail below the issues and problems surrounding the alignment of women with the everyday. While the reservations I express remain, there will be places where the texts addressed raise the question of a special relationship between women and the everyday. However, the important impact of the women's movement in terms of my exploration of dailiness arises both in the inflection of daily experience through one's gender, and in the categorisation of various practices that might make up daily life in terms of their association with a particular gender. Woolf's description of how Jane Austen might have had to hide her manuscript when others entered the room illustrates what I mean here.[9] Writing, a practice acceptable for men, was an unacceptable use of time for women – the same practice takes on a different meaning when performed by different genders. The way in which this differentiation then leads to the categorisation of certain practices according to gender, and a concomitant change in the status of that practice, is suggested in, for example, the way in which the profession of secretary has been downgraded as it has moved from being primarily a profession for men, in the late nineteenth century, to one almost exclusively for women.[10] The increasing visibility of issues of gender during the early decades of the twentieth century raised the question of what women should be able to expect from their daily lives; the increasing recognition of the legitimacy of women's experience throws into question assumptions about what is valuable in a life, what makes up a life.

Increasing gender awareness went alongside, if sometimes in conflict with, increasing class-consciousness. Although an explicit class analysis will not feature heavily in this book, the rapid change in working practices around the turn of the century meant that, as Sara Blair has put it, there was a 'newly visible materiality of this everyday, middle- and working-class life-world'.[11] An increasingly visible, and indeed vocal, working class presented more challenges to any standard model of what constituted a life worth attending to; that is, traditionally, a life with political, historical, or aesthetic potential. Further, rapidly evolving technologies transformed the ways in which people experienced their daily lives, as the innovations of Taylorism and Fordism insisted, for many, on a workplace where time was strictly regulated. Developments in the standardisation of timekeeping, such as the establishment of Greenwich mean time in 1884, as well as the proliferation of gas and then electric lighting already mentioned, made it easier for the working day to be extended beyond its natural bounds – although, as Marx had already catalogued in detail, such natural bounds were by no means respected by employers before this period.[12] In addition, work itself had by-and-large moved out of the private and into the public arena – the working and middle classes were less likely to work from home, although professional people such as the dentist Miriam works for in *Pilgrimage* would often still use their home as a place of work. And yet, alongside this spatial schism between work and non-work or leisure, leisure itself was increasingly being co-opted by capitalist structures, making the time people spent at 'leisure', and the activities constituting leisure, almost as regulated as at work. This is the background against which Stein's 'working' and 'wandering' narrative, Richardson's description of the life of the working New Woman, H.D.'s anxiety about her war 'duty', and implicitly, Woolf's musings on the kind of activity reading and writing constitute, are set.

As Michael Bell puts it, 'the question of living is crucial here since modernist literature is often concerned with the question of how to live within a new context of thought, or a new worldview';[13] a new worldview radically transformed by feminism, technology, class-consciousness and war. This question is indeed at the heart of my interrogation of these literary texts, and brings me to consideration of their aesthetic context. The 'question of how to live' is often answered in modernist literature, at least in traditional critical accounts thereof, in terms of searching for the exceptional moment, the transcendent or the epiphanic, whether in Eliot, Joyce,

Yeats, Baudelaire, Heidegger or Benjamin. Leo Charney usefully surveys the various foundational models of the special relationship between modern life and the moment, instancing among others Heidegger, for whom the 'moment of vision', where nothing can occur and there is nothing but pure sensation, is what allows us access to the sublime; and Benjamin, where the moment as 'shock' is both a symptom of an alienated modern life, and what enables the artistic vision of, for example, Baudelaire.[14] Indeed, Ben Highmore, in his recent survey of theories of the everyday, indicates the centrality of the 'moment' for Henri Lefebvre, who is not only one of the most important theorists of the everyday and thus will provide crucial theoretical context in this book, but was also associated with the Surrealist movement in France and therefore himself played a part in early twentieth-century modernist aesthetics. 'For Lefebvre,' says Highmore, '"moments" are those instances of intense experience in everyday life that provide an immanent critique of the everyday'.[15] Charney characterises these positions as part of 'the modern aspiration to seize fleeting moments of sensation as a hedge against their inexorable evisceration'.[16] By contrast, I will focus on the ways in which the writers I discuss, rather than fighting against the ephemeral quality of the present and searching for the exceptional moment to illuminate the everyday, instead find new ways of imagining and representing the present, life now, ongoing daily time. 'For', as Michael Sheringham says, 'the everyday [. . .] is where we already are: to find it, we cannot "arise and go there", in Yeats's phrase, but have somehow to bring about a transformation that will make it visible or palpable'.[17] These transformations, here understood as the literary techniques these writers develop and make use of to convey the everyday and its temporality, will be the central focus of this project.

The relative critical neglect of the specific temporality of dailiness in modernist literature can be shown by surveying critical perspectives on the temporality of that paradigmatically modernist, and daily, text *Ulysses*. *Ulysses*, Arnold Bennett argued, represents the 'dailiest day possible', the most representative, mundane, unexceptional day that Joyce could have chosen. The paradox of dailiness comes immediately to the fore in Bennett's formulation: the dailiest day is exceptional, exemplary, in its very mundanity. As Lefebvre would have it, the date 16 June 1904 is significant 'by chance and not by chance' (*ELMW* 2); in a formulation which resonates throughout my elaboration of the concept of dailiness, it is 'both-and'.

Critics have tended to address the temporal structure of Joyce's text in one of two ways. Firstly, there is source criticism, focusing on the unearthing or elaborating of the temporal models informing *Ulysses*'s structure. Particularly in the wake of T. S. Eliot's influential essay 'Ulysses, Order and Myth', written only the year after *Ulysses*'s publication, criticism of this kind has tended to view the dailiness of *Ulysses* as the surface matter beneath which lay the real substance of the text, its mythic analogues – primarily, of course, Homer. That none other than Eliot described the method employed in *Ulysses* as having 'the importance of a scientific discovery' would inevitably, to subsequent critics, focus attention on the mythic structure which, in Eliot's words, 'giv[es] a shape and a significance to the immense panorama of futility and anarchy which is contemporary history'.[18] Eliot's construction indicates to the reader that the only way in to this daunting text is through attending above all to this (mythic, Homeric) shape, which orders an otherwise incommensurable, incomprehensible everyday chaos. Further strata of Joyce's temporal system were revealed with reference to, most importantly, Giambattista Vico, as well as other less well-known figures.[19] Vico's model of cyclical recurrence in history intersects interestingly with the questions of the quality of repetition in dailiness, which will be discussed at greater length below. However, critics addressing the influence of Vico have tended to proceed through an increasingly detailed mapping of Vico's system onto Joyce's texts, dissecting Joyce using Vico as a tool, rather than, for example, asking how Joyce's daily structure might speak back to Viconian models.

Secondly, there is a tradition of criticism that focuses on the stream of consciousness in Joyce's text, the mundane psychic development and activity of his characters, developing from interest in the influence of Henri Bergson. This approach was particularly prominent in the 1950s and 1960s – Shiv K. Kumar's *Bergson and the Stream of Consciousness Novel* is probably the most influential of these studies, and the connection between Bergson and modernist literature will be explored in more detail in Chapter 1. However, an Eliotic depth and surface model persists in the work of the important critics of this period. Margaret Church summarises Robert Humphrey's argument, for example, thus: 'the formless nature of the psychic life of his characters forced Joyce to impose exterior patterns on his narrative [. . .] One pattern is, of course, the eighteen hours of one day.'[20] Similarly, Hans Meyerhoff 'pointed out how Joyce injects into the stream of consciousness the hours of the day'.[21] Joyce's text is still figured in a binary fashion: as psychic interiority with exteriority – the hours of the day – imposed upon it, or injected into it. However, while the hours of the day are indeed a relatively artificial pattern, the day itself is not. Indeed, as my chapter on Bergson and William James will show, Bergsonian models of psychic flux are already and inevitably marked by the patterns and experiences of dailiness.

The psyche is not simply a surface text revealing a depth of dailiness, nor is dailiness a grid overlaid on an otherwise uninflected psyche.

'Thus far', Margaret Church summarised in 1983, 'two major temporal patterns have emerged in critical assessments of Joyce's work: a structured Viconian pattern and a more freeflowing Bergsonian one, one socially and historically oriented, the other individually'.[22] It is surprising that the temporal pattern of dailiness itself – both structured and freeflowing – has been overlooked. The anteriority of the day as temporal rhythm to Bergsonian, Viconian and even Homeric temporal structures might suggest that, rather than seeing mythic, philosophical depth overlaid with daily surface, we should rather see Joyce trying to make sense of daily depth by overlaying a variety of mythic and philosophical structures. This idea of daily depth is suggestive for my project in general, although a simple inversion of Eliot's depth-and-surface model will not quite do. Rather, we see how the very idea of depth and surface is challenged in many of the texts under discussion. Stein's texts, for example, with their absolute refusal of any epistemological ground, appear in one sense as nothing but surface, as the infinite permutations of significance allowed by their 'insistence', or their agrammaticality, mean one can never truly penetrate the text to access some depth of meaning; and yet this sliding on the surface of meaning itself reveals the valid, productive, re-creational everyday process of meaning-making. Richardson's geological model of time, by contrast, seems to correspond more strongly to a notion of daily depth, of the profundity of experience lying behind the experience of each day; and yet her archaeology of dailiness refuses to hierarchise everyday experiences, contraindicating conventional assumptions about what is 'deep', profound, significant. H.D.'s palimpsest of texts, each rewriting the others, problematises the concept of a single surface to be penetrated; each textual surface is itself already overlaid with other texts, and has other texts lying beneath it, as every day is already overlaid with the many days which precede and will follow it. There is a constant dialogue in these modernist texts between surface and depth. I find in them a refusal either to participate fully in a search for a specious depth beyond the surface of everyday life – which surface they attend to and valorise – or to reject the idea of depth in dailiness, of there being something, as Virginia Woolf put it, 'that lies beneath the semblance of the thing' (*W* 123).

Finally, it is worth noting the increasing critical interest in the concept of the everyday in literary studies, and the fertile ground this strand of work has found in *Ulysses*. The use of everyday discourses of consumerism in *Ulysses*'s 'Nausicaa', or mass communication in 'Aeolus', and so forth, has been one focus of interest; Garry Leonard's work on Joyce and advertising is exemplary here. However, much work coming out of the sociology of the everyday, including literary criticism, has focused on the spatial. Michel de Certeau, one of the most important recent theorists of the everyday, explicitly says that he 'has concentrated above all on the uses of space';[23] Highmore argues that for Lefebvre, 'the unmanageability of the everyday archive is increasingly managed by spatializing the interrelations of the everyday'.[24] In *Ulysses*, naturally, the importance of space and place is not to be overlooked; not for nothing does Joyce meticulously trace Bloom's and Stephen's steps around Dublin. Nevertheless, I want to distinguish my approach, not only from the depth-and-surface model of the source and psychological criticism characterising approaches to daily temporality, but also from the foregrounding of the spatial, which I discuss further below, in much work on literary modernism's everyday.

'DAILINESS': EVERYDAY LIFE

The everyday: what is most difficult to discover.[25]

Maurice Blanchot lays out in his succinct essay on 'Everyday Speech' the revisiting of the category of the everyday through the 'critique of everyday life', a process most associated with, but by no means instigated by, Henri Lefebvre. 'The everyday', says Blanchot, 'is no longer the average, statistically established existence of a given society at a given moment; it is a category, a utopia and an Idea, without which one would not know how to get at either the hidden present or the discoverable future of manifest beings'.[26] Blanchot describes how what might be called the everyday concept of the everyday, as that which is unmarked, unhistorical (in the sense that it does not enter into dominant narratives of history), average, and reducible (to, say, statistics), is brought from the background to the foreground in the work of Lefebvre, among others. Far from being that which is taken for granted, it becomes that which should not, indeed must not, be taken for granted. Without a critique of the everyday, an examination of what it has come to signify and of why it has come thus to signify, we will simply be unable to understand what it means to *be*, or what it might come to mean. Where I use the term 'critique', then, in my discussion, I intend it to mean a critique in this sense, as a project revisiting the concept of the everyday, rather than in the sense of a criticism or rejection of the everyday.

Two different strands can be detected within work on theories of the everyday. On the one hand, there is the phenomenological strand, including the analysis of the everyday in Martin Heidegger's *Being and Time* as well as, perhaps most influentially, the work of Edmund Husserl. Heidegger's designation of the everyday as 'inauthentic' is on a continuum with Husserl's earlier attempts to parenthesise a *Lebenswelt* of everyday life in order to identify pure phenomenological experience. Husserl's thought has also influenced a wide range of so-called first generation phenomenologists, engaging with the question of how the everyday might be theorised as a kind of system. (Jacques Derrida's deconstructive approach also forms part of this strand of thought; however, where a Derridean influence might be detected in this book, it is in the enabling literary critical tactics suggested by his writing, rather than in his association with this perspective on the everyday.) By contrast, those working from a broadly Marxist perspective, and in particular French sociologists such as Lefebvre and de Certeau, have focused on the everyday as that which precisely evades systematisation. George Perec's writings and activities exemplify the way in which this strand of thought sees the everyday as an arena to be addressed on its own terms, employing strategies and tactics that evade categorisation and analysis by traditional academic methodologies.[27]

My own approach follows the French Marxist tradition, itself related to the earlier work of Georg Simmel and Walter Benjamin, of intervening in the matrix which conventionally relegates the everyday to the realm of the trivial, unremarkable, repetitive and impotent, and of investigating the value-judgements implicit in those associations.[28] Ben Highmore yokes Simmel and Benjamin with Lefebvre and de Certeau by seeing in them all a simple refusal 'to see the realm of the everyday as unproblematic';[29] my work upholds just such a refusal. I will argue that, while the term 'everyday' is most commonly seen as describing a particular range of practices – cooking, washing, gossip, walking and so on – a more appropriate description of the everyday might be as a particular perspective on, a particular kind of attention paid to, the various practices which make up life as a whole. Indeed, Highmore has specifically located the concept of attention as crucial to a formulation of the everyday. Highmore argues not only that 'a different form of attention is needed that can listen to the silences and see the gaps within the archive [of everyday life] as positive signs', but also that 'Perhaps [. . .] the everyday is the name that cultural theory might give to a form of attention that attempts to animate the heterogeneity of social life, the name for an activity of finding meaning in an impossible diversity'.[30] The particular incommensurability of the everyday is here neatly hinted at; it both needs a particular form of attention in order to become manifest, and is itself a particular form of attention. There can be no rigorous distinction between these two ways of understanding the relationship between attention and the everyday; in what follows I will attempt to explore this relationship without reducing it to one or the other definition.

This relationship is particularly important insofar as the question of attention is inevitably connected to that of value, since we supposedly value that to which we attend, and attend differently to things we believe to be of different value. This brings me to the grounding of my argument in a Marxist interrogation of the production of value. My argument challenges, however, the traditional Marxist model in two related ways, following the trajectory of Theodor Adorno's revision of Marx. Firstly, my position takes on Adorno's critique of the traditional Marxist emphasis on alienated labour in general as the source of the exchange process, and thus of the production of exchange value; that moment at which exchange value appears alongside use-value, both coming into play when assessing the value of a particular product. Instead, in *Negative Dialectics*, Adorno posits 'an even earlier origin', as Martin Jay puts it, following Alfred Sohn-Rethel in 'locating the "original sin" in the division of mental from manual labour'.[31] The implications of the posited division between mental and manual labour, and the way in which Marx himself addresses it, will be explored in more detail below. Part of my argument, therefore, is that the texts I discuss invite a reanimation of the question of the division between mental and manual labour.

This aspect of Adorno's revision of Marx forms part of his general critique of the privileging of the mode of production in traditional Marxist thought – the economic element; Adorno insists on giving 'equal weight to psychological, cultural and generically social factors'.[32] These factors necessarily include, I would suggest, gender. Thus my second critique is imbricated with my first, and both stem in large part from Marx's focus on a factory wage-labour system, which while strategically important for Marx, leaves us with some theoretical lacunae. In other words, I would argue that the model from which traditional Marxist analyses of everyday life are drawn takes insufficient account of the place of mental labour in everyday life, and of women's experience of the working day.

We should first, however, turn to Marx himself, and in particular to the ways in which his work engages directly with dailiness. It is neither surprising nor insignificant that Marx devotes a chapter of the first volume of *Capital* to 'The Working Day'. The concept of the working day, its limits (theoretical and actual) and its policing are, as Marx explains in this chapter, of vital importance to the maintenance of capitalism; in his guide to *Capital*, Anthony Brewer makes the general comment that 'Marx usually measures labour power in days'.[33] The concept of labour time is, of course, central to Marx's entire theory of capitalist production. As Ben Fine puts it, according to a Marxist analysis of capitalism, 'exchange is not interested in quality (type) of labour but only in quantity, and that quantity is of abstract social labour. In exchange, the point is not whether the labour-time was expended by a baker or a tailoress, but *if* a certain amount of labour-time has been expended.'[34] It is precisely this quantification of labour time that converts a use-value into a commodity with exchange value. But Fine's paraphrase here neatly encapsulates the trap into which Marx's model falls; not only does it not matter what kind of labour is expended, nor by whom, but the gender of the worker is immaterial (and Fine's choice of the clearly gendered term 'tailoress' must be deliberate). As Adorno points out, even as Marx intends to expose the inequity in the system which abstracts social labour by reducing it to exchange value, by emphasising the economic aspect of the generation of exchange value, he replicates the elision of other factors; qualitative rather than quantitative factors.

What differences, then, might there be between the labour-time of a baker and that of a tailoress – differences that speak to the model of labour proposed by Marx? Perhaps the most important consideration is that women may not, historically, rigorously have experienced the separation between work for wages and work in the home. Marx's model assumes 'work' ends when workers clock off. This would not necessarily have been so for women whose domestic chores may have taken up as much effort and even as much time as their paid work. Indeed, in the case of the tailoress, we can well imagine that the work done in the production of commodities for exchange, and that done in the production of objects for domestic use, may be practically indistinguishable, as, for example, a piece of clothing intended for sale may become, in the process of its production, more suitable for one of her family. Of course, we can also imagine the baker producing bread for his own family's consumption, but the fact that domestic labour was, at the time that Marx was writing, and indeed still is, primarily conducted by women, makes the slippage between these two types of work particularly marked where women's labour is concerned.

On the one hand, then, women's labour extended well beyond the factory. But the 'work' done in the home evades the control of the capitalist – or at least his direct control. Within certain limits, it could be done when the woman chose, how she chose, and with the help of those of the household she deemed most suitable. It may have had sociable elements – communal washing, for example – and would certainly have been considered an arena from which men were excluded. In particular, it gravitates towards consideration of use-value rather than exchange value, and use-value understood in a wider sense than might usually be the case. The act of washing your own family's clothes, for example, or cooking their evening meal, obviously has some use-value, and it is not of a sort that can be converted into exchange value without radically changing the nature of the labour. That is to say, were a baker to agree to bake three extra loaves of bread in exchange for having a shirt mended by a tailoress, the nature of the labour would remain the same in both cases. However, to have another woman cook and serve the family meal in exchange for, for example, washing her floors, has dramatic personal and social implications. The use-value of domestic work is radically resistant to conversion into exchange value, precisely in those social, cultural and psychological aspects to which Adorno draws our attention.

The image which Woolf provides in *A Room of One's Own* of Jane Austen hiding her writing under her needlework encapsulates the relationship between my critique of Marx from a feminist perspective, and my insistence, with Adorno, on the interrogation of the division between mental and manual labour. That this image has become a touchstone for feminist criticism and theory is testament to its power. Yet the focus has up until now primarily been on its vivid depiction of the ideology of the 'Angel in the House', the limitations placed on women's activities, and by association their lack of resources – of 'a room of one's own'. What seems particularly interesting in the context of this discussion, however, is the literal laying of one kind of, socially acceptable, 'work' (which, while hardly producing items which fulfil primary needs, nevertheless would have produced tangible items with a certain use-value), over another kind of work involving, indeed constituted primarily by, intellectual labour. The image Woolf thus generates of Austen engaged in both types of work almost simultaneously returns us to the question of the place of intellectual labour and its incorporation, or otherwise, in traditional Marxist models.

We see Marx's unquestioning separation of manual from mental labour explicitly articulated in his chapter on the working day. In this chapter, Marx's attention to the economic significance of the working day leads him into a more discursive, personally engaged kind of writing than we find elsewhere in *Capital*. As Brewer puts it, 'Almost for the first time in *Capital* these discussions of the working-day reveal Marx's moral condemnation of the system he lived in.'[35] It is signal that Marx's writing becomes so distinctively polemical where the question of the use of time is at its most acute. The structure of the day, announcing its own arrival and departure, reminds us of the particular inhumanity of the abuse of time under the wage-slavery of capitalism; we can in principle get more money, more commodities, but we cannot get more time.

From the very beginning of the chapter, Marx draws attention to the needs, both physical and social, that limit the extension of the working day: 'Besides these purely physical limitations [the need to sleep, eat, wash etc.], the extension of the working day encounters moral obstacles. The worker needs time in which to satisfy his intellectual and social requirements, and the extent and number of these requirements is conditioned by the general level of civilization.'[36] The extent of Marx's indignation at the system's capacity to disregard such limitations is evidenced in his catalogue of exploitative employment practices, under which there is barely time to meet the physical needs of sleep and food, let alone 'intellectual and social requirements'. Although these latter requirements may in practice be secondary, it seems clear that in principle Marx views them as equally important – indeed, the extent to which such requirements are met is precisely a barometer of a society's level of civilisation.

However, Marx maintains a structural and theoretical distinction between labour time, and time outside labour where these other needs are met, which we have already seen challenged through consideration of women's working lives. Evidently, it is crucial to Marx's analysis of the economic structures of capitalism that such a distinction be maintained, since it is labour time which is of most direct interest to an economy. However, pursuing the sociological rather than economic implications of Marxist thought, this emphasis on the time outside work needed to fulfil 'intellectual and social requirements' is suggestive for an analysis of everyday life and daily time. This is time that, like women's domestic work, falls outside the remit of Marx's rigorously economic analysis, while remaining central to Marx's social model. As leisure time itself becomes increasingly incorporated into systems of commodity capitalism in the early twentieth century, such a distinction will of course be problematised; concomitantly, leisure time will thus become more appropriate to a rigorously Marxist analysis. However, it is the extent to which time does not always fall in this way under the control of capitalist structures, the extent to which it evades and indeed resists them, that will be of most interest to me here.

Marx does not account for the possibility that some or even all of a worker's 'intellectual and social requirements' might be met as part of his labour time, while at work. Evidently, in the examples he gives from the factories of Victorian England, this is not likely to be the case. But the possibility that there may be some cross-contamination between the categories of work and non-work, and that the uses of time in each may be less than rigorously distinct, is central to my discussion. For example, my chapter on Woolf takes as a central concern the status of 'thought'; I show how attending to this activity through the lens of dailiness reveals its productive potential not only disallowed by the capitalist system Marx describes, but structurally placed by Marx outside of 'work'. More broadly, my discussion of *Pilgrimage* implies a consideration of the way in which the intellectual labour of the writer contaminates, and is contaminated by, their waged work, in a relationship both potentially damaging and potentially productive. What these observations imply is that women writers of the early twentieth century, 'thinking back through their mothers' both as women, and as writers – engaged in intellectual labour – inherited a notion of work, and indeed of value, which is much more fluid than Marx's definition would seem to allow.

I want to conclude this section on the everyday by situating my approach in relation to perhaps the most important theorist of the everyday for my purposes – not least in terms of the extent to which I deviate from his perspective – Henri Lefebvre. The key specific contributions Lefebvre's work makes to my discussion are twofold. Firstly, there is the general principle of the necessity of an ongoing critique of everyday life, particularly as that which is by definition 'untellable', inarticulable, outside of systematisation. Secondly, there is the idea of the ongoing production of one's own life as a work, possibly even a work of art. As Peter Osborne puts it, Lefebvre's work involves 'a growing consciousness of the need actively to intervene within the everyday, to *produce* – as well as to draw attention to – its utopian side'.[37] Some readings of Lefebvre tend to emphasise his characterisation of everyday life as 'dull routine, the ongoing going-to-work, paying-the-bills, homeward trudge of daily existence' (*ELMW* vii). A more positive reading of Lefebvre's work, however, focuses on the ways in which Lefebvre views everyday life as not simply inauthentic, as Heidegger would argue, or alienated existence. As Ben Highmore puts it, 'however bleak Lefebvre's view of modern everyday life became, the everyday always held out the possibility of its own transformation'.[38] In particular, the idea of 'production' resonates on many levels within my discussion, ranging from 'the possibility of man's self-realization through productive and creative activities', which I address in particular where I discuss the practices of reading and writing in Chapter 5, to the more general concept of an 'art of living' which 'presupposes that the human being sees his own life – the development and intensification of his life – not as a means towards "another" end, but as an end in itself' (*ELMW* 32; *CEL* 199). This view of life is central to my definition of the everyday. To work from a critical perspective orientated in terms of the everyday means to pay attention to activities and practices in these terms; that is, as making up a life which is an end in itself, rather than as contributing to an externally imposed value system. 'Is it not in everyday life that man should fulfil his life as a man? [. . .] Man must be everyday, or he will not be at all' (*CEL* 127).

Lefebvre's language here points at one of two problems with his work on the everyday that will be pertinent to my discussion. Firstly, his use of 'man' in the above quotation sensitises the English reader to the question of gender in Lefebvre. While, in the process of translation into English, Lefebvre's terminology may acquire more clearly gendered associations than were necessarily the case in the original French, Lefebvre's analyses of gender remain problematic. In the later text, *Everyday Life in the Modern World*, Lefebvre explicitly states that 'Everyday life weighs heaviest on women [. . .] Because of their ambiguous position in everyday life – which is specifically part of everyday life and modernity – they are incapable of understanding it' (*ELMW* 73). As Laurie Langbauer says in her feminist critique of Lefebvre, this is a manifestation of 'the old logic that women cannot understand something because they embody it [hence] the contradictions of the everyday, which make it opaque to everyone, make it particularly so to women'.[39] Langbauer indicates how this logic leads Lefebvre into a position where, blaming women for people's unconscious relation to the everyday – for the failure to critique the everyday – 'both women and the everyday come to stand for an overwhelming totality [. . .] women and the everyday in this sense represent that definition of culture as a medium embracing its subjects, one sustaining and shaping them'.[40] Women are both 'more everyday', and are that which precisely defines the everyday, both within and without, in a self-justifying argument which defines each element in terms of the other, closing up the space for critique.

This circular argument is not, however, restricted to Lefebvre. The commonplace association of 'everyday life' with women is an assumption on which many feminist texts on the everyday also rest – in an attempt, perhaps, to redress an emphasis in earlier theorists' work on the urban, masculine everyday.[41] Bettina Aptheker, in her work on women and daily experience, states that 'women have a consciousness of social reality that is distinct from that put forth by men'.[42] While this statement problematically consigns power to 'men' in general, which power not all men may have – not all men are in the position of 'putting forth' ideas about the world – we can concur with Aptheker that, in the patriarchal societies of the West, individuals living with a female gender assignment have their experiences filtered through a society which privileges experiences and systems of thought associated with masculinity. Aptheker identifies the two main factors contributing to this different consciousness among women as the existence of a 'sexual division of labor' and the fact that 'women are subordinated to men'.[43] She defines 'the dailiness of women's lives', then, as 'the patterns women create and the meanings women invent each day and over time as a result of their labors and in the context of their subordinated status to men'.[44] This definition of 'the dailiness of women's lives' is certainly useful, particularly in terms of Aptheker's attention to the sexual division of labour. Nevertheless, the consistent connection of 'dailiness' and 'the everyday' with women in Aptheker's work contributes to a construction of women as somehow more 'everyday' than men. For instance, by quoting Susanne Juhasz as saying 'Dailiness matters most to women', Aptheker begins by assigning a particular range of practices to the everyday, which practices are selected precisely through their being associated with women.[45] An interrogation of the terms 'dailiness' and 'everyday', and the gendered associations they already hold when used in a text, is missing.

My premise, by contrast, is that 'dailiness' describes something forming, by definition, every human individual; indeed most rigorously, the term means something different for each individual – it is both universal, and completely specific. As I explore dailiness, the term 'everyday' will inevitably bring into play the associations it already carries, and my discussion will indeed sometimes make use of these associations; my intention is to make these more explicit. I would agree that women not only generally do participate in the devalued activities described as particularly 'everyday', but that we are socialised to associate these activities with that group. However, it is the question of value which is, for me, most important; rather than beginning by paying attention to women's activities, I want to address activities which are usually devalued, and explore their associations. After all, gender is not the only ground on which labour is divided and according to which domination is asserted; as Aptheker herself concedes at the end of her book, 'Black women [may] have more in common with Black men than they do with white, middle-class women';[46] similarly gay men may experience prejudice placing them in a less powerful position than some straight women, or old men may experience discrimination of a kind younger women do not. The 'dailiness' of those in other oppressed categories can be seen in, for example, Christopher Isherwood's one-day novel *A Single Man*, which (although falling outside of the period under discussion) uses the frame of the single day explicitly to articulate a middle-aged gay man's subject position.[47] Everyone's life is, then, 'daily'; by suggesting otherwise, approaches such as Aptheker's risk staying within the structures of power which construct gender in a binary fashion, by simply changing the polarisation of 'everyday life', making it a good thing rather than a bad thing. To this extent, Aptheker fails in her attempt to interrogate the oppositional structures which have given the everyday – a term suggesting a ubiquitous experience – clearly gendered associations. As Blanchot observes of oppositional thinking and the everyday, 'What is proper to the everyday is that it designates for us a region or a level of speech where the determinations true and false, like the opposition of yes and no, do not apply.'[48]

In focusing on four women writers, then, I do not set out with the assumption that experience of the everyday or of time is necessarily gendered; that there is a 'woman's time' or that the everyday is more 'female'. This is not only because there are such striking differences between these women as individuals – they may have the same gender, but they vary greatly in terms of nationality, class, sexuality, political orientation and so forth, not to mention the style and subject matter of their texts. It is also because to do so would be to fail to understand the way in which the term 'everyday' and its cognates can be and have been used as part of a capitalist and patriarchal system in the West to control the activities of both men and women, to divide and value practices according to their contribution to the production of capital and their capacity to be arrogated by the structures of power. The association of the everyday with women is evidently part of this; women, as a devalued category, will devalue the everyday by being associated with it. However, neither is it merely contingent that most of the writers I address are women. As I have argued above, the idea of women's work, and in particular women's writing, presents a structural challenge to the Marxist tradition in which this work is set; it remains crucial that writing is inflected through gender, whether explicitly or implicitly, consciously or unconsciously. Rather, if it has been assumed that women's lives and their writing are more 'everyday', any critique of the everyday needs to revisit that association; by exploring in detail the instances of dailiness in the texts under discussion I am able to explore the variety and complexity of models of the everyday, problematising the concept of the everyday as either valueless activity, or conversely (as in Aptheker's text) by definition positive through its association with otherwise neglected female activity.

I now turn to the second key problem with Lefebvre's definition of the everyday: the question of what specifies the everyday and rescues it from being so general as to be without significance. This is addressed in Franco

Moretti's commentary on Lefebvre, and Moretti's critique is contiguous with my discussion of gender above. Moretti agrees with Lefebvre that 'there are no limits to what can be incorporated by everyday life' – once again, everyday life is by definition inclusive rather than exclusive – but goes on to argue that 'if we must define a sphere of life, and declare it limitless, then we have not come very far'.[49] In order to make 'everyday life' a category specific enough for it to be of use, Moretti suggests 'we must specify that what characterizes everyday life [. . .] is not the nature or the number of its pursuits but their "treatment". [. . .] We may thus speak of everyday life whenever the individual subordinates any activity whatsoever to the construction of "his own world."'[50] This is not to say that everyday life is about individualism to the exclusion of all other considerations, for, after all, one's own world is defined by personal and wider social relationships. What I mean to emphasise by using Moretti's definition is the everyday as a perspective taken on events and practices, an orientation or, *per* Highmore, 'form of attention' toward them, as well as, or even rather than, those practices in and of themselves. Where Moretti says, 'with Jean Baudrillard, that everyday life is a *system of interpretation*', he emphasises this hermeneutic dimension of the definition of everyday life.[51]

Where Moretti emphasises that everyday life is a way 'of "reshaping" the world of perceiving and evaluating it according to *human proportions*' (my emphasis) the most important project of a discussion of the everyday becomes clear;[52] that is, precisely the process of humanising that which, through systems of patriarchy and capitalism, has been dehumanised. Though we may not be able to believe in the realisation of Lefebvre's utopian 'culture restored by a new preoccupation with everyday life' we can still agree with its aims, 'the restoration of time as the supreme gift (life time)' (*ELMW* 202). The critique of everyday life is, then, crucially bound up with the question of temporality.

'DAILINESS': DAILY TIME

As already noted, Michel de Certeau states that his research in *The Practice of Everyday Life* 'has concentrated above all on the uses of space'.[53] Nevertheless, his exploration of the productive and subversive potential of everyday life also relies on a consideration of our relationship to, and use of, time. Alongside the critique of the everyday as socio-cultural concept, I will want to use the term 'dailiness' as a way of opening onto the variety of possible temporalities which emerge in the literature of the early twentieth century, and which are revealed by the structural features as well as the

explicit content of the texts addressed. In this regard, there are two important general features relevant to daily time in these texts; firstly, repetition,
and secondly, the spatialisation of time.

Lefebvre himself describes everyday life as 'made of recurrences', giving
examples of its many repetitive actions and rhythms (*ELMW* 18). Indeed,
Highmore suggests that 'It is repetition that is crucial to Lefebvre's meaning of the term "everyday life".'[54] There is perhaps no better example of
the relationship between repetition and dailiness than this passage from
Gertrude Stein's 'Miss Furr and Miss Skeene':

To be regularly gay was to do every day the gay thing that they did every day. To be
regularly gay was to end every day at the same time after they had been regularly
gay. They were regularly gay. They were gay every day. They ended every day in
the same way, at the same time, and they had been every day regularly gay.[55]

This paragraph exhibits some exemplary features of dailiness in general,
as well as the dailiness of modernist literature and Stein in particular. As
well as literally articulating the centrality of the day as temporal unit, its
tautologies mirror the sameness that characterises much of everyday life. It
also hints at the inexpressibility ('the gay thing') of everyday lived existence,
what Lefebvre would characterise as the residual, the untellable: the only
way to explain it is to say it again. Its repetitions with minute modifications
(compare the first and second sentence) mirror the pattern of day following almost, but not quite, identical day. Once again, Blanchot provides a
succinct summary: 'the everyday is what we never see for a first time but
can only see again'.[56]

Further, the insistent rhyme of 'gay' with 'day' links dailiness with a
challenge to heteronormativity, adding to a matrix of meaning which hints
at the insubordinate potential of dailiness. The word 'gay' as slang for
homosexual originated in America, and although the earliest citation in
the OED of the term used in this sense is from a text of 1935, there is
no doubt that Stein would have been aware of its resonances at the time
of writing 'Miss Furr and Miss Skeene', living as she did in an openly
homosexual relationship, and with only thinly veiled references to a sexual
relationship between Miss [fur] and Miss [skin] in the text.[57] Finally, the
various other meanings of the word 'gay' place it in a semantic matrix
of play, lightheartedness, even overfamiliarity (as in the American slang
term 'to get gay'). There are also suggestions of other kinds of 'improper'
sexuality, through the nineteenth-century use of the term to designate a
prostitute. Most significations of the term line up in opposition to the
meanings and associations of work, with suggestions of insubordination

and playful mockery, implying a critique of the privileging of labour time in the working day. We see, then, not only that repetition is by no means an unmarked temporal structure, but that the repetitive sameness-and-difference temporal structure of dailiness itself inflects the way in which meaning is created, the way in which value is assigned.

J. Hillis Miller's discussion of two kinds of repetition in his important study *Fiction and Repetition* illuminates the subtlety of the structure of repetition. Citing Gilles Deleuze, Miller explores the manifestation of, and relationship between, what he calls 'grounded' and 'ungrounded' repetition. In the first, 'only that which resembles itself differs' – in this world as icon, art functions as Platonic mimesis; repetition is 'grounded in a solid archetypal model which is untouched by the effects of repetition'.[58] In the second, 'only differences resemble one another' – in this world as phantasm, as simulacrum, everything is intrinsically different, and similarity only arises out of this background of difference. In his discussion of the kinds of repetition found in fiction, Miller shows how 'each form of repetition inevitably calls up the other as its shadow companion'.[59] The quotation from Stein above enacts this imbrication of each repetition with the other, and sets this within the general paradigm of daily time. The effect of the repetition of 'day' relies not only on the similarity of the words but on the assumption that we have a sense of a 'solid archetypal model' of the 'day' (grounded). However, each time the word is deployed it is done so in a context so minutely and yet irreducibly different that any possible originary meaning or signification of the term is undermined, indicating how days are always already different from each other, and thus the 'day' becomes part of a wider ongoing process of meaning-making (ungrounded).

The temporality of dailiness emerges, then, as part of this general temporality of sameness-and-difference, where these two kinds of repetition 'call each other up'. Indeed, it is to be expected that the temporality of dailiness will have a fundamental influence on the ways in which human beings are able to conceptualise time. Peter Osborne suggests that there are three elements constitutive of chronological time: a founding event or zero point; temporal direction; and units of measurement 'derived by astronomy from the observation of cosmic intervals' – the day, month and year.[60] The day, I would argue, is particularly important in that its shorter cycle enables a more direct experience of its repetitive structure; it is more manageable to compare days with each other than months, or years. However, and most importantly, in the texts under discussion dailiness at certain points actually challenges chronology, describing a variety of different temporalities, not least where its imbrication of different kinds of repetition is exploited. Thus, to restate, daily time will be explored in this book not only where daily time is explicitly referred to, but where the kind of repetition it engenders comes into play as a way of opening out different kinds of temporality. Hence there need be no rigorous methodological distinction between texts bounded by the day – one-day novels, for example – and texts which encompass many days, although the specificity of each individual text will of course be attended to at every point. My interest here is in exploring the variety of ways in which a daily temporality informs the writing of the period, rather than separating texts *a priori* according to the temporal structure they employ.

The second aspect of an understanding of temporality particularly relevant to my discussion of daily time, and against which my argument is set, is the idea of the spatialisation of time. As we shall see in later chapters, the relationship between space and time came to be figured in the modernist period as something of a conflict, not least in Henri Bergson's critique of the spatialisation of time in conventional thought, and Wyndham Lewis's subsequent attack in *Time and Western Man* on Bergson's influence on the 'time-based' literature of Joyce and Stein, among others. Indeed, Michael Bell describes the importance of the 'development of spatialized rather than chronological structures' in modernist writers such as Yeats, Joyce, Lawrence and Mann.[61] To this list we might add Richardson: Elisabeth Bronfen's recent work *Dorothy Richardson's Art of Memory: Space, Identity, Text* is one important indication of current interest in spatial tropes in Richardson's work. Woolf's spatial metaphors for the experience of time also feature heavily in Ann Banfield's *The Phantom Table: Woolf, Fry, Russell and the Epistemology of Modernism*. However, while attention to such spatial metaphors is of course crucial to understanding the elaboration of alternative temporalities, excessive attention to the spatial can tend to occlude the extent to which these writers are acutely aware of living in time, of the specific uses of time available or unavailable to them, to their characters, to humanity in general.

Surprisingly, the misogynistic Lewis's emphasis on space over time aligns him, to an extent, with a key strand in feminist thought about temporality over the last few decades. The primary text of this theoretical matrix is Julia Kristeva's essay 'Women's Time'; indeed, Toril Moi argues that 'from a feminist perspective, this is one of Kristeva's most important essays'.[62] In this essay, Kristeva remarks upon the association between women and space, rather than '*time*, becoming or history'.[63] She goes on, however, to say that 'As for time, female subjectivity would seem to provide a specific measure that essentially retains reproduction and eternity from among the multiple modalities of time known through the history of civilizations';[64] or, as Moi puts it, 'female subjectivity would seem to be linked both to cyclical time (repetition) and to monumental time (eternity)'.[65] This is not quite the same as saying that, as Sandra Kemp has put it, in Kristeva's 'Women's Time' 'space (and the things in it) displaces the usual registration of linear time'.[66] Rather, the dominant concept of time as linear is modified by a temporality whose qualities are more closely affiliated to those of space: monumental time is 'all-encompassing and infinite *like* imaginary space' (my emphasis).[67]

I am making these distinctions to draw attention to the way in which all too often there is a reduction of Kristeva's text to a 'woman = space' equation, to the argument that women's time fundamentally means time-as-space. As a consequence, we find rather generalised statements such as, for example, 'the FMF [feminist modernist fiction] substitution of space for time';[68] Sandra Kemp's formulation here elides the complex negotiation between space and time going on in the work of Woolf, Lehmann and Richardson, the writers she discusses. Seemingly as a result of this tendency to view women's temporality as spatialised, issues of temporality and the function of temporal units have tended to be passed over in much work on female modernist writers in favour of discussion of, in particular, the spatial or the optical. Early in Banfield's *The Phantom Table*, for example, we find the footnoted apologia that 'extensive material on time in Woolf's work' has been 'omitted solely for considerations of length'.[69] Jane Marcus articulates what has come to be almost a critical commonplace where she makes the general statement that in Woolf's work 'time is defeated by space'.[70] My intention is not to propose an inversion of Marcus's statement, nor indeed am I suggesting that other critics are somehow wrong to set aside the question of the temporal, or the daily, in their own work. Rather, I wish to bring forward questions of temporality, to check the extent of time's defeat by space in work on modernism, and in feminist criticism in particular. The surprising alignment between Lewis and Kristeva bolsters my case here. If the privileging of space over time was posited by a prominent writer hardly known for his sympathetic views on women, then viewing it as a feminist gesture becomes problematic. This is particularly so given that Lewis was a contemporary of the writers I discuss. It would thus be difficult to sustain the argument that the privileging of space was part of a liberating discourse for women in the early twentieth century without failing to attend to the intellectual context of the time/space debate in modernist thought.

It is important, then, that we find a way of attending to the expression of time through spatial tropes without effacing one aspect in favour of the other. One useful way of so doing is to view the day as what Mikhail Bakhtin calls a 'chronotope'. In his introductory definition, Bakhtin says: 'We will give the name *chronotope* (literally, "time space") to the intrinsic connectedness of temporal and spatial relationships that are artistically expressed in literature.'[71] As might be expected by a somewhat elusive definition such as this – defining the chronotope rather nebulously as a 'connectedness' – the term appears to hold more than one meaning in Bakhtin's essay. On the one hand, there is the chronotope of the kind 'x world in y time' – for example, Bakhtin suggests that the chronotope of Greek romance is 'an alien world in adventure time'. Here, the chronotope appears as a structure that defines a narrative (indeed a genre) as a whole. Elsewhere, however, Bakhtin suggests that the chronotope can also designate a characteristic motif that occurs *within* a narrative: he indicates the chronotope of the road, the meeting, the threshold, and so on, motifs where time and space are indeed intrinsically connected. I want to make use of the concept in the second sense given here, as something that occurs within the narrative but which 'emerges as a center for concretizing representation, as a force giving body to the entire novel'.[72]

Bakhtin argues that the chronotope enables 'the showing forth, the representability of events [. . .] thanks precisely to the special increase in density and concreteness of time markers [. . .] that occurs within well-delineated spatial areas'.[73] Literally speaking, the road has no temporal aspects – it is fundamentally a spatial category, just as the day is fundamentally a temporal one. However, the concept of the road as Bakhtin presents it does involve temporal inflection – this is what makes it a chronotope – since Bakhtin uses the term to imply not just the road as physical object but the progress made along it, which must happen in time. Jean Radford draws attention to this implication in her book on *Pilgrimage*, prefacing a quotation from Bakhtin by describing 'the chronotope of the road (*or journey*)' (my emphasis).[74] Thus, in an inversion of Bakhtin's model, I will argue that the day, as Richardson and others present it, also involves comprehension of its spatial aspects. The day, as 'artistically expressed in literature',[75] takes on a variety of spatial characteristics as a subject exists in it, just as the road-as-journey takes on its temporal dimension from the movement of a subject along it. It is the interrelation between the human subject, having both spatial and temporal dimensions, and the temporal unit of the day, that will interest me in what follows.

It might seem paradoxical that the texts I have chosen appear to diverge strongly from the idea of the everyday specifically in terms of literary style;

they are by no means the most accessible works written in the period. But if, with Highmore, we agree that the everyday can be understood as a 'form of attention that attempts to animate the heterogeneity of social life, the name for an activity of finding meaning in an impossible diversity',[76] then the importance of the wide variety of literary styles, of forms of attention, represented by the texts I discuss, is made clear. My approach mirroring that of my theme, the meanings I find will resonate widely among the 'impossible diversity' of literature, but will also be absolutely unique to each text, attempting indeed to pay attention to the specific qualities of each, to 'animate the heterogeneity' of literature. But what the texts I address have in common is that they all attend to the shifting and multiple temporalities of the human subject, to the complexity of psychic processes and levels of attentiveness which comprise the everyday, and specifically that they enact this in their language and linguistic formulations.

Ben Highmore draws attention to the importance of 'making strange' in explorations of the everyday, since if the everyday is that which is usually taken for granted, we need to shift our perspective in order to detect it[77] – how can we make the everyday visible through everyday language? Or, as Lefebvre puts it, 'What we want to demonstrate is the fallacy of judging a society according to its own standards, because its categories are part of its publicity' (*ELMW* 71). Thus the critique of everyday life in which the texts under discussion participate consists in large part precisely in their critique of everyday language, and involves the reader in actually experiencing that critique, questioning society's standards, through their own everyday practice of reading. As Highmore has put it, 'the everyday might benefit from the attention of purposefully inappropriate forms of representation. Or rather, the everyday might be more productively glimpsed if the propriety of discourses is refused.'[78] Indeed, one of the ways of characterising modernism is precisely that it reacts against nineteenth-century notions of propriety, both in terms of the subject matter it addresses and, crucially, through the challenge it presents to the idea that there are certain naturalistic, 'realist' discourses 'proper' to literature.

Following my two-strand approach to dailiness, I begin in my first chapter by looking at some of the ways in which both the temporal unit of the day, and everyday practices or modes of attention, function in the writing of the psychologists Henri Bergson and William James. I focus on James's *Psychology* of 1892, and Bergson's three major works *Time and Free Will* (1910), *Creative Evolution* (1911) and *Matter and Memory* (1919). Not only have these writers been directly influential, or seen as influential, on some of the literary figures I go on to discuss, but their texts themselves to a certain extent constitute documents of modernist dailiness. In this chapter I suggest how the models of the psyche being developed by these thinkers are inflected through their understanding both of daily time, and of everyday life. I also take the opportunity to elaborate the concept of attention, drawing on recent work by Jonathan Crary, as a term whose significations in this period intersect crucially with my question of what constitutes dailiness.

My second chapter is a detailed analysis of Dorothy Richardson's thirteen-volume novel *Pilgrimage*, published over several decades from 1915 onwards. I begin by exploring how the chronotope of the day features in the novel, the various ways in which the day is figured and the kind of temporality, or rather temporalities, Richardson's text elaborates. I then go on to a related exploration of the working day in Richardson's text, opening the discussion out onto broader questions of the relationship between work and leisure, and ultimately between work and writing. These issues are crucial not only in terms of the social context of rapid changes in working practices, including the increased employment of women, but also because of Richardson's particularly complex relationship to her own writing – as work or leisure, vocation or burden. The question of the kind of activity writing constitutes, its particular temporality, and how a life in which writing features prominently might refigure the idea of everyday life, runs throughout this book, and is central to my chapter on Woolf.

My third chapter takes the issues of work and its relationship to the everyday through two texts by Gertrude Stein, 'Melanctha' and *Tender Buttons*. These texts, while published within only a few years of each other (1909 and 1914 respectively), are written in dramatically contrasting styles, and therefore enable me to do some justice to the wide range of Stein's work. These contrasting styles, different kinds of agrammaticality, reveal the contiguity of linguistic disruption with a challenge to models of work, recreation, and the everyday. My discussion of 'Melanctha' traces a 'wandering' or 'recreational' temporality through not only the figure of Melanctha herself but also through the text's narrative technique. The idea of 'recreation' is also taken through a discussion of the 'recreation of the word' in *Tender Buttons*, and comes to rest on the question of the kind of work, or recreation, the process of reading might itself constitute.

The effect of an experimental literary style in a reworking of temporality is the central focus of Chapter 4, on the representation of war temporality in H.D.'s autobiographical narratives *Her*, *Asphodel*, *Bid Me To Live* and *Paint It Today* (written during the 1920s and 1930s; the first of these to be published was *Bid Me To Live*, in 1960, the year of H.D.'s death). Models of trauma are discussed in order to explore the ways in which H.D.'s narratives express the acute disruption to everyday life effected by the First World War, against the background of the kind of dailiness set up in H.D.'s narratives of the pre-war period; indeed, here I suggest that the temporal structure of dailiness is itself revealed to be contiguous with that of trauma.

Finally, in Chapter 5, I focus on the intersection between the everyday practices of reading, writing and thinking in Woolf's novels. Beginning with an exploration of the relationship between oscillation and dailiness, I go on to show how the complex functioning of memory and repetition in Woolf draws the structure and temporality of reading into the matrix of dailiness suggested by the one-day novel and its concerns, focusing on *Mrs Dalloway* as exemplary text. I work these observations into a further elaboration of a temporality of dailiness with which the everyday practices of reading, writing and thinking are intimately connected, focusing on *The Waves* (1931), *Orlando* (1928) and the essay 'Reading' (1919). In so doing, I indicate how Woolf's texts suggest to us a daily life that takes account of, values and recognises these practices, and, more broadly, where recognition of the value of time in all its variety is central.

CHAPTER I

The contemporary context:
Henri Bergson and William James

INTRODUCTION: DAILINESS AT THE TURN OF THE CENTURY

What is now one of the canonical texts of literary modernism – in particular that strand of modernism that addresses questions of temporality and memory – takes as its foundational event the ineffable moment between sleeping and waking. Proust's lengthy description of the anxious reassembling of self that takes place upon waking, which opens *A la recherche du temps perdu*, draws attention not only to the increasingly prominent question at the time of what constitutes the individual human subject, but also works with the effects of both the normal succession of, and the disruption to, diurnal patterns, day following night following day. The moment of waking, both utterly familiar and deeply mysterious, is used in a similar way by the turn-of-the-century psychologist William James. In his key textbook of the emerging discipline of psychology, the *Psychology: Briefer Course* on which my observations in this chapter are based, James illustrates the way in which we recognise and construct the self as a unity, evoking the fundamental familiarity of the self: 'Each of us when he awakens says, Here's the same old Me again, just as he says, Here's the same old bed, the same old room, the same old world' (*Psy* 215). The unity of the self is demonstrated by the sameness that characterises the dawning of each new day.

Our recognition of sameness, in a moment which is nevertheless utterly unique and unrepeatable as all moments are, contributes to an illusion of homogenous time. Breaking down this illusion was perhaps the central concern of the work of James's contemporary, the 'time-philosopher' Henri Bergson;[1] it is certainly the most important legacy Bergson has left cultural and literary studies. Bergson's insistence that 'the same moment does not occur twice' (*TFW* 200), while in some ways self-evident, is crucial to an understanding of what he was trying to achieve, in particular through his concept of 'duration', from the French *durée*, meaning no less than the

29

temporality of human consciousness.² Some sense of the same is, however –
and as Bergson acknowledges – necessary for society and indeed the individual to function (see for example *TFW* 138–9). Indeed, Bergson states
that 'our daily life is and must be an expectation of the same things and
the same situations' (*CE* 239). This sameness-and-difference of the human
experience of temporality is at its most experientially evident in the rhythms
of day and night. And it is the paradox of the daily, its qualities of sameness
and difference, simultaneity and succession, repetition and differentiation,
that make it a particularly problematic, and revelatory, temporal category.

At the turn of the last century, when psychology was disengaging itself as
a discipline from philosophy and medicine, the concept of time as potentially fluid, emerging from within the human mind rather than fixed in
the external world, began to gain ground. As Jonathan Crary notes, late
nineteenth-century physiology and psychology saw a disintegration of the
distinction between the internal and the external, implying a problematisation of the very idea of objective time.³ This stands in stark contrast to some
of the political developments of the period, most importantly the establishment of Greenwich Mean Time in 1884 which indicated global interest in
establishing an objective, measurable system of timekeeping, primarily to
facilitate the expansion of travel and communications systems. Yet despite
such public-minded developments, the single most important shift in how
time was imagined in this period was, as Stephen Kern puts it, 'the affirmation of the reality of private time',⁴ which privacy is most fundamentally
located in the individual subject.

As discussed in my Introduction, the idea of the unique moment has
been seen as central to the development of a modernist aesthetic. Among the
earliest writers in this tradition was Walter Pater, whose then highly contro-
versial emphasis on 'the moment' is crucially bound up with this question
of what might constitute the present experience of the private individual,
their 'private time'. His 'moment', as glossed by Wolfgang Iser in his commentary on Pater's *Marius the Epicurean*, 'is like a single atom within and
subordinate to the flow of time'.⁵ The paradox of 'the present', with which
thinkers since Augustine have struggled, is here addressed not by dismissing
the present as an illusion, always in the past as soon as it is identified, nor by
privileging it as that from which past and future unfold in either direction.
But by attempting both to identify the present moment and to locate it in
a strict and constantly progressing chronological sequence, Pater's moment
is in danger of becoming impotent: it 'does not even have a potential power
to give form to anything'. Where Iser suggests that 'passivity and enjoyment are the only suitable modes of conduct' through which to exploit

'the moment',[6] his formulation encapsulates the double-bind of the Paterian moment: pleasurable, certainly, but with that pleasure instantaneously extinguished by the moment's transience; and enjoyable only in a form of 'conduct', that is, passivity, which is no conduct at all. Pater's emphasis on present pleasure, famously arguing that '[n]ot the fruit of experience, but experience itself, is the end', that 'to maintain this ecstasy, is success in life',[7] supports Kern's thesis of a shifting emphasis from the public to the private. Public life demands a suspension of this impulse constantly to yield to one's present and passing pleasures; the capitalist and imperialist systems demand deferment of gratification, involving present hardship with the promise (or at least suggestion) of future reward. The anxious denouncing of Pater's arguments by establishment figures indicates the potential programme for subversion contained within his texts.

However, Pater's emphasis on present pleasure runs alongside an anxiety about the isolation that is part of the experience of the moment. The 'Conclusion' to *The Renaissance* describes how dwelling on 'the inward world of thought and feeling' draws us into the 'narrow chamber of the individual mind', 'ringed round for each one of us by that thick wall of personality'.[8] This gloomy image of dungeon-like confinement is in contrast to the effervescent pleasure that, Pater indicates, the moment may bring. Thus there is tension in Pater's moment between the opportunity to valorise the individual and transient private world, and the danger that this is unacceptably closed off to collective experience. Pater's language implies a desire to produce an alternative model of social interaction which emphasises 'experience itself', but enables this to be shared. We will see, in the work of Dorothy Richardson and, in particular, Gertrude Stein, that it is precisely this combination of the unique, individual, and transient, with the collective and indeed productive, that everyday life is able to offer. Indeed, '[n]ot the fruit of experience, but experience itself' could be used to describe Stein's rejection of an ends-driven aesthetic and, by implication, an ends-driven politics. Thus, while the temporality of dailiness is posited as an alternative modernist temporality to the Paterian moment, the sociocultural aspect of dailiness, the everyday, is, rather, contiguous with Pater's emphasis on means, experience and processes.

While by no means all writers of this period will agree with Pater's emphasis on pure pleasure – James, for example, has an explicit ethic of work and efficiency at the centre of his psychology – his 'moment' is a provocative example of widespread attempts to engage with the problem of the present. Indeed, one familiar definition of 'modernity' is precisely that it focuses on the absolutely new – that is, the present, now.[9] However, Pater's moment is trapped (as his language seems to acknowledge) in a passivity which other thinkers would not accept. Woolf is only one writer who invests the present moment with greater potential to cut across chronological boundaries. In the engagements with the daily and the everyday in the texts under discussion, we can see writers addressing the contemporary problem of the present, and in various ways attempting to offer a present whose emphasis on enjoyment of, or immersion in, the immediacy of the everyday, does not eclipse the potential for seeing the everyday as bound up with larger structures of repetition, renewal and progress. Precisely by paying attention to the way in which the present moment of the daily disrupts chronology, and in particular undermines the artificial divisions and strictures of public life, we may reveal a profounder understanding of the ways in which both individual human subjectivity and human communities are constructed and operate; an understanding not just fleetingly glimpsed in the moment of pure present pleasure, but sustained through the ongoing patterns of the daily.

BERGSON, JAMES AND THE DAILY

In this chapter, I focus on two figures whose engagement with the question of temporality, and in particular the origin of temporality within the human subject, were highly influential in shaping the intellectual climate under which the literary texts to be discussed in subsequent chapters were produced. Mark Antliff states that Henri Bergson was 'arguably the most celebrated thinker of his day', and describes the enormous interest that Bergson's theories aroused, his weekly lectures drawing 'an educated public so numerous that it spilled out of the lecture hall'.[10] Certainly, Bergson is probably the most cited theorist in discussions of theories of temporality in the early twentieth century. Specifically in the literary arena, the theories of Bergson and William James are often spoken of together as lying behind the development of the 'stream of consciousness' novel. James coined the phrase in his *Psychology* of 1890, and although writers did not always willingly accept this label – Dorothy Richardson, for example, whose *Pilgrimage* is often cited as an exemplary instance of stream-of-consciousness writing, explicitly rejected the term – the concept clearly lodged in the literary language of the period as a way of describing texts which narrate from within an individual consciousness and depict time as subjective, fluid and qualitative. Shiv K. Kumar's *Bergson and the Stream of Consciousness Novel* gives the most sustained examination to date of Bergsonian influence – direct or, as Kumar puts it, as part of a *Zeitgeist* – on this particular form of literary modernism. Designating the famous Bergsonian concept '*la durée*' as 'psychological time', Kumar goes on to argue that 'The new novelist accepts with full awareness inner duration against chronological time as the only true mode of apprehending aesthetic experience. Only in terms of the emergence of time as the fourth dimension can, therefore, one of the most important literary movements of this century be understood.'[11] However, James's emphasis on the primacy of the practical within the human subject provides a counterpoint to the Bergsonian concept of non-hierarchised *durée*. This is emphasised by Crary's observation that James was 'working with the more act-oriented "thought" instead of "consciousness"',[12] although, as I will go on to discuss, both terms are used in his famous coinage. The volitional aspect of James's theories is made explicit with statements such as 'My experience is what I agree to attend to' (contrasting with Pater's passive enjoyment), as well as, most famously, his statement that his first act of free will would be to believe in free will.

Together, then, Bergson and James's writings on temporality, with their various convergences and divergences, provide an important matrix for an exploration of how the concept of dailiness might emerge from the early twentieth-century literary landscape, not least because the works of these writers constitute both commentaries on, and documents of, modernism. Further, as already suggested, the concepts of the daily and the everyday appear as uniquely problematic for the philosopher. As Lefebvre indicates, philosophy and the everyday are two sides of the same coin: 'The limitations of philosophy – truth without reality – always and ever counterbalance the limitations of everyday life – reality without truth' (*ELMW* 14). The everyday is the surface which philosophy must peel aside in order to gain a more profound understanding of reality; but it is also precisely the object of its scrutiny, the foundation upon which philosophy must build. We will see precisely such a counterbalancing at play in the work of Bergson and James.

The contexts in which these writers use the actual terms 'day' and 'daily' – the ways in which the day appears as chronotope in their texts – will give us an initial indication of contemporary models of dailiness. James's psychology expressly bases itself on the experiential evidence of daily life. Defining and defending his approach to the study of this newly emerging science, James states that 'a student who lives the fulness of human nature will prefer to follow the "analytic" method, and to begin with the most concrete facts, those with which he has a daily acquaintance in his own inner life' (*Psy* 166). From what follows in James's text, from his examples of states of mind, experiences, perceptual illusions, and so on, presented as familiar, we can infer that by using the term 'daily' James is connoting the frequent, the easily recognisable and the usual. Thus 'daily' and its cognates function as normative terms; for example, the expression 'some day' is used with similar connotations, implying any time, unmarked time (*Psy* 263). Indeed, James describes 'the daily routine of life, our dressing and undressing, the coming and going from our work or carrying through of its various operations, [as] utterly without mental reference to pleasure and pain' (*Psy* 443) – in other words, unmarked.

Bergson, however, uses the term differently, in particular as a marker of the most psychologically significant interval of time. For example, 'our consciousness would soon inform us of a shortening of the day if we had not experienced the usual amount of duration between sunrise and sunset' (*TFW* 193–4); 'a feeling which lasted only half the number of days, for example, would no longer be the same feeling for [pure consciousness]' (*TFW* 196). The recurrence of expressions such as 'from day to day', or comparing the perceptions of yesterday and today, even if intended more metaphorically than literally, nevertheless draw attention to the day as the unit of time of most psychological importance, marking the interval after which we might supposedly be able to detect psychologically significant differences in our experience or perception (see for example *TFW* 130, 131). Attempts to identify psychologically significant differences or intervals at this time are exemplified in the work of Fechner and his concept of 'just noticeable difference'.[13] This 'just noticeable difference' forms part of a continuum with the interval of the day; the day appears in Bergson's text as the most useful way of communicating the concept of detectable differences.

Even in Bergson's metaphorical expression 'biologists are not agreed on what is gained and what is lost between the day of birth and the day of death' (*CE* 18), a further important aspect of the meaning of 'the day' is evoked. This particular phrase echoes Ecclesiastes 7:1, 'A good name is better than precious ointment, the day of death than the day of one's birth', and thus biblical resonances with the 'day of judgement' come into play. This last concept, so powerful in Western Christian culture, associates the phrase 'the day' with mystery, that which is beyond human understanding. If we recall here Miller's elaboration of the mutual imbrication of grounded and ungrounded repetition, we might note that Bergson's ungrounded repetition of the day throughout his writing in different contexts also draws on the kind of grounded repetition we see in his metaphorical use of the term; that is, where the term 'day' has resonances of originary meaning, in Christian theology. This example of both grounded and ungrounded repetition reminds us of the uncanny status of the term 'day', signifying both the familiar temporality of human existence and, as in the day of judgement, that which brings the overthrow of human temporality. Throughout his texts, Bergson's use of terms connected with dailiness (*'aujourd'hui'*, *'du jour au lendemain'*, *'la journée'*) suggest ways in which we should return to James's unmarked 'day' and interrogate its apparently entirely neutral, normative function, addressing it as a temporal unit whose significance is worth investigating further.[14]

DAYDREAM

While James states his reliance on the 'concrete facts' of our 'daily acquaintance' for the development of his psychology, he also posits a hierarchy of kinds of human activity where dailiness is subordinate: 'The more of the details of our daily life we can hand over to the effortless custody of automatism, the more our higher powers of mind will be set free for their own proper work' (*Psy* 160). By implication, 'the details of our daily life' are distinct from, and less important than, 'proper work'. This distinction will be important in my exploration of the relationship between 'work' and the everyday, in later chapters on Dorothy Richardson and Gertrude Stein. To be sure, one must agree with James that a human being who had to exercise 'express volitional deliberation' in every daily activity would be 'miserable'. Nevertheless, the principle seems to remain that for James all daily activity is best placed under the control of automatic responses, and that any exercise of the 'higher powers of the mind' on these activities is ultimately a waste of energy. The details of our daily life, once they have yielded us some of the secrets of psychology, can then be left in the shadows; the everyday is no longer important.

The 'higher powers of mind' which James would release through the automatisation of everyday life are exercised most fully in the kind of attention which James describes in his characteristic vocabulary of virility, an 'effort of attention' which constitutes 'the essential phenomenon of will' (*Psy* 446–7). This seems to be clearly distinct from the more general function of attention which James sketches out elsewhere in the *Psychology*. James defines attention as a mechanism of selection: 'out of all the sensations yielded [by an organ, attention] picks out certain ones as worthy of its notice and suppresses all the rest' (*Psy* 184). There are two criteria upon which the attention makes its selection, James goes on to argue: 'first, our practical or instinctive interests; and second, our aesthetic interests' (*Psy* 365). We cannot, however, state what these interests are in themselves, says James;

presumably we can but infer their general tendencies from the objects that the attention picks out. From the references to the daily found in his writing, ('our dressing and undressing, the coming and going from our work', and so on) one can surmise that, for James, the attention characterising everyday life is one in which practical interests are at their most prominent, to the extent that these interests override all other sensation – we conduct these everyday activities 'utterly without mental reference to pleasure and pain' (*Psy* 443), or, ideally, have 'hand[ed them] over to the effortless custody of automatism' (*Psy* 160).

When the 'higher powers of the mind' are released, however, the instinctive imperative is often overridden by an effortful, volitional attention which engages with the question of long-term, often moral, benefit. The cold bath, for example, which practical attention tells us will be unpleasant, is borne in the interests of being clean; or more importantly for James, a sensual pleasure might be foregone in the interests of a greater moral good. This is attention at its most focused, most 'attentive'. At the other end of the spectrum, there is what James calls 'dispersed attention' where 'cerebral activity sinks to a minimum'. This describes a reverie into which, James suggests, 'most of us probably fall *several times a day*' (*Psy* 228, my emphasis). Further, there is at least a conventional idiomatic connection between this state of dispersed attention and the daily, for what is this state if not one of daydream? There is a distinction to be made between normative 'everyday attention', attention oriented to everyday activity, which I suggest appears in James as the practically-driven (in-)attention of habit and instinct, and kinds of attention which might simply arise daily, or 'several times a day' – as a fiat of will might do just as readily as a reverie. However, among the types of attention which cut across our everyday consciousness, James valorises these fiats above all other kinds of attention, as no less than 'the essential phenomenon of will'. For James, the effortful attention is one to which we should aspire; the 'dispersed attention' is one from which we must be rescued, again by some mysterious 'energy [. . .] something – we know not what', which enables us to get on with the activity demanded by the imperative of 'the wheels of life' (*Psy* 228).

The anxiety with which James wants us to avoid falling into periods of 'dispersed attention' is usefully illuminated by Jonathan Crary's thesis in his *Suspensions of Perception*, a study of the construction of the concept of attention in the thirty years from 1879. Crary argues that the concept of 'attention', while having been seen as part of the '"hegemony" of vision within twentieth century modernity', in fact challenges that hegemony, and that attention should be considered in temporal, over and above visual, terms.[15]

As Crary puts it, in this period 'counter-forms of attention are neither exclusively nor essentially visual but rather constituted as other *temporalities* and cognitive states, such as those in trance or reverie' (my emphasis).[16] 'Attention', then, describes not simply an individual's visual relationship to an object or task, but the temporality in which the relationship is sustained. This observation is crucial to my shifting of perspective from emphasis on the spatial and visual in modernist literature toward the temporal. Crary argues that '[d]uring the period I am examining, attentiveness was generally synonymous with an observer who was fully embodied and for whom perception coincided with physiological and/or motor activity'.[17] The privileged form of attentiveness thus defined, that to which the efficient subject should aspire, is a state of mind focused on an end outside itself – specifically for Crary here, on the external physical world, although also in Jamesian terms on a wider moral good. The parallels between this kind of focused, externalised attentiveness and the characteristics of work, which as I will go on to discuss, is at the centre of James's pragmatism, are evident; both involve the explicit aim, expenditure of energy and quantitative measurement conventionally associated with a normative understanding of work. But Crary's thesis makes it clear that in this kind of attentiveness, temporality is also externalised, generated and imposed on the individual according to the demands of the task and its objective. As Crary puts it, the strategy of privileging this kind of attentiveness makes individuals 'isolated, separated, and *inhabit time* as disempowered' (my emphasis).[18] As capitalist economic structures increase their rigor and intricacy throughout the late nineteenth and early twentieth century, so this strategy of divide and rule even in terms of the individual's experience of time will become further entrenched. Throughout the readings of literary texts that follow, this understanding of attention as a temporal category will be crucial.

Crary's critique of models of attention extends to an interrogation of the relationship between attention and distraction, a relationship around which much is at stake in the emerging psychology and sociology of the period. One particular state of 'dispersed attention', of daydream, is of particular interest in this regard since it explicitly marks the point at which the privileged attitude of attention apparently dissolves into its opposite, distraction, a condition seen as negative or even dangerous: Max Nordau linked a state of inattention with sociopathic behaviour.[19] Even well into the century, T. S. Eliot would have 'strained time-ridden faces / Distracted from distraction by distraction / Filled with fancies and empty of meaning' in his *Burnt Norton* of 1936, the first of the *Four Quartets*.[20] There is clear continuity between Nordau's sociopathic distraction and Eliot's 'apath[etic]', 'unwholesome' and 'unhealthy' metropolitan subjects, trapped in a vicious circle of distraction.[21] However, Crary has argued that the privileged state of attention is by no means as stable as theorists such as James and Nordau would have it. Drawing on nineteenth-century physiology and psychology as well as analysis of certain Impressionist and post-Impressionist paintings, Crary argues that attempts to produce attention actually create distraction; there is a flow from one to the other. The dispersed focus, slippages of perspective and play of gazes in the painting of Manet, Seurat and Cézanne, Crary suggests, show that 'looking at any one thing intently did *not* lead to a fuller and more inclusive grasp of its presence, its rich immediacy', but rather its perceptual disintegration, and breakdown as intelligible form.[22]

We see something like this 'breakdown' in Bergson's account of a state that seems analogous to James's 'dispersed attention'. It is detached, dreamlike, and consists of a relaxation or indeed 'scattering' of attention (*CE* 211). Both states are described in terms of passivity: 'withdraw' (Bergson), 'surrender' (James), even 'deficiency' (Bergson). Admittedly, Bergson seems to require an initial effort, if only paradoxically to 'relax my attention', in order to get into this state, whereas James's 'fit' appears as something that comes over one involuntarily – for Bergson, one apparently has to pay attention in order to produce distraction. However, the resultant state appears similar in both authors. The relationship of this state to one's consciousness, however, is read by each as rather different. For James, it is a state that fuses everything together, 'the sounds of the world melt into a confused unity, the attention is dispersed so that the whole body is felt, as it were, at once' (*Psy* 228). For Bergson, however, a relaxation of attention results in an increasing differentiation in the sensations presented to him: 'In proportion as I let myself go, the successive sounds [of a poem being read] will become the more individualised; as the phrases were broken into words, so the words will scan in syllables which I shall perceive one after another' (*CE* 220–1), just as the marks on the canvas in pointillist and post-Impressionist painting are individually visible, drawing attention to the elements which make up the visual whole. And, for Bergson as for James, we are in this state of mind explicitly at the other end of the spectrum from the active fiat: 'this complexity and extension represent nothing positive; they express a deficiency of will' (*CE* 221).

'The daydream, which is an integral part of a continuum of attention', Crary argues, 'has always been a crucial but indeterminate part of the politics of everyday life'.[23] It is literally a site of resistance to imperatives of efficiency and productivity – we might compare it with de Certeau's description of *la perruque*, the 'stealing' of time and materials from the workplace. But it is also the state in which the flowing of attention into distraction becomes clearest – and paradoxically, the dispersal it entails involves us in a kind of attention, whether to differentiated sensations as described by Bergson, or to the world as 'a confused unity' as described by James. There is the potential for this state of daydream, of reverie, to reveal something of the materiality of the symbols which make up the world around us, the sound and shape of individual words and letters; or on the other hand, to reveal the capacity of apparently distinct elements to blend with each other into a whole.

It is not, then, that this state of relaxed attention to which Bergson refers actually involves us in a closer experience of our internal duration. On the contrary, in this state Bergson sees a distancing from duration, a lapse (as he would see it) into the differentiated, homogenous, spatialised external world. Nevertheless the potential reorientation of consciousness toward language which it effects is a suggestive one for readers of modernist writing, with its frequent attention to the materiality of language and suspicion of its purported transparency. James draws explicit attention to the selectivity of the way we conventionally regard language: 'We ought to say a feeling of *and*, a feeling of *if*, a feeling of *but*, and a feeling of *by*, quite as readily as we say a feeling of *blue* or a feeling of *cold*. Yet we do not, so inveterate has our habit become of recognizing the existence of the substantive parts alone, that language almost refuses to lend itself to any other use' (*Psy* 176). Challenges to that refusal are articulated by writers such as H.D. ('What was "now" and what was "doing" and what was "what" precisely?' [*H* 54]), and Stein whose 'word heap' poetry removes the hierarchy of grammar and lays equal emphasis on each individual word, syllable or even letter.

It turns out, then, that this state of daydream enables us to perceive that which we conventionally take for granted – for example, the materiality of the signs which make up the world. It can render opaque, 'visible', the conventionally transparent; although we must be wary of falling into a language of visibility which, as Crary has argued, is problematically privileged. Here is one way, then, in which an aspect of 'everyday' attention, one conventionally dismissed as passive, unproductive, and probably effeminate, might rather constitute an opportunity for an enriching of experience. All the writers I go on to discuss represent and investigate varieties of reverie, or dispersed attention, whether describing its effect on an individual human subject, or producing texts which themselves reflect, even perhaps induce, such a mode of attention. Daydream, dispersed attention, appears in their work as well as in that of James and Bergson as an alternative modernist temporality to the disruptive moment of Pater, Heidegger, Benjamin *et al.*

A discussion of daydream is incomplete without consideration of its gender inflection. In particular, the association of the state of reverie or daydream with women shows how women's perceived lack of mental power, or at least their susceptibility to its attenuation, was essentialised as part of their physiological makeup, and reinforced through an aestheticisation of the daydreaming woman. Freud and Breuer's Anna O., a young woman who, at night, falls into trancelike states during which she elaborately narrates hallucinations she experienced during the day, provides (literally) a case study of the relationship between femininity (and feminine adolescence in particular), reverie or trance, and creativity.[24] Mary Jacobus addresses this intersection in her exploration of Berthe Morisot's portraits of her daughter, which she argues both draw on and challenge assumptions around daydream.[25] Morisot's painting of her daughter in conventionally feminine reverie is compared with Charcot's visual taxonomy of the hysteric; his photographs (often, unbeknown to Charcot, staged and rehearsed) of hysterical women in various states of reverie or trance provide evidence of the entrenchment of the association between women, daydream, the distracted gaze, and passivity, as well as bolstering this association. Morisot's painting, by contrast, attempts to represent the potential for self-containment and control also implied by the state of reverie. The state of 'feminine indeterminacy' in which Morisot figures her daughter, even the hint of auto-eroticism to which Jacobus draws our attention, ensure that the agency in this painting is kept within the realm of the female, although perhaps in a maternal-filial circuit between Morisot and her daughter. As Jacobus puts it, drawing our attention to the potential for aesthetic creativity found when women make interventions into the visual field created for them by the patriarchal: 'This is a portrait in which the maternal *créatrice* finds herself by losing herself in the unfixity of adolescence.'[26] Reverie, then, is not only an everyday temporality which evades the quantifiable, the masculine and the public, but also one where generational divisions can be bridged.

It is worth returning, in conclusion, to Crary's argument that 'spectacular culture is not founded on the necessity of making a subject *see*, but rather on strategies in which individuals are isolated, separated, and inhabit time as disempowered'.[27] The connection between temporality and power is crucial, and the contiguity between the visual, the temporal, and distribution of power and agency at this period can be most readily detected around questions of gender. The gender of the four writers I discuss in the following chapters is of importance in this regard; women were simply more likely to be 'disempowered' than men, then as now. That these writers seem particularly interested in the representation of 'dispersed states of attention' needs, then, to be seen in the context of the association, which is not just contingent, between daydream and femininity. Nevertheless, as this discussion of the state of reverie has shown, this is not solely an issue for women writers; for Bergson and James too, the state of reverie is a particularly fraught and revelatory phenomenon. While presented as undesirable, particularly by James, this 'everyday', banal, useless state is in fact revealed as one in which productive kinds of attention, alternative relationships – even perhaps more empowered relationships – to time, can emerge.

BOREDOM AND IMPATIENCE

'Boredom is the everyday become manifest.'[28]

Both boredom and impatience are states of consciousness that, as described by Bergson and James, function in a similar way to that of the 'daydream' state described above; that is, while these states are conventionally regarded as impotent, Bergson's and James's writing reveals their potential. Indeed, for Bergson, it is impatience that reveals no less than the elusive 'duration' in its absolute form, in consciousness, and he uses a thoroughly everyday example of waiting for sugar to 'melt' in a glass of water. Physics and mathematics may reduce units of time to relationships, to ratios; for the individual human subject, however, watching the sugar in the glass, the time he or she must wait cannot be thus reduced: 'I must, willy-nilly, wait until the sugar melts' (*CE* 10). The period of time which it takes for the sugar to melt, says Bergson, 'coincides with my impatience, that is to say, with a certain portion of my own duration, which I cannot protract or contract as I like. It is no longer something *thought*, it is something *lived*' (*CE* 10).

This last distinction is crucial for what follows. As the twentieth century progressed, the idea of an objective, empirical knowledge was put under more and more pressure – not least through the proliferation of psychological theories – and the relationship between thought and life (life which, as Bergson constantly asserts, is more than the intellect; see for example *CE* 55) is explored, as indeed are the varieties of thought or knowledge available to the human subject. Despite his hierarchy of mental activity, James articulates his desire to move beyond a model of consciousness as perfectible: 'It is, the reader will see, the reinstatement of the vague and inarticulate to its proper place in our mental life which I am so anxious to press on the attention' (*Psy* 179). Indeed, the inflection of the phrase wherein we find one of the most influential coinages of the twentieth century indicates the shifting ground of the relationship between thought and life. James says, in his chapter on 'The Stream of Consciousness', '*let us call it the stream of thought, of consciousness, or of subjective life*' (*Psy* 173). It is as if we can detect James's own stream of consciousness as he works his way through appropriate terms: 'thought' is the most obvious but perhaps too specific and implying too much agency; 'consciousness' too does not embrace all that he wants to convey; finally, it is no less than a stream of 'life'. Writers inspired by the concept of the stream of consciousness have more to convey than simply intellectual processes ('thought').

As we have seen, far from being a wasteful, inefficient state of consciousness, Bergson shows how our feeling of impatience is in fact a crucial window onto our own true internal temporality, our 'lived' duration. James makes a similar observation about the experience of boredom. Impatience and boredom, while by no means synonyms, not only share negative associations of the banal and the imperfect (which are themselves associations of the everyday), but also both involve a particularly heightened awareness of time. As James puts it, '*Tædium, ennui, Langweile, boredom*, are words for which, probably, every language known to man has its equivalent. It comes about whenever, from the relative emptiness of content of a tract of time, we grow attentive to the passage of the time itself' (*Psy* 291). In James's psychic value-system, 'the *odiousness* of the whole experience comes from its insipidity; for *stimulation* is the indispensable requisite for pleasure, and the feeling of bare time is the least stimulating experience we can have' (*Psy* 291). Texts which engage with everyday experiences attempt to represent this commonplace experience of boredom, 'the feeling of bare time', questioning how 'bare' this time can be. The discussion of *Orlando* in Chapter 5 will be particularly pertinent here; Orlando's biographer is frustrated – indeed, bored, impatient – at being required in their conventional biographer's role to depict what is apparently bare time, and becomes distracted by external events, but on returning to Orlando, he or she finds that much has been happening – something is in fact '"Done!"'. That Orlando has been 'sitting in a chair and thinking', a model of apparent inertia, does not mean that the time spent in this activity is bare. Further, the biographer's own boredom and impatience has itself yielded a short, albeit ultimately bathetic, expedition into nature in pursuit of nothing less than 'Life, Life, Life!' (*O* 189).

I want to suggest a refiguring of boredom and impatience, *per* Bergson, as modes of attention which open the self onto itself, demonstrating to the subject its own subjectivity formed through the absolute duration of human consciousness. Siegfried Kracauer, writing in the Weimar Germany of the 1920s, makes precisely this suggestion. In a highly modern city such as Berlin, whose inhabitants are constantly diverted by advertisements, the movies, and the radio, Kracauer advocates an 'extraordinary, radical boredom that might be able to reunite them with their heads'.[29] If sufficiently bored, Kracauer argues, then 'Eventually one becomes content to do nothing more than be with oneself, without knowing what one actually should be doing' – the escape from the social prescriptions and expectations ('what one actually *should* be doing') is implicit.[30] And yet, once more, we note the paradox of this kind of everyday inattention, that an initial effort is required in order to reach this state of lassitude: during the leisure hours allocated him, the urbanite 'would have the opportunity to *rouse* himself into real boredom' (my emphasis).[31] Just as Kracauer elsewhere laments that the distraction offered by the movies is constantly masked by attempts to present the entertainments as 'organic creations' – as unities – rather than giving an audience an honest encounter with fragmented reality, so distraction and attention constantly slide the one into the other, radically undermining concepts of the peripheral and the central, the genuine and the inauthentic.[32] Attempts to isolate attention force the individual to 'inhabit time as disempowered', as Crary has it, to disguise from the individual their own duration, and rather appropriate the time that they have available, requiring it to be 'spent' in certain socially sanctioned ways. States of boredom, impatience and reverie reveal to the individual the passage of time as something which they do not merely 'inhabit', but that unfolds with the unfolding of their own subjectivity, wherein one can 'do nothing more than be with oneself'. Further, these states arise in situations which, by definition, are not privileged or valorised – which are 'everyday'. If, as Blanchot has it, 'boredom is the everyday become manifest', and what is manifested in boredom is nothing less than one's own subjectivity, then what we are left with is the absolute necessity of attending to the everyday as that in which we are, and are most with, ourselves.

HABIT

Like James, Bergson uses the dawning of the day as the exemplary instance of daily routine. However, rather than using it to illustrate how the subject recognises himself ('the same old Me again'), he suggests that as the hour strikes and we rise, 'the act follows the impression without the self interfering with it' (*TFW* 168). So habitual, so automatic, has this conjunction of impression and action become, that the self is in fact bypassed. Admittedly, James is referring to what happens when we *wake* up rather than *get* up, when we initially regain consciousness rather than when we perform our first action of the day. Nevertheless, the use to which each writer puts this example of the human subject at break of day indicates the differences between them, particularly as regards habit, a concept familiarly associated with, or even defining, everyday life. For James, the example confirms subjectivity; for Bergson, it bypasses it. Unlike James, who would encourage the automatisation of the daily, Bergson laments the fact that we perform 'the majority of our daily actions' as 'conscious automat[a]' (*TFW* 168). Bergson's language emphasises the negative light in which he regards these habitual activities; the word 'automaton' goes against the human desire to regard oneself as self-determining and in control of one's actions. Bergson goes on to describe how our habitual ideas and associations form a 'crust' over our ego and it is through 'sluggishness or indolence' that we allow such habits to govern our activity, believing that we are acting freely when in fact we are in thrall to the artificial external outline of ourselves and our feelings that has been built up by habit.

Bergson's 'crust' bears comparison with other foundational modernist models of the subject. For example, there is a parallel in Freud's 'protective shield', which permeable layer prevents our impermeable neurones (our memory) from being constantly submitted to excitations.[33] Although Bergson locates memory in the crust formed by habit, whereas Freud locates it in the neurones beneath, the parallel obtains since in both cases a 'dead' exterior, no longer subject to change but permanently fixed in the facilitation of certain pathways (which form Bergson's 'habit'), effectively controls what the inner organism, the ego or consciousness, receives and processes. However, for Freud, this is a necessary, indeed universal, fact of psychic development; for Bergson, this 'crust' appears as an unfortunate epiphenomenon of human social interaction. Similarly, Simmel describes the specifically modern individual as one for whom the external has come to dominate over the internal: 'Punctuality, calculability, exactness are forced upon life by the complexity and extension of modern existence', and these demands 'favour the exclusion of those irrational, instinctive, sovereign traits and impulses which aim at determining the mode of life from within'.[34] Habit here appears once again as something negative, imposed on the 'sovereign' individual from outside. In the literary texts I address, a perspective on habit, whether negative or positive, as externally imposed (in the metropolitan sections of *Pilgrimage*), or projected from within as a defence mechanism (in the psychoanalytically informed *Bid Me To Live*), frequently inflects these writers' depiction of daily life.

For Bergson, then, habit is predominantly negative. And yet, although throughout *Time and Free Will* Bergson argues that the spatialisation of time and the concomitant 'crystalliz[ation]' of our conscious states in this outer crust of habit suppresses the true duration of our consciousness and thereby occludes our capacity for free will, he does acknowledge that such processes are fundamentally connected with 'the convenience of language and the promotion of social relations' (*TFW* 167). There are practical reasons for suppressing duration; practical reasons which facilitate human communication and interaction. Thus, the practical imperative of the everyday would seem to place it in an oppositional position to Bergson's whole project of revealing duration: far from encouraging absorption in the everyday, Bergson would ask us to break free from it, free from the practical demands of, as Simmel puts it, 'punctuality, calculability, exactness'. Yet we have seen that there are states of mind, of attention, that might be considered everyday, and yet which do not appear to follow directly these practical imperatives – the states of boredom, impatience and daydream. Here, the ambivalent relationship between the everyday and philosophy emerges once more. Bergson states at the end of *Creative Evolution* what his readers might have suspected all along, that the knowledge Bergson seeks, one lodged in duration, 'will be practically useless' even if it is possible, 'but, if it succeeds, it is reality itself that it will hold in a firm and final embrace' (*CE* 362). However, if we examine Bergson's text more closely, we find that the 'practical' is described alongside the 'exten[sion of] our empire over nature', and connected to 'certain natural aspirations of the intellect' (*CE* 362). As we explore the ways in which the everyday is figured in the work of Bergson and James themselves, as well as the writers addressed in later chapters, we find that, rather than representing the dominance of the intellect, everyday life precisely reflects the operation of more than one kind of knowledge. What is practical does not necessarily, as Bergson seems to suggest, mean what is intellectually aspirational and acquisitory, or what complies with the strictures of 'punctuality, calculability, exactness'. As Lefebvre and de Certeau help us to realise, and as my later chapters will show, everyday life finds ways of evading these strictures, of exploring the alternatives to the naturalised ideology of aspiration, of domination – of empire-building, be it intellectual or material.

PRACTICALITY, LANGUAGE AND ATTENTION

Bergson continually reminds us that the externalising of our thoughts into language is both a symptom and a cause of the suppression of duration. For example, Bergson observes that a flavour found pleasant as a child may be disliked in adulthood, and that such an alteration is generally attributed to a change in our taste rather than a change in the sensation itself. However, Bergson suggests, 'What I ought to say is that every sensation is altered by repetition, and that if it does not seem to me to change from day to day, it is because I perceive it through the object which is its cause, through the word which translates it' (*TFW* 131; see also *TFW* 128, *CE* 134). This relationship between repetition and duration is crucial; it is differentiation through repetition which makes the reality of duration apparent. However, in Bergson's view, language tends to occlude this differentiation: 'the rough and ready word', in particular when it is used as a name, 'overwhelms or at least covers over the delicate and fugitive impressions of our individual consciousness'; 'A moment ago each of them [elements of a strong feeling] was borrowing an indefinable colour from its surroundings: now we have it colourless, and ready to accept a name' (*TFW* 132). What we will see in the chapters which follow are the ways in which writers attempt to use language to reveal, rather than occlude, these 'delicate and fugitive impressions' yielded in the repetition-and-duration of daily life.

James regards language in a similar way, as rendering fixed and external our constantly changing conscious state, and again, the name is the greatest culprit: 'We think of the amount [of time] we mean either solely as a *name*, or by running over a few salient *dates* therein, with no pretence of imagining the full durations that lie between them' (*Psy* 290).[35] But it is not only in language specifically referring to time that naming distorts experience, externalising, dividing and reifying the '*moving continuity*' of life, as Bergson has it (*MM* 260). James describes our habitual insistence on a singular quality as defining a particular object, arguing that in dividing the characteristics of an object into those that are essential and those that are merely accidental 'he is himself merely insisting on an aspect of the thing which suits his own petty purpose, that of *naming* the thing' (*Psy* 359). This is amplified in a footnote where James argues against the 'Popular Science' view that 'water is H-O-H more deeply and truly than it is a solvent of sugar or a slaker of thirst. Not a whit! It is *all* of these things with equal reality' (*Psy* 359). James goes on, as is often the case, to produce an instance of such a 'petty purpose' in the moral realm; in the face of a conflict between impulse and what James calls 'the right conception of the case', the intellect is driven 'to find for the emergency *names* by the help of which the dispositions of the moment may sound sanctified, and sloth or passion may reign unchecked' (*Psy* 449, my emphasis).

James indicates how the search for a name arises at a moment of crisis, when conflict with regard to a practice or object comes about. By contrast, the way in which we attend to objects or sensations in everyday life, that is, 'ordinary and even indifferent' life, actually bypasses naming, according to Bergson (*TFW* 170). 'To recognise a common object', Bergson states, 'is mainly to know how to use it' (*MM* 111). Our perception is entirely attendant on 'possibilities of action'; 'the visible outlines of bodies are the design of our eventual action on them' (*CE* 102), or again, 'the question is whether certain conditions, which we usually regard as fundamental, do not rather concern the use to be made of things, the practical advantage to be drawn from them, far more that the pure knowledge which we can have of them' (*MM* 244). When we interact with an object, then, it is immaterial to us, for that moment, what its name is. We do not have to say to ourselves 'paper', to take up an example which James employs, in order to attend to it in an everyday, practical fashion (*Psy* 359).

At this point we should examine more closely the relationship between these observations and the concept of 'attention'. Bergson emphasises the interactive quality of the everyday when he says 'Our daily life is spent among objects whose very presence invites us to play a part' (*MM* 113). But in this interaction, Bergson suggests, 'we commonly act our recognition before we think it' (*MM* 113), which is another way of saying that we don't have to think 'paper' in order to start writing. So here, everyday 'attention' always involves movement of some sort or another, or the potential for movement: 'By the very constitution of our nervous system, we are beings in whom present impressions find their way to appropriate movements' (*MM* 114). However, Bergson states that attention is an adaptation of the body involving initially the inhibition of movement (*MM* 122). In order to attend to something, one must exclude all extraneous activities, a problem to which Crary refers in his description of nineteenth-century psychological experiments, which tried to address the contradiction between 'the aim of stabilizing the world in order to look at it analytically and the experience of a psychological apparatus incapable of such stability'.[36] Thus, as indicated in the section on 'Daydream' above, everyday attention would be characterised by its lack of attention. Attention would irrupt across everyday life, arresting its practical movement, when we came across an object which we could not simply 'recognise', as opposed to those 'perceptions that are dissipated as soon as received, those which we disperse in useful actions', in everyday actions (*MM* 124). Again, it is in the realm of the everyday that the slippage between socially sanctioned attention and supposedly malign distraction is apparent; according to the Bergsonian model, everyday 'attention' would actually seem to involve a lack of attention, failure fully to attend to an object or activity, and rather involves being distracted from some of the aspects of this object in favour of its practical ends. And yet, were we truly, fully 'distracted', we would not be able to 'play a part' in the objects of daily life. The attention of everyday life is a liminal, vacillating one, constantly adjusting, moving between attentiveness and distraction, shifting focus. Paul Valéry's comments on poetic composition are thus equally appropriate to the realm of the everyday; in order to gain control over an object (as we need to do in everyday life) it is necessary to 'forget', to lose focus.[37] Thus everyday consciousness and aesthetic consciousness, conventionally figured as mutually exclusive, have more in common with each other than such a division of psychic labour would suggest, progressing along parallel routes, both exposing the artificiality of certain binaries, such as that of attention and distraction.

If 'attention' is seen as a label attempting to bracket off a particular mode of consciousness, arresting the practical movement which everyday life demands, as Bergson seems to suggest, and if James's model of everyday activities places them, ideally, in the realm of the automatic, with attentiveness at a minimum, then the use of the expression 'everyday attention' might be considered misleading. Alternatives are, however, equally unsatisfactory. 'Everyday distraction' would imply that attentiveness has no part to play, whereas it is the constant interplay of distraction and attention that characterises the everyday. 'Everyday recognition', another possibility, would be equally misleading, as it would occlude the fact that in everyday interaction, the same thing is not recognised in the object time after time, as Bergson has explained – 'every sensation is altered by repetition' (*TFW* 131). Particularly in the context of daily rhythms, the sameness-and-difference of human experience of temporality is foregrounded. Everyday life, specifically corporeal and sensual, is where this duration is manifest – in the irritation felt at waiting for sugar to melt. The body, as 'ever advancing boundary between the future and the past', is the place where duration as 'past and present states' form an 'organic whole' (*MM* 88; *TFW* 100); as Bergson's repeated analogies with music suggest, it is through the senses that we can glimpse duration, through the irreducible materiality of everyday life.

Therefore, I will retain the term 'everyday attention', not only in order to draw on Crary's thesis regarding the strategies of temporal control implied by normative models of attention, but also since I want to emphasise the specific choices of orientation made by some of the writers I will be addressing, retaining this active aspect of the term. H.D., for example, engages with the radical difference of each moment from another, alongside the apparent repetition of certain activities – in particular the important activity of getting up in the morning. Therefore, where the expression 'everyday *attention*' is used here, it is not to be understood as implying an intellectual arrest of perception, as Bergson's definition of 'attention' would have it, or the constant exercise of James's 'higher powers of the mind'. Rather, it is to be seen as an orientation to the world which recognises material, emotional, sensual as well as cognitive aims, but which also, *per* Bergson, attends to the ongoing sameness-and-difference in the duration of psychic life – the ongoing present, rather than the exemplary moment.

IDENTITY AND THE PRESENT

James brackets our awareness of our own identity with our everyday inter-action with objects when he states that 'Yesterday's and to-day's states of consciousness have no *substantial* identity, for when one is here the other is irrevocably dead and gone. But they have a *functional* identity, for both know the same objects, and so far as the by-gone me is one of those objects, they react upon it in an identical way, greeting it and calling it *mine*' (*Psy* 214). (Once more, we notice that the interval between one day and the next is the psychologically significant one.) Hailing our by-gone self as one would a friend in the street, we pick it out as one of those objects we recognise as useful. In his famous chapter on the stream of consciousness, James describes how we recognise our own thoughts as opposed to those of others, and his choice of language emphasises the connection between the question of individual identity and the experience of the everyday. When Peter and Paul wake up in the same bed:

> [Peter] *remembers* his own states, whilst he only *conceives* Paul's. Remembrance is like direct feeling; its object is suffused with a warmth and intimacy to which no object of mere conception ever attains. This quality of warmth and intimacy and immediacy is what Peter's *present* thought also possesses for itself. So sure as this present in me, is mine, it says, so sure is anything else that comes with the same warmth and intimacy and immediacy, me and mine. (*Psy* 173)

James himself defers the question of 'what the qualities called warmth and intimacy may in themselves be [. . .] for future consideration' (*Psy* 173), and yet at no point in the *Psychology* does he return to consider it. His deferral signals a moment at which the text falls back on terms which it cannot logically justify. And, importantly, the terms he chooses to represent the mine-ness of our own thoughts ('warmth', 'intimacy') bind the concept into a discourse far removed from the rigours of philosophy – redolent of the domestic, and strongly connoting the sensual. In other words, the primary problem of psychology, that of the definition of consciousness itself, is best described in terms of corporeal familiarity, homeliness; those aspects of life associated with the everyday. These are irreducible terms which the scientific discourse of psychology cannot reincorporate into its system, and which Freud would go on to explore under the label of the uncanny.

Crucially, it is the matching of the qualities of 'warmth and intimacy and immediacy' in remembered states with those of the *present* that make them recognisable as mine. The present is of course the temporality of the everyday; everyday life is now. But there is more to everyday temporality than just its present-ness, not least because there is more to present-ness than simply 'now'. Towards the end of *Creative Evolution*, Bergson describes how our 'habitual manner of speaking [. . .] leads us to actual logical deadlocks', using the example of the phrase '"The child becomes a man"' (*CE* 329). Here Bergson exemplifies this problem through the use of language at its most 'spatialised', most solidified, that is in cliché. This expression is logically flawed since at no time can the attribute 'man' apply to the subject 'child'. To be strictly accurate, we should say '"[t]here is becoming from the child to the man"'. Then, 'becoming' is the subject, bringing to our attention the duration, the process, of consciousness; as Bergson states in the passage on changing tastes in *Time and Free Will*, 'in the human soul there are only *processes*' (*TFW* 131). Or, put another way, 'You define the present in an arbitrary manner as *that which is*, whereas the present is simply *what is being made*. Nothing *is* less than the present moment, if you understand by that the indivisible limit which divides the past from the future'; the present is 'the invisible progress of the past gnawing into the future' (*MM* 193). In explaining why the terms 'chain' or 'train' are unfit to describe what should more properly be called the 'stream' of consciousness, James uses the same grammatical structure: 'for what we hear when the thunder crashes is not thunder pure, but thunder-*breaking*-upon-silence-and-*contrasting*-with-it' (*Psy* 174, my emphases).

'Becoming', 'being made', 'gnawing', 'contrasting': the present, we might say, should not be a noun but a verb, or perhaps a gerund; there is not the present but there is presenting. However, writing that attempts to express presentness will struggle not only with the fact that language inevitably externalises, divides and spatialises duration (even using the suffix '-ing' creates another unit with its illusion of separateness), but also with the fact that, as both Bergson and James argue, the present 'consists, in large measure, in the immediate past [. . .] *Practically we perceive only the past*' (*MM* 193–4). As James has it, 'it would be difficult to find in the actual concrete consciousness of a man a feeling so limited to the present as not to have an inkling of anything that went before' (*Psy* 174), or (in more Bergsonian terminology) '*The sensible present has duration*' (*Psy* 287). This last problem, of the practical imperceptibility of the present as present, is compounded by the particular pastness of all writing; a reader is always and necessarily reading words after they have been written. Even the writer himself or herself is involved in this process. The only place in which the -ing of writing truly takes place is in the individual consciousness of the writer, and therefore it is incommunicable; writing is a compromise for the sake of practicality, to enable communication. This problem of the temporality of reading and writing will recur in subsequent chapters on Stein and, in particular, on Woolf.

INCONSISTENCY AND ASSUMPTIONS

It is fitting that, as writers whose own internal inconsistency is remarked upon, not least by themselves, Bergson and James will not provide us with a clearly defined concept of dailiness.[38] I echo James, then, as my route through 'dailiness' is picked out, by acknowledging that 'I am always unjust, always partial, always exclusive. My excuse is necessity – the necessity which my finite and practical nature lays upon me' (*Psy* 358). However, as we have seen, these writers can provide productive indications of what might be at stake in the idea of 'dailiness', what problematic regions of the relationship between the subject and time it might indicate, and to what concepts it might be related.

Inconsistency is itself one such concept. Bergson, for example, does not appear to insist on consistency with regard to that most everyday of concepts, 'common sense'. On the one hand, his description of the 'crust' that habit forms over our feelings and ideas would suggest that anything regarded simply as 'common sense' must be placed under suspicion in rigorous psychological and philosophical discourse (*TFW* 167–70). On the other hand, he sketches out an intimate relationship between philosophy and common sense. Throughout *Matter and Memory*, for example, common sense is used as a kind of full-stop to a line of argument. Bergson includes, by way of defending his definition of matter as an aggregate of images, the statement that 'this conception of matter is simply that of common sense' (*MM* viii); in arguing for the existence of spirit, he suggests 'philosophy should here adopt the attitude of common sense' (*MM* 80); defining the present as 'the very materiality of existence', he describes it as 'so evident a truth, one which is, moreover, the very idea of common sense' (*MM* 178, 179). And although Bergson does not use the concept 'common sense' actively in the process of argumentation, we go on to find in *Creative Evolution* that, outside of the domain of geometry and logic, 'pure reasoning needs to be supervised by common sense, which is an altogether different thing' (*CE* 170). However, as when James defines the sense of the present as 'warmth and intimacy and immediacy', what 'different thing' common sense might constitute is left in suspension. These are terms and concepts with which philosophy cannot rigorously engage, even define, yet they are terms and concepts upon which it relies; to quote Lefebvre once more: 'The limitations of philosophy – truth without reality – always and ever counterbalance the limitations of everyday life – reality without truth' (*ELMW* 14).

Inconsistency can also be found at the crux of the relationship between philosophy and the everyday in the form of disorder. Bergson argues that the idea of disorder plays a prominent role in the problem of the theory of knowledge itself, and the idea of disorder is borrowed by philosophy from 'daily life' (*CE* 233). We find an example of this in James where, discussing the apparently random associations of consciousness, he asks 'why, some day, walking in the street with our attention miles away from that quest, does the answer saunter into our mind as carelessly as if it had never been called for – suggested, possibly, by the flowers on the bonnet of the lady in front of us, or possibly by nothing that we can discover?' (*Psy* 263). Throughout the *Psychology*, the street scene is the location for examples of the everyday; like Baudelaire before him and the Imagists after him (among others) the *flâneur* is James's focaliser of the disorder, the incoherence, of modern experience.

The implied audience of James's text comes through most strongly at moments like this, and it is worth dwelling on since it exposes the bias implicit in certain of James's 'concrete facts' with which the reader will have 'daily acquaintance', and on which he will draw to follow the 'analytic method'. For example, James uses the example of a glimpse of the back of a woman's head on two further occasions to illustrate illusions of perception: 'Every bonnet in the street is momentarily taken by the lover to enshroud the head of his idol'; 'Twenty times a day the lover, perambulating the streets with his preoccupied fancy, will think he perceives his idol's bonnet before him' (*Psy* 245, 327). Throughout, the narratee of James's text is a young upper-middle class heterosexual male, aspiring to the 'manly deed', for whom the charms of women will come and go, and for whom 'common duties and common goods' will become more and more important (*Psy* 163, 171). In the introductory pages to his chapter on 'The Self', a whole gamut of assumptions about the aspirations of an individual and the most desirable way in which to live one's life come into play. Among these assumptions are the desire to have a home, wife and children (and the latter are included in 'all that he CAN call his' [*Psy* 190]), the importance of social recognition, 'honor' and power, and the acquisition of material possessions; these are assumptions which again not only interpellate the reader as educated, wealthy, upper-middle class and male, but align that subject position with a whole value-system to which the individual subject might not in fact subscribe. As a range of alternative subject positions are increasingly emphatically articulated in the literature of the period, the question of how we put a value on our daily activity, how we choose to fill the 'becoming' of the present – or where we cannot choose, what effect various enforced routines, time-frames, activities or states of consciousness have on our subjectivity – becomes increasingly prominent.

Above all, then, the young male reader of James's text has his attention fixed on work (just as the human mind itself is constantly oriented to the practical, according to James). As 'we' grow older, 'more zestful than ever is the work, the work' (*Psy* 171). James reassures his readers, in perhaps his clearest exposition of the kind of dailiness to which one should aspire, that 'whatever the line' of his education, no youth need have any anxiety about its upshot, since 'if he keep faithfully busy each hour of the working day, he may safely leave the final result to itself. He can with perfect certainty count on waking up some fine morning, to find himself one of the competent ones of his generation' (*Psy* 165). What constitutes the daily activity of James's implied reader is work: work for its own sake, work in order to acquire material goods and social status, and work as the most important use of time. James's background in the protestant ethic outlined by Weber, where 'waste of time is [. . .] the first and in principle the deadliest of sins',[39] is most apparent here; apparent too is the assumption, the establishment of which Weber describes, that work is necessarily the best use of time – that working is by definition not wasting time. We will see a critique of this assumption in, most clearly, Richardson's *Pilgrimage*.

The meaning of this work is, however, clearly gendered and class-based. Few working-class men or women would have received an education comparable to that of James's middle-class audience, of whatever 'line', and James's own theories preclude class mobility for anyone over the age of twenty (*Psy* 159). Further, although James refers in the *Psychology* to research carried out by female psychologists, and indeed had female students, his text is structured by a clear distinction between the active male, the subject of everyday life, and the passive female, one of its objects. For example, in an anecdote about the maid-servant who props up a faulty clock to make it work, this (working) woman's immediate, practical solution is implicitly inferior to the analysis of the 'educated man', who would have worked out

the 'reason' for the stoppage 'in five minutes' (*Psy* 361). The possibility of
the maid-servant or the bonnet-wearer being readers of this text, hence par-
ticipants in the everyday life to which James refers for his 'analytic method',
is excluded by the assumptions of the text itself.

We should not leave this exploration of James's cultural assumptions
without asking to what extent any such assumptions can be detected in
Bergson's texts. There is a clear stylistic contrast between the two writers.
In James's highly idiomatic style we can hear the voice of James the teacher,
delivering his lectures to a room full of students. There is also occasionally
a conversational tone to Bergson's texts, but it is the literariness of his style
that is most noticeable. Certainly, Bergson makes many fewer references to
concrete examples in the outside world than James; where he does ask us to
imagine, for example, the experience of listening to a poet read his work, or
of waiting for sugar to melt in a glass, these are images with little detail, little
context, as if occurring in a void. James's examples, on the other hand –
the lover's bonnet, the broken clock, and so forth – vividly locate his text
very much in his particular historical and cultural setting.

But because cultural assumptions are not so evident in Bergson's writing,
this by no means implies that they are absent. Indeed, Walter Benjamin critiques Bergson on precisely this point: while applauding Bergson's attempt
to overcome the denigration of experience within a modern culture founded
on obsolescence, Benjamin deplores Bergson's failure to see that his own
thought was in turn historically determined, rather than, as his lyrical, aesthetic style seems to suggest, universally applicable.[40] Crary's observation
that *Matter and Memory* in particular is 'seemingly remote from any social
or cultural polemics' could apply to all three of Bergson's major works
drawn upon here.[41] What I suggest we can detect in Bergson's texts are,
then, assumptions precisely about the primacy of the aesthetic, indicated
not only through his own 'literary' style, but also through the examples he
uses of appreciating music, looking at a painting, and so forth. Implicit in
such examples is the assumption that there is a universally appreciable aesthetic, more or less independent of cultural and historical contexts. Bergson
does not address the extent to which appreciating artefacts might rather
be a product of certain kinds of education, within certain strata of society
where having the leisure to attend to such artefacts is an indication of success and privilege. As such, then, Bergson's texts might be seen as part of an
emerging contemporary debate surrounding the relationship between art
and institutions: whether in modernity the aesthetic can remain apparently
autonomous, unsullied by the vicissitudes of political life or the injunctions
of capitalism; or whether art becomes so thoroughly compromised through

its functioning position as cultural capital that an art praxis acknowledging this institutionalisation of the aesthetic becomes necessary.[42]

In conclusion, I want to address more specifically the relationship between art and dailiness. On one level, the aesthetic is precisely that which is not everyday; attention to the aesthetic quality of, for example, a cup is attention diverted from the practical imperative that it hold liquid. Indeed, for James, art appears as a potentially dangerous diversion. In a tirade against the Rousseauian 'sentimentalist and dreamer', he warns that 'the habit of excessive novel-reading and theatre-going will produce true monsters in this line' (*Psy* 163). Such excesses will produce the habit of feeling emotion without acting on it, an unforgivable waste of energy in James's psychic economy. Bergson, however, is explicitly sceptical on the issue of the principle of conservation of energy (*TFW* 144–6; *CE* 255–6), and this appears to be related to his different position on art and its function in consciousness. Bergson returns again and again to art as a privileged realm where the actuality of duration can be perceived. In one of many such instances, he argues that, unlike a jigsaw puzzle which requires no definite time to complete, 'to the artist who creates a picture by drawing it from the depths of his soul, time is no longer an accessory; it is not an interval that may be lengthened or shortened without the content being altered' (359), just as the time taken to wait for sugar to melt cannot be lengthened or shortened. By implication, Jamesian efficiency will yield nothing here; indeed, it would only damage the aesthetic value of the piece which takes simply as long as it takes to write, or paint, or perform. Creativity, then, is itself evidence of duration, placing it, surprisingly perhaps, in an analogous position to impatience – impatience as, perhaps, the everyday symptom of creativity.

It is not only the maker of art, but also the audience of the artwork, who gains access to a more profound understanding in excess of, or even replacing, the merely intellectual. Art, for Bergson, is again a realm where life's exceeding of intellect is manifested: 'the artist aims at giving us a share in this emotion [the artist's own], so rich, so personal, so novel, and at enabling us to *experience* what he cannot make us *understand*' (*TFW* 18, my emphases). Aesthetic responses arise in a realm, like that of the everyday, involving alternative forms of knowing, of experience. Indeed, 'the object of art is to put to sleep the active or rather resistant powers of our personality', wherein the intellect resides (*TFW* 14). To contrast this view with James's, it is as if James fears that contemplating art takes the individual away from him or herself, whereas Bergson sees art as revealing the individual to him or herself; the novelist who challenges the conventions of 'spatialised' language, Bergson says, 'has brought us back into our own presence' (*TFW* 134). In particular, rhythm is crucial for Bergson, as the movement 'by which the soul is lulled into self-forgetfulness, and, as in a dream, thinks and sees with the poet' (*TFW* 15). Might not this communication, found here between listener and poet, which bypasses intellectual, scientific knowledge, equally be accessed through the temporality of dailiness, rhythm in its most concrete and universal form?

Where rhythm is referred to in literary studies, questions of gender almost invariably arise, primarily as a result of Julia Kristeva's massively influential work on the semiotic and its connection with the feminine. However, Lyndsey Stonebridge has brought into question the sometimes too easy equation of the rhythmic with the feminine specifically with reference to work on Virginia Woolf: 'The collapse of the "feminine" into a generalized concept of rhythmic writing [. . .] risks shoe-horning Woolf's work into a set of gender binaries that do as much harm as good'.[43] I would concur with Stonebridge's caveat against 'shoe-horning' not only Woolf's work, but that of the other writers I will be discussing, into gender assumptions based around the 'rhythm' of their work. In particular, Stonebridge alerts us to the reactionary potential of rhythm; while rhythm has come to be associated with a liberating engagement with the natural, it might in some cases also be a figure of constraint.[44] This possibility is attested to in some of the texts I address; for socially, economically, perhaps psychically disempowered women, dailiness can be a structure as oppressive as it is liberating.

The point at which gender intersects with dailiness is also addressed by Josephine Donovan in her attempts to articulate a 'non-dominative aesthetic'. Donovan argues that the Kantian aesthetic, dominant in Western society, sees art as imposing a form 'redemptive of a threateningly chaotic reality' – art as dominative of everyday life.[45] Donovan brings together Marxist-feminist theory, derived in particular from Woolf's *A Room of One's Own*, with the dialectical aesthetic of Adorno to argue that women's domestic aesthetic practice remains faithful to reality and reveals the 'ontic illuminations that inhere in everyday life'; in other words, providing a non-dominative alternative aesthetic.[46] While Donovan, like Stonebridge, seems to resist a too easy association of the feminine with, in this case, the daily, she nevertheless makes a special case for women's craft or domestic art as offering Adorno's 'negative critique of commodity exchange reification',[47] by participating in a system of use-value rather than exchange-value, and yet remaining non-dominative as, say, autotelic art might not.

I want to draw on Donovan's idea of the non-dominative to elaborate further what I see as the link between the everyday and the aesthetic in Bergson, without implying a gender awareness in Bergson that I do not believe is present. There are of course clear distinctions between Donovan's argument and the kind of perspective articulated by Bergson. Bergson apparently designates the aesthetic as a privileged realm, where a certain kind of particularly gifted individual might offer the suitably receptive reader, viewer or listener a more profound understanding of him or herself. Donovan, on the other hand, indicates how the aesthetic is inherent within the objects of everyday life, drawing on authors who propose 'an aesthetic theory where art remained embedded in and arose out of conversation with the contingent, everyday world'.[48] However, as I have been arguing above, Bergson's theories suggest that we approximate the authentic temporality of human consciousness of duration not only through contemplation of the aesthetic but also through such everyday states of (in)attention as daydream and impatience. Such states of mind bypass the cognitive processes we might indeed associate with a Kantian dominative aesthetic. Although Bergson might not perhaps agree with Woolf that as much aesthetic value may be gained from 'a scrap of newspaper in the street, [. . .] a daffodil in the sun'[49] as from a psychological novel or oil painting, his theories of human temporality nevertheless suggest to us that it is through a partial relinquishing of the strictures of attention and intellectual convention that our understanding may be enlarged, and that such a relinquishing takes place not only in the contemplation of a poem, but also while waiting for sugar to melt.

The novelist in particular has a privileged role, according to Bergson – but only the 'bold novelist, tearing aside the cleverly woven curtain of our conventional ego'. He commends the novelist who tries to show us the 'infinite permeation of a thousand different impressions' (*TFW* 133), who resists the homogenisation of duration. The privileged role of the novelist is worth considering further in relation to my choices of texts for analysis. The novel, in a fairly simple way, incorporates an ongoing temporality in a way that other art forms (usually) do not. Not only does it literally take more time to read a novel than a poem (again, usually), but, as Frank Kermode argues, novels cannot 'banish time [. . .] even to the degree that poems and criticism can'.[50] Change and repetition over time – which might be one way of describing duration, as involving both these elements – are the concern of the novel above all other genres. The novel cannot 'banish' time, as Kermode puts it, and nor does it want to, generally speaking, but neither can it 'banish the form we like to think of as spatial', seemingly posing a problem for Bergson's privileging of the genre. As Kermode observes, we need 'geometries [. . .] to measure change'.[51] Yet Kermode echoes Bergson where he observes that '"spatialization" is one of those metaphors which we tend to forget are metaphorical'.[52] Since we cannot hope to eliminate all spatialising tendencies from language – indeed, language could not function as such were we to – the best we can hope for is to be reminded that such spatialising is metaphorical. The novelist attempts to render the complexity of internal duration, and the explosion in technical experimentation in the literature of the early twentieth century draws attention to such attempts; further, in a familiar paradox, we are thereby made aware of the ultimate futility of such attempts. Nevertheless, the value of such experimental literary texts lies in their potential for enabling the reader to observe the struggle with language; it is the novelist who makes us *reflect*. We are briefly able to see what was to us transparent, that is, the artificiality of our ego as constructed through language, and thus a more authentic selfhood is glimpsed: the novelist 'has brought us back into our own presence' (*TFW* 133). Again, it is through the temporality of the return, the rhythmic, the repeat ('brought us back') that this glimpse of our complex subjectivity is made possible.

CHAPTER 2

Dailiness in Dorothy Richardson's Pilgrimage

INTRODUCTION: RICHARDSON, BERGSON, TIME AND GENDER

While the resurgence of interest in the work of Dorothy Richardson is thanks primarily to her reassessment by feminist critics, from Sydney Janet Kaplan in the 1970s to Joanne Winning's recent study *The Pilgrimage of Dorothy Richardson*, feminist responses to Richardson have by no means been unreservedly positive. Both Elaine Showalter and Rachel Blau DuPlessis reserve some unusually intense criticism for Richardson's thirteen-volume novel *Pilgrimage*, and their criticism focuses on, or seems related to, what DuPlessis calls the 'really excessive' length of the text.[1] Similarly, Showalter's general frustration with Richardson for not producing the progressive feminist text that she, Showalter, believes Richardson might have done centres on Richardson's lack of courage, as Showalter sees it: specifically, 'Most of all, Richardson's art is afraid of an ending.'[2] What is particularly surprising about this kind of criticism is that the crimes of which Richardson is accused, of fear and of excess, are the kind of feminised traits – feminised and therefore conventionally seen as negative – which feminist criticism has a tradition of reappraising. Here DuPlessis and Showalter deploy these terms in voices resonant with precisely the kind of patriarchal ideology they want to challenge. One might respond to DuPlessis's criticism by asking: *Pilgrimage* is excessive as compared with what, nominally appropriate, length? What does it mean to say that the appropriate length of *Pilgrimage* is any shorter than precisely the length it is? And in suggesting what Richardson might (indeed should) have done had she been less fearful, Showalter is not only being fruitlessly speculative, but also seems to want to create a concrete ending, aim, achievement, where Richardson herself constantly and deliberately avoids it.

Richardson's biographer notes that poets were much less perturbed by the structure and length of *Pilgrimage* than novel-readers, reminding us that part of Richardson's project involved a reworking of the genre of the novel – itself an important feminist gesture. In her essay 'Dorothy Richardson Versus the Novvle', Gillian Hanscombe elaborates on precisely this point; Hanscombe's detailed attention to Richardson's technical and stylistic innovation implicitly affirms the length of the project as intrinsic to Richardson's broadly feminist agenda, rather than a symptom of writerly intemperance.[3] Evidently, then, the question of time, in terms of the length and structure of the text, as well as its stylistic reworkings of and explicit statements on temporality, is closely connected to the question of the text's feminist potential. That the 'excessive' length of *Pilgrimage* is in one sense its most anti-teleological, and therefore anti-patriarchal, aspect, and yet that its length is an aspect of the text to which feminist critics seem particularly to object, is only one indication of the highly complex and ultimately undecidable nature of the temporality of *Pilgrimage*, in all senses of the phrase.

The contradictions of *Pilgrimage* are made particularly apparent on considering its relationship with Bergson. Kumar's *Bergson and the Stream of Consciousness Novel* devotes a chapter to Richardson, despite the fact that, as we have seen, Richardson both rejected the term 'stream of consciousness', and when approached by Kumar denied being aware of any influence of Bergson on her work.[4] Yet the association between the narrative strategies of *Pilgrimage* and Bergsonian models of temporality is common in writing on modernist texts, and it is necessary to engage with this tenacious association. Further, recent writers on Bergson have sought to distinguish between what they call 'Bergsonism', the inherited and filtered view of Bergson as 'simply the "time philosopher"', and a fuller understanding of Bergson yielded by a return to his work.[5] Paul Douglass, for example, comments on Richardson's apparent attitude to Bergson expressed in a letter to Kumar: '"No doubt Bergson influenced many minds, if only by putting into words something then dawning on human consciousness: an increased awareness of the inadequacy of the clock-time as time-measurer." That is the view of one who has experienced Bergsonism, but not Bergson in his profound entanglement with the troublesome issues presented by science and psychology in the years before the war.'[6] While acknowledging the existence of a presumed relationship between Richardson and Bergson, or indeed between Richardson and 'Bergsonism', I aim to take a step back from this presumption by returning to the texts of each and to look afresh at the extent of any consanguinity between these writers.

There do indeed seem to be close similarities between the approaches of Bergson and Richardson in the crucial area of their understanding of the relationship between past, present and future (the Bergsonian 'flux' of time). There are numerous passages in Richardson's text that articulate temporality in what seem to be classically Bergsonian formulations. For example, Miriam states in *Interim* that 'The present can be judged by the part of the past it brings up. If the present brings up the happiness of the past, the present is happy' (*P* 2:402).[7] This constitution of present perceptions by the elements of memory with which the perception is associated, 'the part of the past it brings up', is precisely the relationship between present perception and memory that Bergson articulates in *Matter and Memory*. Or again, in *Revolving Lights*, 'She was once more in that zone of her being where all the past was with her unobstructed; not recalled, but present, so that she could move into any part and be there as before' (*P* 3:322); this articulates the thoroughly Bergsonian suggestion that the past is real, has never ceased to exist, and in remembrance we enter entirely into the past in order then to make our selections among it. When Miriam exclaims, in response to Shatov's attempts to explain his previous sexual experiences, 'Can't you see that there is no past?' (*P* 3:211), she does not mean that the past does not exist, that the past is nothing, but on the contrary, that nothing is past, the past never ceases to be.

Beyond explicit articulations of Miriam's concept of temporality, it is of course the style and structure of the text which has led many to draw comparisons between Richardson and Bergson. Of central importance here is the facility with which Miriam's consciousness moves between present perception and recollection of the past, and the opacity with which temporal locations are presented, such that the reader may often be unsure as to which point of the temporal oscillation of a particular passage is the present, and which the past. (For a particularly clear instance of this, see the first chapter of *March Moonlight*.) The entire text of *Pilgrimage* could be read as an elaboration of the Bergsonian theory that 'our previous psychical life exists for us even more than the external world, of which we never perceive more than a very small part, whereas on the contrary we use the whole of our lived experience' (*MM* 188). The emphasis on use-value draws together not only Bergson and Richardson but William James also, with his emphasis on practicality – although perhaps each would have different criteria for usefulness – and relates to the use-value model of aesthetics discussed in my introduction; Bergson suggests that the past has not ceased to exist, it has only ceased to be useful (*MM* 193). When we only discover a year after the event, during a conversation with Shatov, that Miriam has had a potentially fatal cycling accident, we must accept that the use-value of this event is most fully realised here, as it is discussed with Miriam's lover-to-be, and not, as we might expect, at the time – that is, when it was present rather than past. It is only now that this element of Miriam's past is 'ready to reveal its quality for the first time' (*P* 3:83). Such radical disruptions of the usual priorities of narrative question assumptions about individual and cultural priorities, and are part of an attempt to articulate the complexities of human temporality – complexities so often, as I will go on to discuss, obscured by socio-cultural and economic structures. The questioning of individual and cultural priorities implied by the narrative disruptions of *Pilgrimage* forms precisely part of the critique of everyday life, the reappraisal of what makes up a life and what should be valued therein, that can be detected in these texts.

On the general question of the intermingling of past and present, and the functioning of memory, then, we find a great deal of similarity between Bergson and Richardson. Within this general tendency, however, contrasts emerge, some of which turn out to be more dramatic than others. Firstly, Bergson continually rails against what he calls the 'spatialisation' of time, the human tendency to measure time such that we externalise, quantify and ultimately reify and make lifeless the internal flux of human temporality, or 'duration'. Externalising time, we create and accept the illusion that time is a 'homogenous medium' (*TFW* chapter 2 *passim*). On one level, then, we might suggest that Richardson falls into precisely the kind of trap that Bergson warns against – of emphasising spatial models in her construction of human consciousness – as I shall go on to discuss. Indeed, the very title of Elisabeth Bronfen's rigorous phenomenological reading of *Pilgrimage* in *Dorothy Richardson's Art of Memory: Space, Identity, Text* posits a fundamental connection between memory – the relationship of human consciousness with the past – and space, in *Pilgrimage*. However, Bronfen's elevation of space over time, contending that 'performing space in and through language is the shared issue, the common concern subtending and gathering together the various textual layers of *Pilgrimage*', tends to occlude the issue of temporality which, one might just as well argue, is the 'common concern' of the text.[8] Certainly, Richardson's spatial language may often 'enact an attempt "to be in two places at once"';[9] Bronfen's analysis is invaluable in drawing attention to the importance of spatiality, both literal and metaphorical, in the development of Miriam's subjectivity – in particular in the paradigmatically modernist space of the city. However, it risks overstating the prominence of spatial models, and of simultaneity, in the text. Just as often, the language of *Pilgrimage* insists on the irreducibility of temporal experience, its ineluctable processes; and indeed, at a structural level, as Kaplan puts it, 'the very bulk of the novel is largely taken up with those very "associational processes" which require the passage of time',[10] in other words, which involve succession (a process only truly at work, Bergson argues, in human consciousness).

That Richardson uses spatial categories to express temporal states by no means implies that she thereby effects a total quantification and reification of time. On the contrary, I will argue that precisely through using such spatial categories, indeed by problematising spatial metaphors for time with which we might be familiar, Richardson draws attention both to the potential of spatial models for representing time, and to their limitations. By bringing into close proximity the language of time and of space, Richardson requires us to rethink the relationship between the two. Simply employing the language of space does not necessarily imply a spatialisation of time – that is, in Bergsonian terms, a homogenisation and quantification of time. Rather, by using an unexpected vocabulary, Richardson is able to question conventional ways of expressing time; to articulate the fluid, contradictory and subjective nature of human temporality. Hence the usefulness to my discussion of the chronotope (as elaborated in my Introduction), a concept involving equally and inextricably both spatial and temporal categories.

Part of what I hope to do in this chapter, then, is to contribute to a critical landscape where an emphasis on the spatialisation of temporality has resulted in a neglect of how temporal terms operate and circulate in *Pilgrimage*, and how, as the text draws our attention to alternative models of temporal experience, it also encourages us to consider more deeply that in which experience of time consists. Specifically, I will argue that while the mystical, that which is beyond the material, plays a crucial part in Richardson's worldview as expressed in *Pilgrimage*, the text also requires us to attend to the ways in which social and economic structures distract the subject from his or her relationship with time, and paradoxically, do so precisely by demanding that the subject attend to certain sanctioned activities, ways of operating and of perceiving the world.

The closest critical precedent for my understanding of temporality in *Pilgrimage* can be found in the work of an early 'second wave' Richardson critic, Shirley Rose. Of particular note is Rose's 1974 article 'Dorothy Richardson's Focus on Time'. Here, Rose concludes by suggesting that *Pilgrimage* expresses 'two necessary movements in temporal existence',[11] the first oscillatory, the second cyclical. For Rose, these movements, and in particular the 'greater compass' of the cyclical movement, are signalled by Richardson's emphasis on Christmas in the novel. Drawing attention to the importance of annual patterns in the novel, Rose argues that '[u]ltimately, Christmas becomes both the example and focal point of her theory of stasis within flux'.[12] Rose's article relates to my argument in several important ways. Firstly, Christmas is itself, of course, both a day like no other, and just another day among many ('both the example and focal point'). I want to expand this observation to explore how days in general function as both unique and unremarkable in *Pilgrimage*. Secondly, the significance of Christmas is both mystical and socio-cultural, each aspect informing and modifying the other. The relationship between these two discourses will be central to my elaboration of the dailiness of *Pilgrimage*. Further, I want to overlay Rose's temporal map with a more finely calibrated grid (or perhaps a closer metaphor would be, to add a second hand to her clock): within the cyclical and oscillatory annual pattern, both the cyclical and the oscillatory are to be found at the level of the day, for just as Christmas comes around every year, so dawn, for example, comes around each day. *Pilgrimage*'s particular depiction of time grounded in this daily structure aids its articulation of the ways in which time is experienced.

Returning to consideration of the relationship between Bergson and Richardson, we find a second, and more profound, point of conflict, around the tension between being and becoming. Bergson famously argues that, in our concept of 'being' (indeed, in the very language which we use to express this concept), we occlude the 'duration' of the human subject. 'Becoming', Bergson argues, more properly describes human consciousness (*CE* 329–30). 'Nothing *is* less than the present moment' (*MM* 193); the present moment is not that which is but that which is being made: in all these formulations the concept of 'being' is replaced with that of 'becoming'. Richardson, by contrast, explicitly rejects 'becoming': 'it is certain', she argues, 'that becoming depends upon being' (*P* 4:362). Indeed, her rejection of the expression 'stream of consciousness' would seem to be related to this distinction, since a stream implies some kind of process, or forward movement. A more appropriate expression, she suggested early on in her writing career, would be 'an agglomeration, a vital process of crystallization grouped in and about the human consciousness'.[13]

In a useful contemporary explication, Evelyn Underhill's *Mysticism* of 1911 draws attention to the distinction between vitalism, of which Bergson was seen as an exemplar, and mysticism, with which Richardson seems more closely affiliated, precisely by stating that vitalism's focus is on 'not Being but Becoming', whereas 'Being, not Doing, is the first aim of the mystic'.[14] Although it would be overstating the case to categorise Richardson as mystical in opposition to Bergson's vitalism, Richardson's work certainly expresses a sympathy with, and experience of, mystical aspects of life. Indeed, as Suzanne Raitt has indicated, there is a literary tradition of the mystical in women's autobiography in particular, which tradition Raitt detects in

Pilgrimage.[15] However, these sympathies remain generally unarticulated and certainly unformulated in Richardson's work as a strict system of belief, as one would expect from one so fluid in her affinities. For example, although Richardson became friends with and went for treatment from a young man who apparently suddenly discovered a gift for healing powers, nowhere does Richardson explicitly refer to the 'mystical' aspect of his healing.[16] Even direct statements that might sound like articulations of faith, whether in *Pilgrimage* or elsewhere, must, as always with Richardson, be held in suspension, since alternative positions can and almost always will be articulated at another time or place.

However, there is one thread of association which appears relatively consistent throughout *Pilgrimage* and throughout Richardson's life; that is, the association of being and the mystical with women, and becoming and science with men.[17] Writers on Richardson have noted this association in various different ways: Bronfen musters a useful array of quotations to draw attention to the association between the feminine and the spiritual in *Pilgrimage*, but importantly reminds us that, particularly in the early volumes, Miriam's own gender identification is profoundly ambivalent;[18] Radford clearly articulates the 'being/women', 'becoming/men' distinction with reference to Miriam's discussions with Hypo Wilson, by which time Miriam's gender position has become more entrenched.[19]

It is not only that women are singled out as more strongly allied with the mystical than men. The whole question of sexual equality for Richardson is a question of faith, of the spiritual. We find this most clearly expressed in a phrase from Richardson's short 1914 book on the Quakers (who, she reminds us, belong to 'the family of the mystics').[20] Richardson describes the Quaker concern for, and actions to bring about, the equality of men and women as 'the result, not of any kind of feminism, any sort of special solicitude for or belief in women as a class. Nor was it the result of a protest against any definitely recognized existing attitude', but rather 'an act of faith'.[21] Here, the emphasis on 'faith', or the transcendental, rather than any 'existing attitude' or contemporary context, crystallises Richardson's own essentialist beliefs. Although she was associated with feminist groups through her involvement with the Fabians in the 1890s and 1900s, and has Miriam associate with them too, she also has Miriam rail against feminism for assuming that women had ever been, indeed could ever be, 'subject'.[22] Belief in the transcendental nature of femininity overrides the argument also present in Richardson's work that the condition of women is contingent on socio-cultural contexts. Richardson's writing gives expression to what she views as the already unassailable mystical essence of feminine consciousness, distancing her from the first generation of feminists as mapped by Julia Kristeva – those whose project would include 'the rejection, when necessary, of the attributes traditionally considered feminine or maternal in so far as they are deemed incompatible with insertion in [history as political, linear time]'.[23] Attributes such as the compulsory wearing of long skirts even for bicycle rides might indeed be rejected in *Pilgrimage*, but essential qualities of the mystical feminine will be clung to; for Richardson, they are irreducible, and cannot be rejected even were she to wish it.

My contribution to this aspect of Richardson's work is, then, to draw attention to a manifestation of the, otherwise potentially rather intangible, relationship between women's 'being', and the mystical, specifically in the activities of everyday life. This matrix will arise at later points in my discussion, in particular where I discuss the importance of Sundays in *Pilgrimage*. For the moment, no better indication of the connections I want to bring out can be given than Miriam's suggestion that '"A woman's way of 'being' can be discovered in the way she pours out tea"' (*P* 3:257); even the most everyday of situations is suffused with the mystical.

THE 'DAY' IN *PILGRIMAGE*

When she rattled her key into the keyhole of number seven, she felt that her day was beginning. It would be perpetually beginning now. Nights and days were all one day; all hers, unlimited. [. . .] her own life of endless day. (*P* 2:30)

The term 'day' is far from being a simple signifier of a period of time in *Pilgrimage*. The variety of ways in which the term is used draws attention to the importance of the day to the text's figuring of temporality in general. Days are described as if they were rooms, as clothing, as types of counter, moving out of their strict chronological sequence and able to take on different qualities as units of time. Attention is drawn both to the uniqueness of each day as it takes on its particular qualities, and also the sameness of any given day, its congruity with other days (and here spatial and arithmetical metaphors are particularly important); the two kinds of repetition identified by Miller, grounded and ungrounded, can clearly be seen at work.

Some of the spatial metaphors Richardson employs in phrases involving the term 'day' are reasonably familiar – the idea of time as elastic, for example, is evoked in expressions such as 'The day stretched back long and eventful' (*P* 3:441). Here, time retrospectively takes on a particular quality according to the individual subject's experience of it: this day 'stretches' because of the pleasurable activity which has filled it. What is perhaps less familiar, at least in the striking way in which Richardson expresses it, is a model of the day as a kind of receptacle or container, already in place regardless of the subject, which the subject must then enter, with a sense of volition. Such expressions are particularly prevalent in passages depicting Miriam's working life at the dentist: Mr Hancock had 'gone on into his day' (*P* 3:385); Miriam herself 'floated off into her day' (*P* 3:482), as if they had physically moved into a particular space or room.

This use of the room as a figure for the day is striking in a text in which, as Elisabeth Bronfen argues, the room is a particularly important reflector of Miriam's subjectivity.[24] Here, however, rather than the qualities of the room being entirely contingent on Miriam's state of mind, as Bronfen suggests, the day/room has an objective, external existence independent of the subject's position with regard to it. Her working life at the dentist is marked (as her days in Germany, for example, are not) by routine; they are knowable in advance, and are so predictable that they function as if they indeed were already in existence in advance of the subject's own movement into them.

Such a model is not restricted to the working episodes of the central volumes. Toward the very beginning of *Pilgrimage*, Miriam's sense of her imminent estrangement from her family's everyday life is described thus: 'There would still be blissful days. But she would not be in them' (*P* 1:16). Again, the day is figured as a kind of room-like space, present even if it is not visible or otherwise present to the senses, having an existence of its own without the subject who can be absent from or present to it. Most explicitly perhaps, a passage in *The Tunnel* describes Miriam 'mov[ing] eagerly about amongst the strange angles and shadows of her room, the rich day all about her' (*P* 2:78). Here, the two clauses invite an identification of the day with the walls of the room, and not just the walls, but the furniture, the books, the towel – all the objects described. Again, the day encloses Miriam as if it were something already complete. *Pilgrimage* expresses an understanding of the future as experientially part of the past, as even our projections of the future become past thoughts as soon as we make them; here too, that which is apparently in the future, the complete day, is nevertheless experienced by Miriam as a comforting, enclosing whole. Here, to paraphrase Bakhtin, the 'increase in density and concreteness of [space] markers [. . .] that occurs within well-delineated [temporal] areas'[25] (e.g. here, the day) makes the day not simply a temporal unit, but a chronotope of the text, involving both spatiality and temporality as a subject moves within, lives through, its particular form.

The chronotope of the day in *Pilgrimage* takes on, however, a variety of very different spatial characteristics, or 'space markers'. It can surround Miriam as if it were a room that she enters; it can also enclose her as if it were a kind of fabric or clothing. Again, Richardson sometimes uses a familiar phrase: summarising the changes Miriam experiences as a result of Julia Doyle's arrival at Banbury Park, she explains 'The fabric of the days, too, had changed' (*P*1:278). When this idiomatic expression functions conventionally, it is only certain characteristics of 'fabric' that are important, in particular its texture. It is, perhaps, a symptom of Richardson's professed distrust of metaphor that she elsewhere unsettles our taken-for-granted understanding of this expression by taking it further, by bringing into play the various other kinds of signification implied by 'fabric', those that involve focus on its practical, or cultural, aspects.[26] Phrases such as 'She wrapped her evening round her' (*P* 3:40) or '"A to-morrow that will wear for ever and make a petticoat afterwards"' (*P* 3:364) remind us that fabric is used to keep us warm, or to make clothes which, for the sake of economy, must be hard-wearing. Indeed, throughout *Pilgrimage*, Miriam is often acutely aware of what she and others are wearing, of how she feels in her clothes, both physically, if they cause her discomfort – for example when her shoes crack as they dry out in the heat of Mag and Jan's fire – and psychologically, as she displays awareness of what certain clothes mean socially and culturally. She is often conscious, for example, that her clothes display her financial hardship. Mag and Jan's bicycle ride wearing knickers rather than skirts draws attention to the physical restraints placed on women by cultural conventions regarding clothing. Once more, Richardson's more unusual ways of expressing the qualities of the day form part of important thematic and linguistic threads within the text: of the room, of clothing; which themes are themselves constant indicators of the particular material context of the novel.

As one might expect in a text so ready to express conflicting positions, days are also expressed in ways almost diametrically opposed to those dis-cussed above. And once more, familiar idioms or concepts, such as the synecdoche of the day for a longer period of time (the experience of 'to-day's long lifetime' [*P* 4:102] at Oberland), are extended and magnified. For example, after a visit to Miss Dear in hospital: 'This kind of day lived forever. It stood still. The whole year, funny little distant fussy thing, stood still in this sort of day. You could take it in your hand and look at it' (*P* 2:255–6). Rather than enclosing Miriam, she herself can enclose this day in her hand, hold it as if it were a small object; further, the whole year is accessible through this manageable, finite object, with clear boundaries – with an end. Distance is gained between the subject and his or her time; a *mise-en-abyme* structure is created where Miriam can observe the day comprising the year wherein she herself must be.

Far from it being a disorientating experience to feel oneself at a distance from the flow of time, distance is comforting, connected with the stillness for which Miriam strives – see for example the first paragraph of chapter IX of *Deadlock* (*P* 3:188–9). A degree of control is also implied by the ability to 'take it in your hand and look at it'. Here is one moment where the double temporality of the narratorial voice of *Pilgrimage* is clearly detectable; we can imagine Richardson literally able to hold in her hand and look at the days and years that she describes, in the paper on which she is writing. Moments such as this remind us that Miriam's experiences are filtered through Richardson's narratorial voice, at a distance, try as the text might to express these experiences as immanently and unmediatedly as possible.

The clearly defined boundaries of the day, marked by the distinction between darkness and light, render it highly susceptible to being figured as just such a small, manageable, limited object, from which one can gain distance, since it has boundaries in the way that, say, an hour or a week does not. By placing the physical boundary of her hand against the physicalised boundary of the day, Miriam is able to extricate herself from her experiences in time, imaginatively if not actually. The variety of ways in which days are figured as separate from each other contributes to a kind of arithmetical model of time which emerges in *Pilgrimage*. While Frank Kermode has, as we have seen, suggested that we need 'geometries [. . .] to measure change',[27] we are presented in *Pilgrimage* with an arithmetic that measures temporality. This is by no means, however, a conventional arithmetic.

The limits of the day are expressed in *Pilgrimage* in a strongly felt distinction between day and night. Perhaps the most explicit expression of this sense of distance comes early in the novel, when Miriam wakes in the night and is comforted by the sound of fluttering foliage: 'It was enough . . . and things happened, as well, in the far far off things called "days"' (*P* 1:461). Night is not just part of the ongoing flow of time; it is qualitatively different from day, it is 'the neutral zone between the two days' (*P* 3:165) where, again, days become 'far-off strident irrelevancies, for ever unable to come between her and the sound of the stillness and its touch' (*P* 3:165). Spaces between days or groups of days are readily imagined in the text, usually constituted by a break in a particular routine: 'To-day, in the space between the week's work and the week-end with its pattern ready set, was serenity immeasurable; given by autumn' (*P* 3:445). The experience of a 'solitary excursion' one day in Oberland creates 'a gap in the sequence of days. Those standing behind it were now far away, and yesterday had failed to bridge the gap and join itself to their serenity' (*P* 4:103). On one level, clearly, it is the fact that during this particular day Miriam would 'break the snare' and go for a walk in the Swiss mountains on her own that gives it this quality of being an unbridgeable gap in time. At the same time, however, the way in which days are figured as a 'sequence' to which yesterday failed to 'join itself' creates a sense of time as piled-up days, as if one's progress through time constituted something like the transfer of counters from one pile, in the future, to that of the past.

Indeed, the specific vocabulary of arithmetic is employed in the text with reference to the experience of time. During a visit to Eve and Harriett in their new positions as shopkeeper and landlady, Miriam finds that 'the early days flowed up, recovered completely from the passage of time, going forward *with today added to them*, forever' (*P* 3:97, my emphasis). And again, a moment on a tram while on holiday with the Wilsons finds her 'out in eternity, gliding along, *adding* this hour to the strange sum of her central being' (*P* 4:265, my emphasis). An arithmetical model of sorts is also indicated by phrases that express in visual terms Miriam's perception of the future. During a walk with Rachel Mary at Dimple Hill, Miriam suddenly finds herself at the turning point between past and future; the 'long weeks' of the past are 'swept away' and 'Ahead, vanishing into the far distance, lay an untellable number of days' (*P* 4:529). This occurs as the walkers reach the rise of a hill, adding to the visual aspect of the expression. A new heap of counters, although 'untellable' in number, have come into play.

However, as the passage on the tram suggests, at the most profound level (of the 'central being') time is being added to something that does not alter by its being added to; in this process of addition, nothing is rendered redundant or left behind. Even that which might seem to have been left behind, such as the 'early days' referred to during the visit to Miriam's sisters, can be recovered, or rather, recover themselves; the days which are left in the past are still 'standing' (*P* 4:103), far away although they be. The coexistence of a sense of the fundamental demarcation of past and future with a geological unity of time is expressed in this passage from *Oberland* (a chapter-novel where Miriam's experiences constitute both a complete disruption to her normal, everyday life, but also quickly take on a dailiness and routine of their own):

To-day was an unfathomable loop within the time that remained before the end of Eaden's visit, his short allowance that added, by being set within it, to her own longer portion. His coming had brought the earlier time to an end; made it a past, expanding in the distance. And beyond his far-off departure was a group of days with features yet unseen. Looking back upon that distant past, it seemed impossible that the crest of her first week was not yet reached. (*P* 4:96)

'To-day' is an 'unfathomable loop', literally incomprehensible, not susceptible to cognitive understanding or to being contained, within a temporal system. Eaden's coming, like Rachel Mary's confession in the Dimple Hill passage above, marks the turning point between past and future. The earlier days are now not simply 'earlier', they are 'past'. Yet the days to come are still seen as to a certain extent homogenous; they are 'a group'. Further, there is still a kind of 'adding' involved in the model of time: Eaden's portion of time cannot extend, elongate, Miriam's 'portion', but can render it more profound. In Bergsonian terms, it is rendered not more extensive, but more intensive. Here we see how space, as pure extensity, will not provide a structure subtle enough to express the temporality of Miriam's experience.

Gilles Deleuze's reading of Bergson provides us with a useful way of further opening these observations about *Pilgrimage*'s counter-logical arithmetic of dailiness onto the question of spatiality. 'Number', says Deleuze, 'and primarily the arithmetical unit itself, is the model of that which divides without changing in kind. This is the same as saying that number has only differences in degree.'[28] Described thus, then, we can draw a direct parallel between the arithmetical and the spatial, since 'the principal Bergsonian division: that between duration and space' locates space as that 'which never presents anything but differences of degree'.[29] On this Bergsonian model, then, Richardson's presentation of temporality is anything but spatial. Its 'strange sum' certainly involves a sameness, an identity between units (or difference only in 'degree', in number), that permits them to be part of an arithmetic. But it also involves very clearly the uniqueness of individual days, such that they radically disrupt this arithmetic. Further, as we have seen, this addition does not alter that to which it is added; it does not effect a difference in kind. This discussion recalls Miriam's reflections while sleeping outside at the Wilsons: 'A difference in degree is also a difference in kind? Yes. But the *same* difference' (*P* 3:358). Such elliptical phrases appear to be an attempt to negotiate the sameness-and-difference which pervades *Pilgrimage*, not least at the level of this temporal 'strange sum'.

The distinction Miriam makes between paying rent to her boarding-house landlady Mrs Bailey, and to her landlord at Flaxman's, not only crystallises oppositional kinds of temporal arithmetic, but also involves this opposition with Miriam's distinction between genders, and also expresses her radicalised political consciousness. Paying Mrs Bailey 'had marked, not the passage of time, but its rest, at an unchanging centre. Paying rent to this man [the Flaxman's landlord] would be counting off time; and a weekly reminder of the payment for life going on all over the world' (*P* 3:448). While the rent paid to Mrs Bailey adds to the '*unchanging* centre' (my emphasis), forms part of that 'strange sum' where addition does not alter what it adds to but forms part of the ongoing 'being' of the feminine, the rent paid to 'this man' brings with it associations of change, time passing, 'becoming', as well as a political awareness of power differentials and a sense of solidarity with those, like Miriam, who do not own their dwellings and who thus are obliged to make 'payment for life'. As suggested in my discussion of the relationship between Bergson and Richardson, Richardson's text (indeed, one might argue, her life) revolves around a feminine 'unchanging centre'; temporal differences are ultimately ways of articulating Richardson's conception of a fundamentally eternal humanity, of women in particular. Further investigation of the temporality of a specific day, Sunday, will bring me back to these observations.

Not only does *Pilgrimage* add days to each other, but it also divides days up into their constituent parts. As with the spaces between days, days are most often described in this way during periods of leisure (although the temporal divisions of the working day are also in evidence during the 'day at the dentists' passage early in *The Tunnel*). While on holiday with the Wilsons, Miriam takes pleasure in feeling 'each day in four long bright separate pieces, spread out ahead, enclosed' (*P* 3:340); with the Brooms, she anticipates the 'evening portion of the long, shared day' (*P* 4:406). And yet, once more, this division is by no means conventional. During a Sunday with Selina Holland at Flaxman's: 'Sunday morning stands in eternity [. . .] until the late afternoon, when tomorrow will pour in over the surface of the hours' (*P* 4:185). This Flaxman's Sunday expresses the flexibility of the division of the day. Sunday morning is clearly divided from late afternoon, as a separate and defined element of the same day, and yet both elements exceed their boundaries to participate in alternative temporalities: Sunday morning as part of 'eternity', Sunday afternoon as a recipient of Monday morning, already making its presence felt. It is, indeed, around Sunday that some of the text's most complex explorations of dailiness arise.

For obvious reasons, Miriam looks forward to Sundays as a relief from her week of work: she sees 'the week of working days, standing between her and next Sunday's opportunity' (*P* 3:135). Walking through London on a

Sunday, Miriam observes that the 'bright week-day names lost meaning in
the Sunday atmosphere' (*P* 3:310); while visiting the Wilsons, Miriam finds
'There was no feeling of Sunday in the house', but returning to her room
'she found it waiting for her' (*P* 3:345). The effect of the 'Sunday atmosphere' is here described in more detail. In particular it involves stillness; it
is both all-encompassing and heightens boundaries and definition, creating
a kind of self-sufficiency: she finds the 'feeling of Sunday [. . .] pouring into
the room from afar, from all over the world, breaking her march, breaking
up the lines of the past and of the future, isolating her with itself; and, 'The
sea sparkled *to itself*, refusing to call the eye' (my emphasis). On Sunday, all
is sufficient unto itself; there is a freedom from external demands. Yet this
is not simply a result of the socio-cultural fact of Sunday being a holiday.
'Sunday is in the sky', concludes Miriam; it is a kind of metaphysical, essential entity. We can of course suggest that it has taken on this mystical quality
as a result precisely of its socio-cultural significance, but that Miriam insists
on its being bound up with the natural world further intensifies our sense
of days in *Pilgrimage* as temporal units available for inflection through,
yet ultimately having existence beyond, socio-cultural and historical
contexts.

The capacity of Sunday, as a kind of exemplary day, to 'break[. . .] up
the lines of the past and the future', is emphasised. Miriam's last Sunday
spent with Selina Holland at Flaxman's joins with all other Sundays, out of
weekday time: 'Sunday morning stands in eternity and gathers all its fellows
from the past. Now that it is here, it is no longer the last Sunday with Selina
but an extension of all our Sundays together' (*P* 4:185).[30] Sunday enables
pure presence, the pure present: it is only 'now that it is here', not through
anticipation or remembrance, that Sunday can extend itself thus, be joined
to the alternative temporality of Sunday. Sundays involve a dailiness that
is both absolutely anchored in Sunday's location as one of a succession of
days, but also involves participation in an extra-ordinary time. Dailiness,
then, as a temporality, has many more complex inflections than simple
twenty-four hour rhythmic sequentiality.

Miriam's involvement with the Quakers, particularly in the chapter-
novel *Dimple Hill*, requires her to reappraise her feeling about Sundays,
since Quakers do not mark the sabbath. And yet, this does not mean that
Miriam loses her 'feeling of Sunday'; on the contrary, she sees the Quaker
life as 'A perpetual Sunday' (*P* 4:491). The passage in which she makes this
observation is crucial in crystallising Miriam's feelings about Sunday and
its dailiness which is outside of weekday time. The double inflection of

Sunday, formed both through socio-cultural forces and also through some more mysterious, metaphysical force, is intensified as Miriam reflects on the difference between those who mark Sunday, and those who do not, yet who seem to perpetuate the qualities with which it is associated throughout every day. Again, as Miriam describes the Sunday feeling from her childhood in Babington and Barnes, the qualities of separation, stillness, and primarily here distance, are to the fore. Even the activities of Sunday involve this careful selection and separation: 'one went out to watch pater *cut* the sacred asparagus [. . .] carefully *detaching* a few peaches' (*P* 4:490, my emphases). And again, this quality of distinct isolation and sufficiency – 'the part one was in, belonging to itself' – is combined with an all-encompassing universal experience; it 'sent one's mind gliding over the whole' (*P* 4:490). Miriam equates the Quaker life with this Sunday feeling: 'Living always remote, drawn away into the depths of the spirit, they see, all the time, freshly. A perpetual Sunday' (*P* 4:491).

Here, then, Miriam is at her more mystical, articulating her experiences on a spiritual level. Yet she goes on explicitly to link the Quaker's 'perpetual Sunday' with economics:

I understood why Friends make no separation of days and wondered whether, since only those who are not exploited by others can spend all their days sabbatically, Friends all work together, Friends for Friends, keeping their firms apart, unexploiting and unexploited, engaging only in honest trades? For most workers, especially for those helplessly employed in dishonest enterprises, only Sunday is at all comparable to a game or a dance whose rhythm lets one immediately into an eternal way of being. (*P* 4:491)

Oscillating in this passage between socio-economic and spiritual discourses, Miriam articulates the mutual shaping of Sunday between these two forces. What both forces create for her, or should do ideally, is a hiatus in time on Sunday; but this can constitute such a hiatus 'only so long as the day keeps people upright and apart, as in a dance or game; by having an invariable shape, and therefore in all its parts unfathomable depths' (*P* 4:491). Miriam's tendency to shape days, into rooms and wraps and pebbles, is found here in her insistence that Sundays have an 'invariable shape'. And what this shape resists – what Miriam avoids – is 'skat[ing] over its surface [. . .] passing the time'; forward movement is not what Sunday is about. Miriam's Sundays are to be plunged into (as Mrs Dalloway plunges gleefully into her June day), one suspends oneself in them, and here it is precisely through everyday sounds that the day is given its invariable shape:

[. . .] solitary Sundays in London, kept in shape by the audible surrounding world, the recurrent church bells and the sound of the traffic unburdened by the ceaseless heavy rumble of commerce, and admitting, between the passage of lightly running wheels and echoing hoof-beats, stillness and distance, held a depth no other day could provide. (*P* 4:491)

The image is of Miriam held suspended in a matrix of sounds, bells and wheels and hoof-beats, as if caught in a web, 'alighting nowhere' as she puts it in her description of her childhood Sundays. The partial suspension of the machinery of ongoing everyday life in which people are exploited and exploit, where one's time belongs to another, enables a kind of ecstasy, where by being kept still and apart in one's own time, one is able to absorb a universal perspective; or rather, such stillness and distance enables a heightened perception spread over the sensations and experiences of the surrounding world.

Miriam's time with the Quakers, then, enables her to experience a life of 'perpetual Sundays', to realise that the freedom and stillness given by Sunday need no longer be tied to the conventional, commercial weekly structure – part of what Crary calls 'the disciplinary organization of labor, education, and mass consumption',[31] rapidly increasing during the years described in *Pilgrimage*. Thus, very near the end of *Pilgrimage*, when Miriam has effectively been given a year's leisure (a year of Sundays?) through a financial gift, Miriam anticipates the unfolding of the year she has ahead of her as 365 days 'each with a morning, an afternoon, an evening. Three eternities. Yet they are not three eternities but one eternity' (*P* 4:609). If we compare this with the Flaxman's Sunday, where 'Sunday morning stands in eternity [. . .] until the late afternoon, when tomorrow will pour in over the surface of the hours' (*P* 4:185), we note that, with 365 days of Sunday ahead, 'tomorrow' (i.e. Monday) no longer makes its presence precipitately felt. Miriam again imagines the day as minutely and distinctly divided, here into three parts; yet with each part utterly sufficient and complete in itself, each an eternity; and yet again, with each eternity itself part of one eternity, each element available to be added together to make nothing but itself. Indeed, the whole text of *Pilgrimage* mirrors this structure; chapter-novels are gradually added over many years, and yet *Pilgrimage* as a project remains fundamentally the same; after each addition it remains as it was beforehand, as no more nor less than *Pilgrimage*. We see how Richardson's insistence that her text was projected as a single novel, rather than a series of novels, both reflects and provides a structure for the playing out of the 'strange sum' of the text's temporality. In other words, this temporality at which Miriam now arrives, at the moment where the writing of *Pilgrimage* itself is about to begin within the text, is the temporality of *Pilgrimage*. Such elliptical formulations are the only ways, in our ultimately externalised and linear language, to attempt to express the internal folds and layers of the temporality of Richardson's text.

The ways in which days are described in *Pilgrimage* seem, then, to open up a distinction between Miriam's life, and the days in which this life takes place, which mark it out. As their particular characteristics are elaborated, a distance appears between them and the narrative voice that observes them. Indeed, Miriam explicitly states that 'Day, not night, is forgetfulness of time' (*P* 3:357); time can be disguised by the forms which days take on. The subtleties of this distinction are played out in particular around the relationship between work and leisure, and will therefore also arise when I address this relationship in more detail below. And yet, as I hope the foregoing discussion has indicated, by having forms unique to themselves, days become manageable, enabling the articulation of that dailiness in general in which human temporality consists. One everyday form around which the day coalesces, that of the bar of soap, provides a particularly condensed expression of the dailiness of *Pilgrimage*, and a useful conclusion to this discussion of the forms of days in Richardson's text.

The organisation of the day around everyday objects (hairpins, books, dining tables) is a recurring theme in *Pilgrimage*. Particularly striking in this regard is Miriam's 'passion for soap' which arises in volume 4, recalling the appearance of soap in *Ulysses* to evoke a matrix of associations around the everyday – femininity, domesticity, sexuality and corporeality, commodification and advertising, and so on. Soap is banal, certainly: waking up one Sunday morning at Flaxman's, Miriam finds that 'the scent in the air that had brought memories of flowers was turning out to be the faint scent of soap' (*P* 4:177). But in being thus mistaken, soap is linked to Miriam's earliest and most potent memory, what various critics have called the 'bee-memory' (a memory of a garden scene involving a bee and a flower, which recurs throughout *Pilgrimage*), and therefore a further layer of significance is already added to this domestic item. Later in the volume, upon her arrival at Dimple Hill, Miriam finds escape from the watchful eyes of the portrait hung on her bedroom wall by placing herself 'at the wash-stand within whose rose-pink cake of fresh soap were safely stored the days to come' (*P* 4:435). Soap is a sign of hope, of the assurance that day will follow day, and as it gradually diminishes it is a visual and material reminder of the passing of days; Miriam is comforted by its presence. Soap here functions as a kind of container or guardian of days, releasing them carefully one by one, holding them 'safely stored'. However, Miriam's first important encounter with soap, occurring in the earlier chapter-novel *Oberland*, emphasises that days are not just within soap, as here, but that soap is also within days; it is itself an everyday object.

Arriving in Oberland in the Swiss mountains, to convalesce from what has apparently been some kind of nervous breakdown, Miriam goes shopping – for its own sake, it seems, as she vacillates between buying a box of biscuits or a bar of soap. Here she finds the effects of the international marketplace in evidence. Both products are brands identical to those found in England; indeed, deciding on the soap, Miriam leaves the shop 'in possession of a replica of the tablet she had unpacked last night' (*P* 4:61). This is a signal moment of modernity: wishing to purchase something to mark her arrival in Switzerland, and just for 'the excitement of shopping', a very modern phenomenon, Miriam finds that commerce has erased national differences, as well as the physical distance, between the England from which she is briefly fleeing, and the Switzerland where she hopes to find rest.

The 'mystery of her passion for soap' is explored in the paragraphs that follow. It is not only the physical, sensual pleasure it brings, in particular its variety of evocative scents, but 'the secret of its power was in the way it pervaded one's best realizations of everyday life. No wonder Beethoven worked at his themes washing and re-washing his hands' (*P* 4:62). Soap is a leveller – 'all great days had soap [. . .] Every day, even those that are called ordinary days, with its miracle of return from sleep, is heralded by soap' (*P* 4:62–3). But this by no means involves a neutralisation of the meaning of the day; soap is 'with you when you are in that state of feeling life at first hand that makes even the best things that can happen important not so much in themselves as in the way they make you conscious of life, and of yourself living' (*P* 4:63). Every day, no matter how important the things that happen in it – its contents – is first and foremost about 'yourself living', for no matter if you are a great composer or dentist's secretary, you still use soap. As we will see, Miriam has a sense of the things in life – one's work, one's friends – as constitutive of everyday life, and yet fundamentally these things are superposed on a background of 'her own life of endless day' – 'yourself living'.

Soap, then, reveals at least three crucial and imbricated aspects of the dailiness I am exploring in this text, and throughout this book. Firstly, days appear as stored up – as in the room-day chronotope discussed above, they are always already there. The comfort to be found in the reliable progression of days, particularly related here to that which washes clean, implying the opportunity for a fresh start, is expressed – 'the illusion of beginning, as soon as you have finished, all over again as a different person' (*P* 4:62). Yet the soap will itself be 'in' every day; attention is once more drawn to the *mise-en-abyme* structure of dailiness, where every day is different, and yet each mirrors, even contains, all that have gone before. Secondly, soap is part of an increasingly commodified everyday life; whether Miriam is disturbed or comforted by her ability to purchase a bar of soap in Switzerland precisely matching that which she bought at home is not clear, but what is evident is the eclipsing of difference, of cultural and geographical space, in this gesture. The commodification of everyday life risks running against the Lefebvrian desire to return each individual's life to him- or herself, to render what is unique in each life. Finally, and relatedly, the most unusual association of soap in *Pilgrimage* draws attention to 'yourself living', to the everydayness of all lives. This is precisely the kind of levelling gesture which I have argued in my Introduction should be implied in a critique of everyday life. According to the dominant values of Western culture, the life of Beethoven is given greater value than that of other people. But he too washed his hands; fundamentally, his life was just as 'everyday' as that of anyone else, it just so happens that for him, everyday life included the composition of symphonies that would become major cultural landmarks. The ritual of soap enables Miriam to see her life, just as much as Beethoven's, as part of a Lefebvrian 'art of living', 'not as a means towards "another" end, but as an end in itself' (*CEL* 199), attending not so much to 'things that can happen' as 'the way they make you conscious of life, and of yourself living'.

PILGRIMAGE AND EVERYDAY LIFE

> For what astonished, and still astonishes, me more than anything else was the existence, anywhere, of anything at all.[32]

The everyday and the daily are often defined in *Pilgrimage* in a normative sense, as the banal, the tedious, and the unremarkable. Particularly in the early volumes, the 'everyday' is the unmarked and the ordinary, but most suggestively it is both reality, and that outside of which the real is to be found. For example, thinking of Bob Greville and his London club life, Miriam seems to break off her train of thought to note, in a phrase given a paragraph to itself, 'But in some way he was connected with that strange thing outside the everyday things' (*P*1:469). As Miriam's experiences widen, moving out from the limited horizon provided by her suburban childhood in Barnes, so her concept of the extent of reality extends. The idea that there is something 'outside the everyday things' is a product of her own new experiences – differing wildly from anything she had ever expected to experience. Before Miriam even begins her independent life in London, then, she is becoming aware of the alternatives to what she regards as 'everyday things'. And by the time of *Interim*, Miriam has had her consciousness explicitly raised by her contact with 'Bohemia'. Her sudden vision of a Europe integrated through intellectual exchange brings 'a comfortable assurance that somewhere beyond the hurrying confusion of everyday life something was being done quietly in a removed real world that led the other world' (*P* 2:342). Here, as in the quotation regarding Bob Greville, the everyday is background, unremarkable; however, what is now going on elsewhere, in this 'removed real world', is no longer 'strange', but on the contrary brings comfort.

In formulations such as these, then, Miriam seems to view the everyday in the way Bakhtin suggests it functions in *Madame Bovary*, as 'a contrasting background for temporal sequences that are more charged with energy and event'.[33] Describing the provincial town setting of *Madame Bovary*, Bakhtin suggests that 'such towns are the locus for cyclical everyday time. Here there are no events, only "doings" that constantly repeat themselves.'[34] Indeed, the term 'day' here proliferates in Bakhtin's own prose, 'A day is just a day [. . .] Day after day', and so on, emphasising the commonplace association of dailiness with inactivity and banality. And yet, Emma Bovary's passionate desire precisely for 'events' in this endless round of 'doings' indicates that certain locales are not inevitably shackled to certain temporalities; that life is never, as it appears to be in *Madame Bovary*, only going on elsewhere. Indeed, it is Emma Bovary's assumption that this is the case that precipitates her tragedy.

The realisation that life is not to be found elsewhere is played out in *Pilgrimage*. For while Miriam is seduced by the idea of the 'strange', the 'real', going on outside her everyday life, what the text itself draws attention to is the strangeness and reality of Miriam's own 'everyday' life, and implicitly validates it simply by existing as a narrative of this life. Certainly, Miriam continues through the 'consciousness-raising' chapter-novels of volume 3 to view strangeness as the underside of dailiness, as she does during her first experience of London on a bank holiday: 'Daily London grown invisible, incredible' (*P* 3:501), indeed dailiness retains notions of the banal, even the tawdry, as she senses the dailiness of her weasely landlord Perrance's 'den' (*P* 3:509). Yet it is at about this point that she articulates the realisation that 'This scene that she persisted in seeing as a background, stationary, not moving on, *was* her life, *was* counting off years' (*P* 3:484). Emphasis on the spatialisation of temporality in *Pilgrimage*, or *Pilgrimage* as a primarily 'spatial' text, can have the effect of suppressing this central insight; that time, albeit cyclical, oscillatory, elliptical, sedimentary, is nevertheless never going on in another place, in the supposedly strange, real elsewhere. Earlier in the volume, Miriam had reflected with frustration and distaste on people 'who talk about "ordinary everyday life" and approve of "far horizons", and desert islands and the other side of the moon, *as if they were real and wonderful and life was not*' (*P* 3:19, my emphasis). Everyday life is precisely what life is; as my discussion of Miriam's attachment to the use of soap has explored, even the most extraordinary events, persons, experiences, are as much the same as they are different, sharing both the definitive ordinariness and the 'strangeness of the adventure of being, of the fact of the existence, anywhere, of anything at all' (*P* 4:638).

To emphasise the centrality of everyday life is not, of course, to deny that it is often tedious, difficult, or painful. Had this not been the case for Emma Bovary, she would have had no need to try to escape it. Miriam's own experience as a working woman attests to the discomfort and hardship of her everyday life. However, the way in which Richardson records this everyday working life precisely emphasises such physical and mental hardship by paying attention to it not as background to Miriam's 'real' life, but as 'the thing itself', life itself. Textual space, and therefore a reader's time, devoted to the details of this everyday working life, metonymically drives home the fact that these hours make up Miriam's life as much as her intellectual exchanges with Mag and Jan do, as her combative relationships with Shatov and Wilson will. In particular, the passage in *The Tunnel* where the events of a single day at the dentists' surgery are transcribed over many pages is, as we shall now see, an example not of everyday life as 'a contrasting background for temporal sequences that are more charged with energy and event',[35] but as just such a charged temporal sequence.

Richardson spent many years in conventional, waged work before she began work as a writer, which in turn preceded her novelistic career. The fact that Richardson's working life began in the 1880s, that she chose explicitly to describe her non-literary work in her writing, and that she was a woman, marks her out among modernist writers. Throughout *Pilgrimage*, there is a continual ambivalence regarding Miriam's working life. While she feels great pride in her ability to support herself – particularly after she arrives in London and is able to live independently on her salary – Miriam also resents the physical and mental demands of her work. The limits of her tolerance and the extent of her principles regarding the level of control employers have over their employees are displayed in Chapter 8 of *Deadlock*. Following a grumbling complaint from her employer regarding his library books, organisation of which Miriam has begun to take responsibility for of her own accord although it is not formally part of her job, Miriam finds herself delivering 'a whole long speech' to Hancock:

About unfairness. And to prove my point to him individually I told him of things that were unfair to me and their other employees in the practice; about the awfulness of having to be there first thing in the morning from the country after a week-end. *They* don't. They sail off to their expensive week-ends without even saying good-bye, and without even thinking whether we can manage to have any sort of recreation at all on our salaries. (*P* 3:179)

The fact that Miriam even has country weekends does, of course, mark her out from most employees – her class and social privileges extend thus far – but her speech still legitimately draws attention to the inequality between employer and employee. However, Miriam cannot afford to pass up the opportunity of 'put[ting] it right' (*P* 3:183) and regaining her employment – 'I have no training for any other work, and no resources' (*P* 3:180). And despite her earlier vociferous protests, Hancock insists that '"You must clearly understand that I expect you to fulfil all reasonable requests whether referring to the practice or no, and moreover to fulfil them *cheerfully*"' (*P* 3:185). Not only, then, can an employer demand absolute control over an employee's time, requiring that they spend a morning arranging flowers in addition to their formal duties, for example (*P* 3:179), but they even regard it as within their authority to control their employee's emotional state – Hancock does not simply want Miriam to appear to be cheerful, but actually to *be* cheerful. This Miriam cannot guarantee. What she must assent to, however, is the absolute control her employers assert over her time during working hours, and their rigorous maintenance of the limits of those hours – there is no subsequent mention of any relaxation of the rules regarding appearance at work the morning after a country weekend.

Miriam's sense of agency within time, which we have seen is profoundly mutable, conflicts with this rigid demarcation of temporality. Her experience of days which range around her, which she dons like a cape or holds in her hand, is pitted against a system where one's time literally belongs to someone else. No wonder that Miriam feels, even early on in her London life, that 'nothing that happens in the part of your life that is not free, *the part you do and are paid for*, is alive' (*P* 2:215; emphasis in original).[36] Morag Shiach's commentary on Gissing's *The Odd Women* of 1893 reveals a similar ambivalence towards the work which the New Woman had so vociferously argued for the right to undertake; the extent to which work, far from constituting a liberation, involves a repression of the individual subject: 'The element beyond "the work by which I earn my money", the element that Rhoda experiences as integral to her self, cannot be articulated.'[37]

Chapter 3 of *The Tunnel* describes in detail, from beginning to end, a single day in the dentist's surgery where Miriam works – the part of her life that she 'does and is paid for'. Spatially speaking, Miriam's work day operates primarily on a vertical axis, as Miriam runs up and down stairs to her office, the surgeries, the workshop in the basement, and the domestic rooms where meals are served. The forty-two pages devoted to this day are almost pure description with relatively little reflection by Miriam; the third person narrative is full of reported speech, pays great attention to the minute physical details of Miriam's work (the various instruments she must maintain, the materials required for her to wrap a parcel, and so forth), and is divided into numerous short passages of no more than two pages, the longest being those that describe mealtimes, with a concomitant relaxation of pace. The overall effect is one of constant industry; the passing of time is not reflected upon save to note, say, whether the late incidence of tea is likely to make Leyton miss an appointment. The relief felt by Miriam as the day reaches its close, at the end of the chapter, is shared by the reader, emerging from the densely descriptive prose of the long penultimate paragraph into the clarity of the three simple sentences which make up the final paragraph. But as the door closes and Miriam's day 'scroll[s] up behind her' (*P* 2:74), the reader encounters the white space of the end of a chapter which reminds him or her of the extensity of the chapter which has just come to an end. The chapter, like the day, may now be over, instantaneously coiling up and thereby apparently losing this extensity. The vertical spatial axis of the workplace may encourage a reading which excludes temporal progression. But this moment of pause at the end of the working day enables the reader to perceive the length of this day, the time it constituted – both for the reader, since Richardson has given this day palpable temporal extensity by devoting a whole chapter of forty-two pages to it, and for Miriam.

At this early point in her employment at Orly's dentists' surgery Miriam, like the reader, is caught up in the details of her work. Miriam, in good William Jamesian fashion, learns working habits which allow her (and hence the narrative) to reduce the energy spent focusing on the details of her work. Nevertheless, in a moment of insight toward the very end of *Pilgrimage*, Miriam describes the whole ten years of working life at the surgery as 'One long moment of attention, more or less strained, day and night' (*P* 4:386). This part of Richardson's text takes us back to the key question of the status of attention at this period, and specifically Crary's argument that 'attention and distraction cannot be thought outside of a continuum in which the two ceaselessly flow into one another, as part of a social field in which the same imperatives and forces incite one and the other'.[38] One particular passage from this chapter is signal here. As Crary reminds us, '[d]uring the period I am examining [from 1879 to the very early 1900s], attentiveness was generally synonymous with an observer who was fully embodied and for whom perception coincided with physiological and/or motor activity'.[39] As part of her duties, Miriam must look after and clean the dental instruments. This process is described using a series of present continuous verbs, in one long sentence with one verb per clause: 'drying and cleansing [. . .] freeing [. . .] polishing [. . .] repolishing [. . .] scraping [. . .] scraping [. . .] clearing'. Thereby, the 'tedium of the long series of small, precise, attention-demanding movements' is heightened (*P* 2:40). And yet, this period of minute attention to the physical task at hand flows into a psychological state of what could best be described as distraction, as Miriam's thoughts turn from *her* work to work in general, all the other 'drudgery workers, at fixed salaries', and the system which keeps them there. However, despite Miriam's mental distraction, we assume that she continues with the 'series of small, precise, attention-demanding movements', since by the end of her period of reflection – daydream, perhaps? – the work is done.

Here we find a confirmation of Crary's main hypothesis, namely, that attention is less a visual and a more temporal state. While the attention Miriam pays to the work of cleaning the instruments participates in a chronological, external temporality, a distracted temporality is also apparent, where her thoughts allow her an escape from her own drudgery (i.e. these thoughts are not focused on the demands of the office schedule). This passage shows Miriam as a subject who primarily '*inhabit[s] time* as disempowered' (my emphasis),[40] her time at work belonging to her employers, and who is yet able through the slippage between attention and distraction to evade the temporality of work, in a temporal version of de Certeau's *perruque*. Indeed, it seems to be precisely the minute attention demanded by the task of cleaning, and its tiny repetitive movements, that allows such a period of distraction. Finally, the content of these thoughts reflects Miriam's insubordination against her employers, as she sympathises with those wage-slaves in the same position as her. Her sense of disempowerment is emphasised as she makes a distinction between the 'Blessed' drudgery of housekeeping, and 'someone else's drudgery'. Later in life, as a writer, she will be doing her own work; here, regardless of what she is doing, the work is fundamentally someone else's.

One final remark here ties these observations back into contemporary discourses on gender. A 1913 article asking 'Are Men Better Typists than Women?', quoted by Shiach in her discussion of the development of the association of women with typewriting, surmised that, given the evidence of some aptitude tests, men are 'inferior to women, perhaps, in power of sustained attention'.[41] The emphasis on 'sustained' is interesting here; while men work more quickly, presumably passing more rapidly from one thing to the next, women appear to be aligned with the kind of prolonged attentiveness associated with more serious activity. We find explicit reflection of such observations in *Deadlock*, where Miriam finds herself indignant at a lecturer's 'assertion that it is curious that the human faculty of attention should have originated in women' (*P* 3:29); her indignation is not at the assertion itself, but at the lecturer's apparent surprise that so important a faculty should have arisen originally in women. Attentiveness was seen to have 'originated in women', and a 'sustained' attentiveness at that; and yet the kinds of attentiveness culturally associated with women – daydream, distraction, superficiality – apparently run counter to the definition of proper attention as externalised, ends-driven, efficient. It is not surprising, then, that the slippage between attention and distraction here appears particularly manifest at a moment of something like daydream, one of those liminal and feminised states which presents the greatest challenge to any attempted regulation of psychic energies – which regulation, as we have seen, Miriam vehemently resents and attempts to resist.

Particularly when seen in the context of what comes before and after it, the 'day at the dentist's' chapter provides evidence of the hypothesis that by being made to pay attention to a limited range of objects and tasks, we are distracted from the fact that daily life is the thing itself, life itself – the insight toward which Miriam progresses throughout volumes 2 to 4 of *Pilgrimage*. This chapter, as noted above, consists in large part of pure description; unusually for *Pilgrimage*, the chapter begins with several pages devoid of explicit textual transcription of Miriam's reflections. By contrast, the previous chapter ends with an extended passage of Miriam's personal reflection on her thoughts and feelings, a typically Richardsonian flow of association around the smell of syringia. Similarly, the next chapter plunges the reader back into a vision of London very clearly inflected through Miriam's individual associations and feelings. This chapter now sees Miriam at leisure, that 'recreation' which she holds so dear in her later tirade against Hancock. Chapter 3, by being 'about' working, focuses Miriam's attention, and that of the reader, with its details of the state of the address books, a broken denture, and so on. By doing so, it distracts one from the realisation, reawakened with the scrolling up of this long day and Miriam's plunge back into her London leisure, that it is the same person, no less real and no less important, who lives through the tedious routine of the work-day, as she or he who lives through their free time. What Crary calls 'the disciplinary organization of labor, education, and mass consumption'[42] – here specifically of labour – nascent at the turn of the century and now fully entrenched, tries to enforce a distinction between the subject at work and the recreational subject, between the attentive and the distracted subject. Indeed, Miriam will continue to view this part of her life as not 'alive' (*P* 2:215); it is the coexistence of this view of the work-day in *Pilgrimage*, along with passages such as Chapter 3 of *The Tunnel* where the extent and complexity of this temporal unit is dwelt upon, that emphasises the inhumanity of a system which makes the subject feel, by implication, dead, during vast stretches of their life.

While, as we have seen, the work-day involves an attempt strictly to regulate the working subject's time and attention, leisure in the late nineteenth and early twentieth century was also becoming more and more regulated and organised as a system outside of, but having increasingly strong parallels with, the world of work.[43] To further complicate this increasing correlation between work and leisure, one of the more frustrating aspects of her work-day, as Miriam sees it, is the expectation that certain activities usually categorised as leisure activities – for example, accompanying a singer at the piano, arranging flowers, or dealing with library books – form part of her responsibilities as an employee. Elsewhere in *Pilgrimage*, we will see Miriam taking great pleasure in playing the piano; here, it can only be seen as an encroachment on the time allocated to her by the labour system to complete her official tasks. Leisure is, then, not so much defined by the activities in which it consists, but rather the time in which it takes place.

An implicit privileging of work over leisure, where certain activities are seen as valid where others are not, is expressed in Miriam's reflection on a habitual exchange between herself and her sometime lover, Hypo Wilson. Miriam predicts his question: '"Well, what have you been up to since last week?" and she should answer, as a hundred times she had answered: "Living".' Hypo recasts this response, 'what he considered an evasion', as 'agreeable loafing that leads nowhere' (*P* 4:220). The contrast between Hypo's ends-driven view of life, of the use of time, and Miriam's, where leisure or 'loafing' is just as much 'living' as other mode of existence, also inevitably takes on a gendered aspect, since so much of Miriam's reflection on the relationship between men and women takes place in response to her relationship with Hypo. This returns us to Richardson's distinction between women's 'being' and men's 'becoming'. As the distinction implies, men are seen as driven by a goal, moving toward something, away from where they are now; hence Hypo's criticism of Miriam's loafing that '*leads nowhere*'. And this masculine model, the 'determination to see life in terms of certain kinds of activity' (*P* 4:318), is of course dominant: 'Even in Bohemia people thought it was necessary always to be doing some definite thing' (*P* 2:368). Miriam is not interested in 'kinds of activity' per se, but in the forms which they take, the role they have in producing and informing individual consciousness. Kaplan's view of the relationship between Hypo and Miriam is pertinent here. Kaplan argues that, despite Hypo's explicit belief in equality of treatment and opportunity for men and women, Miriam cannot accept his insistence on rationality and logic, his pursuit of 'scientific goals' and organisation, and his refusal to acknowledge 'the feminine way of thinking – intuition, mystical perception, multi-leveled consciousness'.[44]

This disagreement between Miriam and Hypo, as well as enabling an articulation of gender distinctions, is relevant to a larger debate around the status of the human subject in modernity, and in this period of modernity in particular. In his study of the *Bildungsroman* in European culture – a literary tradition *Pilgrimage* continues and modifies – Franco Moretti presents the following definition of 'modern personality':

It designates what renders an individual unique and different from others. But this distinction [. . .] never applies to a single activity or a single characteristic. The modern individual feels that no occupation, be it work or family life or whatever, ever permits one to 'express fully' one's personality. [. . .] It would prefer never to have to bend for anything, never to be the means toward an end, whatever that end might be.[45]

Thus, and remembering perhaps Lefebvre's insistence on the incorporation of work, leisure and family life in everyday life, Moretti states that 'modern personality [the place through which all these elements demand equally to be realised] lodges at the centre of everyday life'.[46] Miriam's resistance to the idea that her life must be realised in one activity, 'some definite thing', directly relates to her feeling that 'nothing that happens in the part of your life that is not free, *the part you do and are paid for*, is alive' (*P* 2:215). Indeed, Moretti notes, drawing on such important theorists of modern life as Lukács, Simmel and Weber, precisely that 'it is fairly difficult for modern "personality" to reach its goal in a professional occupation alone, that is to say, in work'.[47] A faultline in twentieth-century capitalist society is once more opened up. While there is pervasive pressure to be doing something that leads somewhere, some definite thing – to be 'taking something up', as H.D.'s peers will demand of her – in order to validate one's existence, precisely this emphasis on 'a single activity or a single characteristic', an 'end', is at odds with the fulfilment of modern individual personality as it has been constructed alongside, indeed as a necessary part of, the entrenchment of bourgeois capitalist values and structures. These structures have produced (or rather, are at this period in the process of producing) a model of the human subject as a complex, self-determining, unique individual, ultimately defined not by any collective identity but by the exercise of his or her (supposedly unfettered) free will – a model finding its ultimate expression in the consumer freely able to choose between buying a tin of biscuits and a bar of soap. When Hypo accuses Miriam of 'loafing', then, he fails to understand that this loafing, or 'idling' to use Moretti's phrase, 'does not mean doing *nothing*, but rather not entrusting the definition of one's personality to any *one* activity';[48] that Miriam, far from failing to do herself justice, is in fact pursuing the kind of life most likely to enable full expression of her personality.

For Miriam it is 'living' that is an end in itself. In an earlier exchange, Hypo has argued that 'You think too much. Life's got to be lived' (*P* 3:377), but his formulation excludes the possibility that thinking is living too. Indeed, the very innovation of Richardson's style is to reflect the fact that an individual life is lived through a particular consciousness, through particular ways of thinking. Hypo argues that Miriam will have to make decisions to avoid 'miss[ing] things'. When asked how one can 'miss things', Hypo responds that '"Mere existence isn't life"', but Miriam comes back with '"Why *mere*?"' (*P* 3:237–8); why, Miriam suggests, should an existence which eschews 'taking definite steps', leading somewhere, becoming, be any the less full than one which does so? Further, how can it make any sense to say that one has 'missed' things? – since there is a sense in which the only experiences one can have are those that one does have; one can only live one's own life.

A similar angle on the relationship between subject and world is expressed as Miriam reflects over dinner at Mrs Bailey's boarding-house that 'There is no need to go out into the world. Everything is there without anything; the world is added' (*P* 3:67). 'Everything is there without anything'; this is not only an example of Miriam's belief in predestination, but a reflection on the world as having qualities, existence, regardless of our 'going out into' it, of our 'taking definite steps', as Hypo puts it, rather as it is figured in the room/day analogy discussed above. And earlier in *Pilgrimage*, just before the chapter at the dentists', Miriam clearly states the quality of that which is 'there without anything': 'It would be perpetually beginning now. Nights and days were all one day; all hers, unlimited. Her life and work at Wimpole Street were something extra, thrown in with her own life of endless day. Sarah and Harriett, their lives and friends, her own friends, the Brooms, the girls in Kennett street, all thrown in' (*P* 2:30).

On one level, this might be seen as contradicting my previous argument, that the chapter in the dentists' draws our attention to the reality and extensity of Miriam's daily life, 'her life and work at Wimpole Street'. It seems here, rather, that Miriam sees her work as just a contingent aspect of her life, not central, but 'extra'. However, it is not only her work which she categorises in this way; every element of her life, all the parts of her life that are most important to her (her sisters and her friends as well as her work), are viewed as equivalent, '*all* thrown in'. No single element is central; they are all superposed over the background of an 'endless day', and as such are all equally important. Herein, indeed, lay Katharine Mansfield's criticism of Richardson's work in her review of *The Tunnel* and *Interim* in *The Athenaeum* of January 1920, stating that if everything was of equal importance in these novels, everything equally must be of 'equal unimportance'.[49] And yet, as noted above, in years to come Miriam will feel that 'This scene that she persisted in seeing as a background, stationary, not moving on, *was* her life, *was* counting off years' (*P* 3:484), the scene of herself as dentists' secretary. *Pilgrimage* does not allow us to conclude that what one does with one's life – in particular, what one does for a living – completely defines one's existence, absolutely constitutes the dailiness of one's life; in one sense, these contingent aspects are less fundamentally constitutive of the subject than the very fact of dailiness, of life going on in an ineluctable, rhythmic fashion. Neither, however, can we conclude that what one does with one's life, the way in which one is obliged to 'take definite steps', is entirely irrelevant. As Miriam puts it, indeed, this pattern of the working week and the longed-for leisure of the weekend '*was* her life, *was* counting off years'. That the text devotes more and more time to the description of Miriam's leisure time disguises from us, as it has been disguised from Miriam, the amount of time actually spent at work. This is a narrative necessity perhaps, in order to maintain the reader's interest, since if the narrative was divided between Miriam's working life and leisure time in their precise proportions, no doubt the reader would become as weary with the text as Miriam becomes with her work. But it is also a common strategy in daily life, where the individual subject may define themselves more strongly through their leisure activities, seen as truly 'individual', than through their work – disproportionately to the amount of time devoted to these conventionally separated areas of life.

When Hancock says that '"I think a man who can make a hobby of his profession is a very fortunate man"' (*P* 2:139) he is precisely emphasising the fact that these two realms are generally considered to be mutually exclusive. Even when they are apparently brought together, as when Miriam plays the piano at the dentists', the dominant economic impetus and cultural ethos of work renders this leisure activity simply a part of the working day. However, there is a third category of activity which Hancock does not consider – that of vocation. It is through considering Miriam's, and Richardson's, vocation as a writer, that we can start to address the complex question of what kind of 'work' or occupation writing might constitute. Miriam has distanced herself from the 'writers' of the Wilsons' circle, people who Miriam observes 'gradually making themselves into writers' and thereby gaining access to 'the world of clever writers' (*P* 4:147, 148). Clinging to the vision of herself alone in her room in Chapter 4 of *March Moonlight*, spending her 365 days in an eternity which is beyond the sanctioned divisions of 'work' and 'leisure', Miriam eschews the socially sanctioned figure of 'the writer', instead insisting upon writing as a vocation outside of, and anterior to, the world of hobbies and professions, and their attendant associations and social status.

The idea of life expressed as vocation is again illuminated with reference to Richardson's personal spiritual context. Describing the beliefs of the founder of the Quakers, Richardson says: 'For Fox, we cannot keep too clearly in mind, the relationship of the soul to the Light was a life-process; the "inner" was not in contradistinction to the outer. For him, the great adventure, the abstraction from all externality, the purging of the self, the Godward energizing of the lonely soul, was in the end, as it has been in all the great "actives" among the mystics, the most practical thing in the world, and ultimately fruitful in life-ends.'[50] The Quaker life shows how spiritual fulfilment is indeed to be found in the process of action in the world, but that one need not seek fruitful practical actions or 'life-ends' outside the compass of one's own everyday 'life-process', one's everyday activities and interactions. The Quakers see active intervention in society as contiguous with their apparently passive, solitary contemplation or inwardness; both are part of their everyday lives: 'The "inner" [is] not in contradistinction to the outer.' 'Loafing' and 'taking definite steps', as Hypo would put it, no longer constitute distinct activities under this model. Both constitute the fulfilment of the individual's vocation. It is thus as vocation – being both active and passive, involving both 'loafing' and taking definite steps – that the activity of writing is best understood for Richardson.

The paradoxical aspects of Miriam's feelings about writing are explored during Chapter 4 of *March Moonlight*, the text's most sustained meditation on what it might mean to write, and to be a writer. During a train journey, Miriam muses on the potential now open to her thanks to the financial aid of a benefactor. She expresses her almost involuntary impetus to write, envisaging 'a choice of experiences, any one of them presently returning of itself with power to move me to put it into words'. Experience is crucial in order to write. Yet 'To write is to forsake life' (*P* 4:609); time spent writing is time spent not 'living' (although we will see this challenged in Woolfian models of daily life). Writing a novel, Miriam feels, 'would mean spending enormous pieces of life away from life' (*P* 4:614). And yet, evidently, Miriam/Richardson does go on to write this novel, to spend this time away from life. To this extent, then, writing is like the kind of work done in the dentists' surgery, that keeps one away from 'life', leisure, recreation, one's own time.

Certainly, the writing of *Pilgrimage* seemed to become, over her lifetime, less of a choice and more of a chore to Richardson. There were practical and economic factors involved here; the chapter-novels of *Pilgrimage* were never going to earn Richardson much money, whereas her journalism was a more reliable source of income and therefore more immediately attractive. Fromm observes of the years 1927 to 1930 that 'in three years she had man-aged to write only half a novel [which would become *Dawn's Left Hand*], and she blamed her lack of progress on all the other work she had done instead'.[51] Fromm suggests that Richardson seems to have been avoiding work on her novel (consciously or otherwise). Short stories, forewords and even translations were relatively manageable projects, with an aim, purpose and, importantly, an end in sight. Indeed, as shown in the foregoing discus-sion of the shapes of days, *Pilgrimage* expresses the comfort to be found in that which is bounded, clearly formed, that has an end and clear purpose, as well as the restrictions imposed by the setting of boundaries and ends. The writing of *Pilgrimage*, by contrast with these shorter writing projects, was neither work nor leisure, but became Richardson's spiritual vocation. It appeared to be leisure in that she chose to do it, it would not necessar-ily make her any money, and she was apparently prevented from doing it because of 'work'; yet it also appeared as work in that it defined her (as 'a writer'), that it involved (at least nominally) being paid, and that it was very often painful. Sean Latham has recently asserted that key modernist writers such as Woolf and Joyce 'understood that their literary art was also a social and business practice, that is, an attempt to secure both symbolic and economic capital for themselves'.[52] Richardson, by contrast, while far from being exempt from economic concerns, produces a modernist text that resists at every point – in the process of its making as well as its consumption – assimilation to received notions of 'social and business practice', of participation in a capitalist labour economy. It was quite simply, to return to her paraphrase of Fox, her 'life-process'.

Understanding the writing of *Pilgrimage* alternatively as a vocation, then – as indeed the title invites us to do – we might be able to understand more fully Richardson's being 'afraid of an ending', for an ending to *Pilgrimage* would thus quite literally constitute an end to Richardson's life. Paul Ricoeur's commentary on Proust might just as easily be applied to Richardson: 'The fact that the time of the hero's story approaches its own source, the narrator's present, without being able to catch up with it, is part of the meaning of the narrative, namely, that it is ended or at least broken off when the hero becomes a writer.'[53] Indeed, there is a strong connection between the two texts, in their scope, ambition and form; Richardson eagerly anticipated reading Proust, and 'read and re-read' the first two volumes of *Swann's Way* when she was given them at the end of 1922; she was sent further volumes by the literary patron and writer Bryher in 1924.[54] Fromm articulates a key similarity between the two writers thus: 'for both of them the past was a world to which they went forward rather than back, thus making of it a future that would one day be the present';[55] this convoluted construction precisely articulates the mobius strip which both Proust and Richardson make of time.

It is painful, then, that *Pilgrimage* must not end; that Richardson can never give herself the pleasure of concluding – which pleasure must not, in a critical context which emphasises circularity and eternity in Richardson's work, be occluded, and to which pleasure the text consistently draws attention. But overriding this pleasure is a more profound impetus, to resist ending, which is the most vital aspect both of the text, and of Richardson's life and work. Just as days end, but dailiness does not, *Pilgrimage* includes the comfort of endings, of the manageable and material, but also gestures toward the liberation of a temporality beyond beginnings and ends.

CHAPTER 3

Re-creation, work and the everyday in Gertrude Stein

INTRODUCTION: STEIN AND WORK

Gertrude Stein once wrote that 'what is known as work is something that I cannot do'.[1] For so prolific a writer, this may seem an unlikely statement. What it asks us to do, then, is examine more closely the meaning of 'what is known as work' for Stein. In this chapter I will suggest that internal to Stein's texts we find positive values attached to a kind of temporality or attention which does not involve the accepted attributes of 'what is known as work'. The term 'work' bears certain standard associations, at the time of Stein's writing as now: involving some kind of labour or expenditure of energy, and based on an epistemology of logical cognition, it has a particular aim, usually explicit, and it involves a temporality of sequence and chronology, in particular one where time is valued quantitatively rather than qualitatively. Thus defined, 'work' also describes the conventions of reading, and writing, implied by a standard text. Stein's texts, however, challenge these assumptions. Her texts do not necessarily require laborious working-through; indeed, they resist it. They articulate and require the activation of alternative 'ways of knowing'. They resist a teleological structure of origin and end, and they encourage exploration of alternative models of temporality, resisting the quantification of time.

Stein's textual techniques resonate with the improvised, fluid, sensual and evasive operations that we have come to associate with the everyday, particularly through the work of Lefebvre and de Certeau. I aim to reappraise the relationships between the terms 'work', 'recreation' and 'everyday' – terms employed suggestively by Stein herself (who once described herself as being engaged in 'the recreation of the word') and by critics of Stein. In a conventional figuration, 'work' might seem to define the everyday as its opposite. Within capitalist political economy and from a bourgeois perspective, power is located in work, in production, in 'industry'. Work is the valorised system of operations, against which every other mode of operating is measured; any mode of behaviour or perception which does not fully comply with its injunctions is seen as trivial, and that would include recreation and the everyday. Such suspicion and trivialisation of the everyday within structures of power lends credence to Lefebvre's and de Certeau's affirmation of the everyday as precisely that which has the potential to evade and subvert structures of capitalism. However, the actual experience of 'work' is more likely to place individuals in a position of *dis*empowerment, or, to use the conventional Marxist terminology, alienation. By destabilising the category of work, not only questioning its value but broadening its signification to suggest that it also describes a certain kind of psychic activity, Stein allows us to explore the extent to which excessive emphasis on work does indeed disempower, particularly in terms of the individual's experience of time. While bourgeois capitalist systems enforce the division of time, creating a hierarchy of activity within the day (as suggested in my discussion of Richardson's days of work and leisure), Stein's texts, in their exploration of non-privileged (i.e. non-'working') modes of behaviour, explicate how work is one of a number of everyday activities, and resituate working alongside various other equally valuable, productive, creative activities. By drawing attention to the value to be found in non-working practices, Stein's texts gesture towards a reinscription of the subject as empowered in time, in all aspects of their everyday existence.

As we have seen, Lefebvre insists that everyday life involves the elements of both work and leisure. Further, he specifies that the critique of everyday life 'involves an investigation of the exact relations' between the terms of various binaries including 'triviality and splendour – seriousness and play – reality and dreams, etc.'; the couple 'work' and 'recreation' could also obviously be included in Lefebvre's inexhaustive list (*CEL* 251). Stein's texts will be explored here in terms of the extent to which they constitute just such a critique of everyday life, an investigation of its apparent binaries. I will argue that Stein's restitution of the everyday as the context within which work and recreation both find their place does not involve an outright rejection of 'work', since she eschews the binary model upon which its assertion of primacy is predicated. Rather, 'work' forms a dialogue with 'recreation' within the context of the everyday. To this extent, there is contiguity between Stein's writing and the theoretical orientation of de Certeau, in particular his inflection of the Lefebvrian investigation of binaries. Ben Highmore says of de Certeau that 'What de Certeau's work employs are non-oppositional binary terms. Not only do the terms "production" and "consumption", for example, fold back on each other, but each provides the other with the very essence that would define them'.[2] Substituting the words 'work' and 'recreation' for 'production' and 'consumption' in this formulation provides a useful indication of the relationship I am positing between the two terms.

Further, the productive potential of 'recreation' itself, particularly as it is understood as re-creation, is revealed in Stein's work. To put Stein into the genealogy of the everyday as sketched by Michael Sheringham, for Stein, '[as later] for Lefebvre, as later for Michel de Certeau, the level of the everyday is associated, "*malgré tout*", with creative potential'.[3] And yet, crucially, as de Certeau puts it, 'The "everyday" arts no more "form" a *new* product than they have their own language' (my emphasis).[4] Stein's writing, I argue, intensifies our understanding of literary writing as just such an everyday art, which can never appear as absolutely novel ('*new*'). Rather, whether in the 'insistent', repetitive style of Melanctha, or the word heap style of *Tender Buttons*, Stein's texts involve the reader in a continuous, fluid *re*-creation of meaning – one which mitigates against the temporal suspension involved in the discourse surrounding 'work' – as they involve precisely the recreational activity of reading. Stein's own antipathy to 'what is known as work', despite her evident personal commitment to her own work as a writer, provides a biographical indication of possible motives for this redistribution of value among the conventionally serious 'work' and conversely frivolous 'recreation'. Further, and perhaps more importantly, the sentiment Stein expresses raises the question of what kind of work writing, and indeed reading, constitute. Much of the following is contiguous with this question, which has already surfaced in my chapter on Richardson and which remains open, shifting its ground with the texts under discussion.

There are various biographical threads one might pick up *en route* to an examination of Stein's representation of work in her writing. Stein studied for eight years at Radcliffe College and Johns Hopkins School of Medicine; she then worked as a psychological researcher in the laboratory of William James in the late 1890s, and as such experienced something approximating work as it is conventionally described, conducting experiments on the automatic responses of human beings. Nevertheless, that Stein abandoned this career and moved to a different continent to begin life as an art collector and writer certainly indicates an incompatibility with this particular lifestyle; the everyday life of the working scientist was not, then, for her.

Stein's mature working life as a writer was spent almost exclusively in France, and mainly in Paris. Her attachment to the artistic, bohemian communities centring around the Parisian salons, indeed her installation at the centre of one such community, signals one way in which she literally moved away from an American work ethic. Texts such as Henry James's 1903 novel *The Ambassadors* indicate a perceived contrast at the time between the successful American business world of new money – Mrs Newsome's 'big brave bouncing business' – and a European tradition of family money and 'old accumulations'.[5] The prevalent American view of European society, as populated by sophisticates and degenerates by whom naive Americans might be ensnared and corrupted, is corrected in this novel. Furthermore, the supposedly honest and decent American business is undermined by the apparently unspeakable nature of its products. Stein, then, moved across the Atlantic from an America which, it seems, already viewed Europe as in some ways frivolous; though serious in its heritage and tradition, neverthe-less not in keeping with the efficiency of America's 'great production' and 'great industry'.[6]

Stein's own domestic arrangements, a constant source of controversy, themselves indicate a further rejection of 'what is known as work'. It is true that, in some senses, 27 rue Fleurus (where Stein lived with her lifelong partner Alice B. Toklas) was a conventional household, with Alice, the 'wife', ruling in the kitchen, while Stein and the other 'men' discussed books and paintings. As Lillian Faderman has shown, there was an accepted cultural precedent for two women living together, a relationship variously defined as 'romantic friendship' or, more pertinently to Stein's era, the Boston marriage, although Faderman also argues that during the early years of the twentieth century, this kind of relationship was an increasing focus of social and cultural anxiety as sexology and the discourse of psychoanalysis drew attention to the sexual aspect of such relationships.[7] Stein's categorical distinction between her realm and Toklas's (blurred though this may have been in practice, as recent critical attention to Toklas's role as amanuensis as well as muse has shown) suggests a certain approximation between their relationship and the heteronormative model of marriage. And yet Stein professed her dependence on her regulated, domestic, everyday existence, which is articulated through the preoccupations of her work (*Tender Buttons* is only the best known example; texts such as 'Pink Melon Joy', 'Susie Asado' and 'Ada' are other important instances of the domestic in Stein's writing). This intermingling of the domestic and the professional challenges a conventional definition of work as something defined in part (at least since the industrial revolution) by its taking place away from the home – the two realms being perceived and constructed as distinct and mutually exclusive. Indeed, the figure of the writer is a problematic one for this distinction, as, conversely, it would be seen as more unusual for a writer to work outside the home (though they may have a room set aside for writing). Because their work does not take place in a location spatially or indeed temporally distinct from the domestic, and because many hours of work do not necessarily produce a concomitantly great number of pages, such work is often seen as frivolous, not serious – indeed, merely leisure or recreation.

Stein's earliest published text, *Three Lives* (1909), provides a useful starting point for an exploration of work in her writing. All three stories in *Three Lives* describe the working lives of their characters. The eponymous protagonists of 'The Good Anna' and 'The Gentle Lena', the shorter first and third stories, are both in domestic service. However, the longest of the three stories, 'Melanctha', is of particular interest since it contrasts two distinct personality types, the 'working' Jeff, a doctor, and the 'wandering' Melanctha of the title, drawn together through their relationship as lovers. Not only does 'Melanctha' explicitly refer to the working lives of its characters, but the text's particular use of non-standard grammar, and its temporal shifts and loops, sketch out differing temporalities, tied to personality, of work and of recreation. It is both a case, as Stein herself put it in *Composition as Explanation*, of 'the time *of* the composition and the time *in* the composition' (my emphases);[8] the temporalities the text describes, and that in which it participates. It shows precisely, as Lefebvre puts it, 'the everyday as the confluence of disparate temporal rhythms'.[9]

In the first part of this chapter, I will explore the everyday temporality of 'Melanctha', and suggest how this intersects with the concept of recreation as a crucial aspect of everydayness. I will then broaden my claim by addressing a very different text from Stein's second distinctive phase of writing, her *Tender Buttons* of 1914, and shifting the focus from the temporality of dailiness to everyday attention – while continuing to insist on the imbrication of the two. Working with Crary's thesis that in this period 'counter-forms of attention are neither exclusively nor essentially visual but rather constituted as other temporalities and cognitive states, such as those in trance or reverie',[10] my reading of *Tender Buttons*, which forms the second part of this chapter, emphasises the ways in which this text involves precisely such 'counter-forms of attention', which do not conform to the definition of attention as work, as an ends-driven, chronological process, focused on the external object over and above the perceiving subject. I will suggest precisely that *Tender Buttons* involves, on several levels, a certain kind of attention paid to everyday objects, constituting a re-creation of these objects with each moment and as they become incorporated into the consciousness of the observing subject, in a dialogue or conversation between object, text, writer and reader.[11] It is a kind of recreational attention that I want to reclaim within the terms of the everyday, one which in liberating the subject from reading as work, enables them to experience more fully their relationship with time, rather than 'inhabit [it] as disempowered'. Indeed, this improvisatory, fluid, living attentiveness has clear parallels with the kind of temporality recovered and explored by Stein in 'Melanctha'. Finally, the human scale and sensuality of *Tender Buttons* further inscribes the text in the matrix of the everyday, counterbalancing the true with the real, the perfect with the useful, the conceptual with the concrete.

The contiguity of the reworking of temporality in 'Melanctha' with the reworking of attention in *Tender Buttons* is, then, explored through viewing both from the perspective of the everyday. Both texts reveal a mode of perception and behaviour within the everyday that may be covered by the term recreation, or re-creation. The term recreation should here be read as retaining its two primary meanings: as 're-creation', a creative, and perhaps specifically aesthetic, act; and also as another word for leisure activity. I also, however, want to keep in mind the signification which lies behind its having first been drawn into the semantic field of leisure, namely, recreation as the gesture of restoring oneself.[12] This internalising aspect of the term 'recreation' contrasts with the externalising gesture of attentive work as explored above. Recreation, then, has a centripetal as well as a centrifugal force: it implies becoming more oneself, restoring the same to the same, as well as producing, proliferating, re-creating. As this chapter progresses, it will become clear that I am using the term 'recreation' as a tool through which to yoke together a number of significations, temporal, psychic, epistemological and literary. Yet as the semantic field associated with this term expands to encompass attention to the present continuous, a kind of 'wandering' knowledge, a non-teleological epistemology, and so on, nevertheless the usefully ambivalent specific meanings of 'recreation', as I have just defined it, should not be lost. Finally, to recover the value to be found in the everyday modes that will come under the term 'recreation' is not necessarily to privilege this term above its complement, 'work', nor to imply that Stein does so; as suggested above, such a move would simply reinforce a binary structure which Stein's writing attempts to evade. Fuller articulation of a neglected everyday mode, in order then more profoundly to understand the complex of which it is a part, is the overarching gesture of this chapter.

'MELANCTHA'

The extent of the influence of Stein's time as a psychological researcher under William James on her subsequent writing has been consistently contested by readers of Stein. Indeed, Stein herself vigorously denied, for example, B. F. Skinner's assertion that *Tender Buttons* was an example of automatic writing, no more nor less, and, as Tim Armstrong puts it, '[h]er official position was that the most important thing that she inherited from her period as a psychological researcher was a sense of the different types of human character'.[13] The exploration of types, which is discussed at greater length below, is clearly visible in *Three Lives*. Yet other critics have read James's influence running deeper than this in Stein's texts. Lisa Ruddick, for example, provides a convincing interpretation of 'Melanctha' as both homage and challenge to Jamesian models of psychology. As Ruddick notes, according to this model, the figure of Jeff is plainly the more positive of the two; indeed, quite apart from his approximation to Jamesian ideals of perceptual selection (the ability to reflect on, distinguish between and hierarchise experience and perception), his narrative reward is the greater, since he returns enriched to his already established professional life, whereas Melanctha returns to her 'wandering' which will lead, directly or indirectly, to her death. However, as Ruddick argues, Melanctha's end could equally be read as 'a protest against the entire notion of mental success represented by Jeff', and points out ways in which Stein's text provides models which challenge the Jamesian ideal, describing the text as 'a meditation on conflicting ways of knowing'.[14] Of particular interest here is Ruddick's idea of Melanctha's "way to know" that has no bearing on practical life but is more elevated than mere sensory abundance', together with her sense of how this is reflected in the structure and syntax of the text itself.[15] I want to build on Ruddick's model to argue that Melanctha's way of knowing is more bound up with 'practical life' than Ruddick suggests, in the sense that it comes from and feeds into the practices and rhythms of everyday life which are themselves reflected in the structure and syntax of Stein's texts.

The first few pages of 'Melanctha' build up a sense of Melanctha as a strongly emotional character, lacking in rationality, and driven by sensual pleasure. She is 'the complex, desiring Melanctha' in contrast to the 'careless' and 'lazy' Rose (*TL* 60); both sensual, but Melanctha's sensuality drives and moves her where Rose's encourages lethargy and passivity. A paragraph early in the text describes the oscillating, inconsistent and illogical emotional state which Melanctha inhabits:

Melanctha Herbert always loved too hard and much too often. She was always full with mystery and subtle movements and denials and vague distrusts and complicated disillusions. Then Melanctha would be sudden and impulsive and unbounded in some faith, and then she would suffer and be strong in her repression. (62)

The terms of this description suggest a bodily location for Melanctha's emotional life: adjectives such as 'too hard' and 'strong' imply physicality, as does the formulation 'she was always full'. This is a character bounded and driven by her sense of the physical; hence when she is emotionally damaged, she feels it physically: when Rose rejects her Melanctha feels 'all sore and bruised inside her' (166). Melanctha also 'loved to be with horses; she loved to do wild things, to ride the horses and to break and tame them' (63); this affinity with animals and the desire to do battle with them physically ('break and tame them') emphasises, albeit through a clichéd image, her sensuality. Further, 'the real power in Melanctha's nature came through her robust and unpleasant and very unendurable father', a 'big black virile negro' (63). Melanctha's 'nature' is defined, then, with reference to this emphatically physical, sensual, indeed sexual, racial stereotype.

The question of how Melanctha's sensual epistemology ties the text in with contemporary racial discourse is an important one. Richard Bridgman's suggestion that '[t]he important stylistic innovations of "Melanctha" have nothing to do with the Negro' seems both accurate and misleading;[16] given that Stein changed her upper-middle class white characters in *Q.E.D.*, the autobiographical text on which 'Melanctha' was based, into black characters in the published text, we are bound to ask what 'the Negro' has to do with this story (beyond being one way for Stein to disguise the personal origins of the story, perhaps). But there are stylistic similarities between all three stories in *Three Lives* – specifically in their use of what Chessman calls an 'oral discourse' associated with a marginal social position.[17] Stein's text was written at a time when, according to Kenan Malik, the systematisation of racial difference was in progress. But, according to Malik, 'the discourse of race arose out of perceived differences within European society and only later was it systematically applied to differences of skin colour'.[18] Melanctha is black, but Anna and Lena are servants of German extraction, and the other girls who befriend Lena are Irish; these are other racial types – all of which one might, bearing in mind the aesthetic context, call 'primitive' – which are not, however, distinguished by skin colour.[19] The stylistic innovations of 'Melanctha' may, then, not just be to do with 'the Negro', if we accept that *Three Lives* as a whole makes use of racial stereotypes, and associated speech patterns, that are not just to do with skin colour but ultimately develop from social stratification.

It has already been noted that, as Bridgman puts it, Stein's desire to 'classify people' continued through her work under William James and the interest in 'types' she developed there.[20] Yet this desire to classify need not be seen as a purely restrictive and repressive trajectory. Malik suggests that in fact 'the discourse of race developed as a way of understanding the changing relationship between humanity, society and nature';[21] however stereotypical her models, an incipient racial discourse enabled Stein to draw on the associations of the 'primitive' with alternative modes of human social interaction, perception and knowledge. To illustrate the association of certain racial and social strata with certain kinds of perception, Malik cites the French writer Gustave LeBon (whose theories were highly influential to Freud). LeBon's distinction between an élite capable of reason, and the mass, 'controlled wholly by instinct', is only one example of a theory which was prevalent in various forms around the turn of the century.[22] The imbrication of the lower classes, racial difference and, I would suggest, femininity, in this discourse of the instinctive and the unreflecting, seems clearly evoked by Stein's depiction of Melanctha's 'wandering', her inability to reflect, and her sensual responses to her surroundings. This is not to say that Stein attempts necessarily to ascribe this alternative model of action and cognition exclusively to 'primitive' individuals. Rather, we can read Stein using the discourse of the primitive to explore non-standard narration and its concomitant non-standard models of knowledge.

Although it now appears crudely unquestioning of an anthropology of the primitive, Michael Bell's book *Primitivism* nevertheless gives further suggestive indications of the kinds of associations the 'primitive' might have had at the time of Stein's writing. In particular, Bell suggests that, for 'primitive man', 'time is conceived in its psychological aspect, that is to say, as it impinges on the individual's possibly varying state of mind, rather than as a fixed and objective category'.[23] This description fits well with the kind of temporality I will argue is sketched out by the narrative of Melanctha, which resists any sense of time as 'fixed and objective' as the narrative follows the psychological vacillations, lapses in memory, and deviations, of daily experience.

One of the most striking aspects of 'Melanctha' is its lack of events, or subordination of event to character or dialogue. Telling the 'story' of Melanctha

would take very little time; we are given only a very few specific singulative events occurring either before or after the main body of the story,
which concerns itself with the conversations between Melanctha and Jeff as
their relationship develops, progresses and eventually dissolves.[24] Further,
where they do occur, Stein subsumes many of these specific events into
a broader depiction of ongoing patterns of behaviour, further obscuring
a clear chronological storyline. Stein consistently uses the impressionistic
time loop, of which Ford Madox Ford is usually cited as the exemplary
exponent, where a particular passage of text begins by describing an event,
then goes on to describe what led up to that event, and ends by repeating
the initial event. A good example of this is the description of Melanctha's
father's intervention in her relationship with the horseman John Bishop,
beginning: 'One day James Herbert came to where his wife and daughter
lived, and he was furious' (*TL* 64). The narrative does not then explain
what happened next, but rather loops back to describe James Herbert, his
relationship with his daughter, Melanctha's relationship with John Bishop,
and the fight between the two men which results in the visit referred to
above. The words James Herbert utters on coming to visit his wife and
daughter are then repeated, but with minute modifications; as Ruddick
has it, 'for Stein to allow exact repetitions would be to falsify the small
mutations of consciousness'.[25] In fact, all three narratives in *Three Lives*
follow what Marianne DeKoven calls this 'characteristically impressionistic temporal structure'.[26] In 'Melanctha', the narration begins with the
birth of Rose Johnson's child, an event that takes place after Melanctha's
relationship with Jeff; the narration then loops back to begin describing
Melanctha's life from childhood onwards, eventually leading back to the
moment of Rose giving birth. The effect of such narrative loops is to give
an event depth and resonance beyond its momentary occurrence; by the
time of its repetition (or to use Stein's own terminology, its 'insistence') it
is irreducibly set in the context of the ongoing experience of, in this case,
Melanctha's life. Here indeed we find, in Bell's terms, 'time [. . .] conceived
in its psychological aspect'.[27] Any particular event's apparent importance is
attenuated as the other events, experiences, characteristics and so on which
inform it are elaborated. Stein's work constantly resists attempts to extricate single moments, images or attitudes to represent the whole of everyday
experience, its ongoing temporality.

Despite its temporal loops, the narrative leaves few gaps; the continuous
flow of time is not forgotten, even in the periods when there is not much
to report:

Now for a little time there was not any kind of trouble between Jeff Campbell and Melanctha Herbert. They were always together now for long times, and very often. They got much joy now, both of them, from being all the time together.

It was summer now, and they had warm sunshine to wander. [. . .] (*TL* 108)

That it is difficult to know where to end a quotation is an indication of the way in which Stein's prose relies on its patterns of iteration and reflection, within and between sentences and paragraphs, to create this sense of a ceaseless duration. The love affair between Jeff and Melanctha does not arise suddenly; both the build up to and disintegration of their relationship are full of hiatuses and inexplicable withdrawals or swerves away from the romance plot – again, the random everyday disruptions to or subversions of what is conventionally depicted as a standard sequence with carefully plotted obstacles are foregrounded. And yet we are given both beginning and end of the affair – we see life going on before and after. As at dawn and dusk, where the transition from day to night and back again is gradual, Melanctha's life without Jeff blends into her life with him, and back out again, such that he is almost gone before we notice it. This smooth textual surface is a fundamental aspect of the famous 'continuous present' of Stein's work.[28]

It is not only through the overall structure of 'Melanctha' that the all-embracing continuous present of the everyday is revealed. At a more minute level, the syntactic structures characteristic of Stein are crucial in building up and sustaining the particular ongoing temporality through which the text functions. For example, Melanctha has an ardent desire to evade her father's attempts to control her, and dreads that her mother will speak to her father about her 'wanderings' (of which more below). Her fear is expressed thus: 'Melanctha with all her hard courage dreaded that there should be much telling to her father' (*TL* 68). Rather than expressing the act of telling as if it were a single, if repeated, event (for example, 'dreaded that he should be told' or 'that her mother should tell him'), the *duration* of the act of telling is emphasised. Later Stein texts such as 'Miss Furr and Miss Skeene', discussed in my Introduction, and others from the 1922 *Geography and Plays* collection in particular, as well as *The Making of Americans* of 1925 (composed from 1906 to 1908), provide further examples of this quotidian temporality where, in contrast to traditional narrative where the tense in which events are described often implies that they take no time at all – 'something happened' – the duration which they would almost always occupy in the lived experience of the everyday is emphasised – 'something was happening'. This is just one of the textual innovations which draws attention to the iterative qualities of the quotidian, its gradual changes within a structure of sameness and continuity, focusing on the individual's ongoing existence in time and the way in which they live through that time. For example, from 'Miss Furr and Miss Skeene': 'They were both gay there, they were regularly working there both of them cultivating their voices there'; 'She was not lonesome then, she was not at all feeling any need of having Georgine Skeene'; 'she was regular in being gay, she always was living very well and was gay very well and was telling about little ways one could be learning to use in being gay'.[29] Further, in this text, the revelation of what I will call a recreational temporality (and here we might remember, incidentally, that the story apparently concerns two women at music college, not at 'work') is explicitly connected to the rhythms of dailiness:

To be regularly gay was to do every day the gay thing that they did every day. To be regularly gay was to end every day at the same time after they had been regularly gay. They were regularly gay. They were gay every day. They ended every day in the same way, at the same time, and they had been every day regularly gay.[30]

We are, then, building up a model of experience sketched out in Stein's work which is grounded not, as the structures of traditional narratives might imply, in a series of individual, discrete, sequential events, but in the ongoing, repeated, shifting temporality of the everyday, from day to day. The lack of specific dates or periods of time in 'Melanctha' further indicates this. Although specific time periods are sometimes referred to, usually at moments of particular stress or uncertainty in the relationship between Jeff and Melanctha, in the majority of cases the time periods or frequencies of occurrence involved are not specified; the terms 'often' and 'sometimes' proliferate. In particular, 'now' is used to cover a broad spectrum of temporal periods, often serving to confuse the distinction between simultaneity and succession, as in this paragraph:

Jeff Campbell never asked Melanctha any more if she loved him. Now things were always getting worse between them. Now Jeff was always very silent with Melanctha. Now Jeff wanted to be honest to her, and now Jeff never had much to say to her. (*TL* 133)

It is impossible to decide whether these 'nows' all refer to one ongoing state of affairs, during which Jeff felt and acted in all these ways, or whether each 'now' indicates an additional emotional state which developed after, as an intensification of, the previous ones. The very process of reading means that such a dilemma is inescapable; we cannot help but read successively.

What Stein's parataxis seems to suggest is precisely the misleading nature of a rigorous distinction between simultaneity and succession; it constantly insists on the imbrication of the two. The relationship between simultaneity and succession, and the valorisation of one over the other, is an important focus of much modernist thought and innovation. For example, the Italian futurists, as well as Wyndham Lewis and his circle, strove to find ways of expressing absolute simultaneity in visual and verbal terms. This valorisation of simultaneity was, explicitly in Lewis's case, in opposition to Bergson's theories and his insistence that in human psychological time there is nothing but succession; for Bergson, simultaneity is simply impossible, and the positing of its possibility is a result of our erroneous tendency to express temporality in spatial terms. In her disruption of the distinction between these two positions, Stein is characteristically complicating one of the most contentious binaries in the thought of her period.

Another key aspect of Stein's work which evokes and mimics this everyday temporality, in which simultaneity and succession both participate, is her blurring of the distinction between the singulative and the iterative narrative event. Take for example the paragraph that begins:

Melanctha now never wandered, unless she was with Jeff Campbell. Sometimes she and he wandered a good deal together. [. . .] Sometimes Jeff Campbell teased her about not talking to him. 'I certainly did think Melanctha you was a great talker [. . .]' (*TL* 94)

Here we find a number of Stein's characteristically non-specific deictic markers: 'now', 'sometimes', 'a good deal'. Yet by the end of the paragraph, this iterative event, presented as an example of a type of conversation occurring we know not how often ('*Sometimes* Jeff Campbell teased her [. . .]'), has become a singulative one:

'[. . .] Good-by, Jeff, come see me to-morrow, when you get through with your working.' 'Sure Melanctha, you know that already,' said Jeff Campbell, and then he went away and left her. (95)

Stein has begun by taking emphasis away from this particular conversation here and now, placing it within an iterative context; yet, and crucially, her use of reported speech retains insistence on individual speech acts and the specificity of their patterns and rhythms, and the narrative comes to rest on a singulative narrative event. Further, the temporality of reading – that is, that it will take a reader a certain amount of time to read from the beginning of the paragraph to the end – forms part of the subtle rendering of this shift. If the two moments, iterative and singulative, were placed more closely together, as above, the reader would be more disturbed by this conflation. As it is in the text, reading the paragraph puts temporal distance between the two, demonstrating through the reader's own experience how substantial changes can take place almost imperceptibly over time.

In her retrospective account of her writing in *Composition as Explanation*, Stein describes *Three Lives* and *The Making of Americans* as an 'elaboration of the complexities of using everything and of a continuous present and of beginning again and again'.[31] Again, as in the passage with the succession of 'nows' discussed above, this paratactical phrase operates on a number of levels: the construction of the continuous present itself relies on the strategies of 'beginning again and again', and of 'using everything'; all three elements are implicated in each other. Stein goes on in the *Narration* lectures to indicate how this gesture of inclusivity is bound up with a sense of the daily or everyday: 'I can say it enough but can I say it more than enough that the daily life is a daily life if at any moment of the daily life that daily life is all there is of life.'[32] Unlike the 'moment' of modernity with which other writers struggled – the moment never sufficient unto itself, always cognised after it is sensed – the 'moment of the daily life' is synecdoche for 'all there is of life', and all there is of life is that daily experience. Stein's texts eschew attempts to isolate this moment, separate it from its past and future, and rather constantly emphasise a flow of one moment into another, strongly reminiscent of Bergsonian *durée*. Rather than screwing up her eyes tight, working hard to try to locate the now, Stein relaxes, broadens the perspective, and in doing so the constant recreation of the continuous present out of itself comes into focus.

The contrast between the two main characters in 'Melanctha' intensifies the questions of temporality and everydayness suggested by my discussion so far, as a particular incident in the text shows. As their relationship begins moving toward its end, Melanctha berates Jeff for his way of 'remembering', speaking of an earlier incident in the narrative:

[. . .] that day in the summer, when you threw me off just because you got one of those fits of your remembering. No, Jeff Campbell, its real feeling every moment when its needed, that certainly does seem to me like real remembering. [. . .] No, it certainly is me Jeff Campbell, that always has got to be remembering for us both, always. (*TL* 128)

The incident to which Melanctha here refers, when Jeff remembers what he had been told about Melanctha and her 'wandering', stands in stark contrast to Melanctha's sensual remembering 'every moment when its needed'.

Recalling de Certeau's elaboration of the 'tactical' is useful here; one of the most crucial terms in his vocabulary of the everyday, de Certeau describes the tactical as 'procedures that gain validity in relation to the pertinence they lend to *time* – to the circumstances which *the precise instant* of an intervention transforms into a favorable situation' (my emphases).[33] We can see how this concept resonates with the recreational everyday mode I am uncovering in Stein by agreeing that Melanctha's memory – 'every *moment* when its *needed*' (my emphases) – appears as precisely tactical, precisely, *contra* Ruddick, having 'bearing on practical life': pertinent to this 'precise instant'. This kind of remembering deepens our sense of Melanctha's grounding in the ongoing, continuous present of the everyday. By contrast, Jeff's introduction of his note of doubt, suspicion, ugliness and disgust in his 'fit of remembering' is incongruous in its moment – intempestive, one might say, in relation to the idyllic rural setting, which had the couple 'resting, with a green, bright, light-flecked world around them' (109). Even the narrator, whose preference for Jeff's interiority over Melanctha's suggests a bias in his favour, is baffled by Jeff's remembering: 'What was it that now really happened to them?' (109).

The narrator's commentary does, however, indicate, if not *what* it was that sparked off Jeff's incongruous remembrance, then *how* it was sparked off. The commentary makes it clear that there was no verbal communication involved in Jeff's change of emotion. Rather, the narrator asks 'What was it that Melanctha *felt* then, that made Jeff remember all the *feeling* he had had in him when Jane Harden told him how Melanctha had learned to be so very understanding?' (*TL* 109, my emphases). The duality of the verb 'feel', signifying both the emotional and the physical, mirrors the aspects of Stein's textual style which itself creates meaning through alternative epistemologies. Stein's text encourages the reader to engage with the sound and the look of the text – in this case, its long paragraphs, proliferating '-ing' endings, repetition and modulation – not to supplant, but to supplement the meaning created through standard cognitive verbal interpretation. The reader of Stein learns about the sensuality of the text just as Jeff has learnt through Melanctha a sensual communication of feeling, or everyday way of knowing.

Further, the text's repetition of the fact that Melanctha 'had learned to be so very understanding' through her 'wandering' draws attention to just such alternative epistemologies. 'Wandering' is the term that most characterises Melanctha, just as 'working' is most often used to describe Jeff. Certainly, 'wandering' has sexual connotations: 'Melanctha liked to wander, and to stand by the railroad yard, and watch the men and the engines and the switches and everything that was busy there, working' (*TL* 68); and she does not only watch, but 'begin to learn to know this man or that' (67). However, Melanctha's distance from the world of work is emphasised by her initial position as a watcher, and then, by her transformation of this world of work into one of play (albeit dangerous play, breaking her arm during participation in the dares and challenges set to her by these working men). Further, the aim of Melanctha's wandering is 'wisdom' (70). Yet it follows a liminal, sensual, sinuous path to a wisdom that will not be found through the rigour and direction involved in, by contrast, Jeff's dogged pursuit of knowledge, his constant reading and thinking, activities inextricable from his 'working': 'He thought and thought, and always he did not seem to know any better what he wanted. At last he gave up this thinking [. . .] and began with some hard scientific reading' (91). Wandering might be compared to Moretti's 'idling', discussed in Chapter 2, '[which] does not mean doing *nothing*, but rather not entrusting the definition of one's personality to any *one* activity'.[34] 'Multilateral and prismatic, personality remains a constantly unsatisfied idol', says Moretti;[35] wandering is a suitably multilateral and prismatic activity, yet it is precisely in being thus multilateral, indefinable, constantly shifting, that it fails ultimately to construct a clear path for that personality.

'Wandering', then, is the name for an everyday way of knowing associated with, but not reducible to, the sensual, as well as the cognitive – an epistemology of 'feeling'. It is, in more ways than one, a way of knowing that reveals and valorises the recreational aspect of everyday life. At a straightforward level, Melanctha's 'wandering' is precisely the kind of 'undifferentiated global activity' which Lefebvre regards as the first level of 'leisure' activity – recreation in one of the straightforward senses discussed in the introduction to this chapter (*CEL* 32). Further, however, the term 'wandering' is itself recreated in Stein's text as it is repeatedly deployed with various different connotations – sexual, spatial, emotional, epistemological. The reader's work becomes re-creation, being required to read the term anew or with a new inflection each time it appears; one cannot 'work out' what wandering means, one can only follow its own wandering.

Melanctha's psychic development – her 'wandering' – is never static or detached, but follows a spontaneous, felt, meandering path that unfolds from itself, sometimes leading back to itself. By contrast, Jeff's sudden incongruous remembering is just one example of the way in which the narrative establishes a pattern in his development consisting of periods of suspension in scepticism, detachment, 'thinking', periodically interrupted and dramatically overthrown by moments of crisis. The paradox here is that Jeff's destructive 'remembering' – despite Melanctha's insistence on the difference between their kinds of remembering – occurs as a 'Melancthan' sensual response. Jeff learns, implicitly from Melanctha herself, the value of an everyday recreational epistemology of sensuality, a system of knowledge or 'wisdom' for which she is always searching. Thus we see that in some cases, the individual has to re-learn everydayness, be reintroduced to the multivalent, shifting, corporeal world in which they live. It is, then, not so much the quality of this particular experience as Jeff's habitual temporal mode of experiencing and assimilating the world – that is, by holding it in suspension as an object to be observed and reflected upon – that causes the disruption, by contrast with Melanctha's constant assimilation of each moment to her physical and psychic state. Jeff's inability to be spontaneous, and his being 'slow-minded', creates a crisis in him when a spontaneous sensual response is aroused which he cannot assimilate by 'thinking'.

The kind of responses Jeff and Melanctha have to their experiences cannot, then, be separated from the temporality through which those responses are assimilated. Melanctha's assimilation of each experience to the present continuous is indicated in her model of remembering, not as a cognitive activity which reanimates a feeling from the past, but a constant affirmation of each present moment in relation to the totality of all moments, and crucially, as a practical, tactical, everyday response to emotional need – 'real feeling every moment when its needed' (*TL* 128). Jeff, by contrast, creates a temporal distance between himself and what he is feeling. In saying, for example, 'I can't say things like that right out to everybody till I know really more for certain all about you, and how I like you, and what I really meant to do better for you' (90), Jeff is positing a moment in the future when he will know how he feels about Melanctha, a moment presumably arrived at through 'thinking', and proceeds on this basis, rather than on the basis of what he does feel at the present moment. This, I would argue, is precisely the kind of 'inhabit[ing] time as disempowered' that Crary suggests is the outcome of the working attentiveness imposed by the structures of capitalism. Melanctha's question early in the development of their relationship draws attention to this problem: '"Don't you ever stop with your thinking long enough ever to have any feeling Jeff Campbell"' (92); being suspended and isolated in the temporal mode of thinking and working alienates Jeff from the present reality of his emotional life, only available to him in flashes and crises.

I want now to make a connection between the model of experience as suspension of the present moment represented through Jeff, and the temporality of work in a very general sense. It may be more helpful to approach this from the other direction; that is, to posit Melanctha's temporality in opposition to a temporality of work. Ruddick speculates that 'From the vantage point of James's psychology, Melanctha's mind is deficient because it does nothing but drift.'[36] Ruddick makes the important point that, although James is often assumed, as the originator of the expression 'stream of consciousness', to have been a proponent of this particular model of perception, 'James's chapter on the stream of thought is meant to describe an overlooked dimension of mental experience, not to champion it'.[37] Conversely, I would not argue that Stein champions Melanctha's temporality over Jeff's; rather, she draws attention to the validity of alternative models through her change of focus and concomitant stylistic innovation. Rather than remaining within the 'working' model as the privileged structure, governing the construction of identities and texts, Stein reorients this matrix, viewing both working and wandering as everyday modes of operating.

Ruddick's vocabulary at this point in her discussion is itself highly suggestive. She states that 'In James's scheme of things, wandering is the meanest possible use of the mind. It is a species of *rest* – something that occupies us between one focus and the next, or overcomes us in moments of fatigue' (my emphasis).[38] By inference, then, if we are not wandering (or resting) then we are working (focusing) – which is indeed what Jeff is most occupied with. Melanctha, by contrast, although often very busy and occupied with the care of her mother or of Rose Johnson, is rarely described as 'working', further supporting the sense that the term 'work' as used in 'Melanctha' is uniquely associated with Jeff.

The term 'work' is also important in the other texts in *Three Lives*. The central characteristic of the good Anna is that she is hard working even in defiance of the desires of those around her: 'she worked away her appetite, her health and strength, and always for the sake of those who begged her not to work so hard' (*TL* 19); 'Yes, taking care of Miss Mathilda were the happiest days of all the good Anna's strong hard working life' (42), states the narrator, reinforcing the idea that being 'hard working' is precisely what defines Anna's life. It is not, then, that Stein's idea of 'work' is gender-specific, nor even class-specific, as Anna is a housekeeper and Jeff a doctor. It does, however, seem connected in both cases with a sense of there being a lack of enough time, a pressure on time – 'I am always so busy with my thinking about my work I am doing and so I don't have time for just fooling', says Jeff (86). A further complication to arriving at a definition of 'work' in Stein's text comes in 'The Gentle Lena', where the early period of her working life is described as 'all a peaceful life for Lena, almost as peaceful as a pleasant leisure' (172). There is no suggestion here that Lena is not busy – she too has 'good hard work all morning' (171). So it is not simply the extent to which one is occupied that defines an activity as work; rather, as Stein's text with its repetition of 'peaceful' suggests, it is the quality of the relationship to time – since being peaceful excludes any sense of the pressure of time, not having enough time, and so on, that would define one's activity as work. This reinforces the suggestion made in my Introduction that viewing work through the perspective of gender problematises the category itself. In describing Lena's objectively hard work as yet in some senses 'a peaceful life', Stein is exploring the extent to which the alienating tendency even of waged work might be mitigated where the situation is a domestic one, gendered as female, and inescapably inflected through emotional ties, making this labour inapt to be assimilated to exchange values. By contrast, Jeff's approach, with its extended suspension of the present followed by sudden crises, could not be described as 'peaceful' over the long term. And paradoxically, although Melanctha is described as always finding 'new ways to be in trouble' or 'get excited', this is not reflected in Melanctha's psychic state which, despite external excitations, seems remarkably constant.

Work might be read in *Three Lives*, then, as a name for something that is certainly necessary, but that may prevent one from experiencing the present continuous. It is not that, for example, Stein disapproves of Jeff's work as a doctor, but she contrasts it with another kind of living that is grounded in the present as it is lived. Through an excessive emphasis on 'working' and its concomitant verb 'thinking', Jeff is unable to experience his transformations except as crises, suddenly and all in one go. However, he *is* transformed by his experiences. Melanctha, on the other hand, only goes on becoming more and more herself by assimilating each moment to the present moment of her being; if emphasis on work involves suspension of the present moment, emphasis on wandering involves immersion in the present moment. In Melanctha's case, her tactical temporality is undermined by her inability to have even a short term or limited aim, rendering her experience entirely contingent on its momentary setting, and so psychically unavailable to her to re-examine and build on with hindsight; her experiences are, then, ultimately unable to initiate change. Melanctha's early and bathetic death might be seen as part of this impotence – which impotence, it must be remembered, might be more concretely grounded in her cultural context as a black woman, excluded from socio-economic structures of power and production.

The specific textual, temporal characteristics of 'Melanctha' the text, then, reveals an ongoing 're-creation' in Melanctha the character: time spent becoming more oneself. Here I differ from DeKoven in my reading of Melanctha; DeKoven says that 'Melanctha is defeated by what is emerging as the fatal flaw *par excellence* of heroines in women's fiction: a divided self. At crucial times in her life [. . .] she acts against her own best interests [. . .] "Melanctha Herbert was always seeking rest and quiet, and always she could only find new ways to be in trouble".'[39] I would argue that, conversely, it is Melanctha's excessively unified self that means she is unable to act in her own best interests; the Melancthan temporality of constant re-creation, with no room for distance, inevitably involves a repetition of old patterns – Melanctha can only become more Melancthan, which means 'finding new ways to be in trouble'. Melanctha asks Jeff to come and see her when he 'get[s] through with [his] working': by contrast, the reader cannot 'work' their way through this text; and one is never 'through with' recreation. It is through paying attention to the day-to-day experience of everyday life, and how the temporalities of work *and* of recreation configure that experience, that this rewriting of work within the everyday has been possible.

TENDER BUTTONS

Where Lisa Ruddick's work provided the jumping-off point for my reading of *Three Lives*, Marianne DeKoven's will do the same for my reading of *Tender Buttons*. It is DeKoven's scepticism regarding arguments for 'interpretable coherence' in *Tender Buttons*, her belief that there is no 'way of writing a critical account of *Tender Buttons* that will be recognisable as such', and in particular her assertion that 'Stein went beyond the book in this period', that are important here.[40] DeKoven not only provides a useful way of addressing the methodological problems that arise when approaching this particular text, but in doing so, also suggests ways in which a text such as *Tender Buttons* draws attention to and modifies the very experience of reading. DeKoven's take on *Tender Buttons* is indeed seductive, not least because it seems to let the Stein reader off the hook. She echoes the sentiments of many in asking 'how do we plough through the thirty-five pages of *Tender Buttons*', a text which resists a cohesive reading at every moment. DeKoven herself responds that 'Reading [*Tender Buttons*] entails giving up altogether the idea of the book, of the coherent work. We needn't plough through it at all. We need pay attention only as long as the thrill lasts, the tantalizing pleasure of the flood of meaning of which we cannot quite make sense.'[41]

Ruddick makes an objection to DeKoven's stance which I would echo, in saying 'I believe that a text can be polysemous [as DeKoven insists] and still have themes, or "patterns of meaning"'.[42] And yet, although I do explore patterns of meaning, I would resist emphasis on such patterns in Stein's text. Rather, I want to pay attention to the processes by which meaning is made in *Tender Buttons*, and suggest that the rewriting of reading that takes place through the text might usefully be elucidated through its everydayness. As stated above, my reading of *Tender Buttons* will foreground a model of everyday attentiveness that crucially involves an empowered relationship with, rather than disempowered inhabiting of, time; and yet this recuperation of a contingent, spontaneous, oscillating attention (oscillating between subject and object) will nonetheless always be counterbalanced by a need to recreate useful meanings, by the need to come to an end in order productively to communicate and explore our feelings about our everyday life.

I want to preface my discussion of *Tender Buttons* with a consideration of the implications of its stylistic innovation for a critique of everyday life. *Tender Buttons* has long been understood as a challenge to the 'pointing system' model of language, the referential model where words unproblematically refer to an object in the world; rather, it proceeds as a 'compositional game', resembling a Jakobsonian 'word heap'.[43] Why this pushing of language to one of its extremes, the extreme end of the 'vertical or metaphorical axis of their discourse',[44] should be seen as language particularly revelatory of everyday life is not immediately apparent. This apparent contradiction can be unpicked with reference to Lefebvre's discussion of the relationship between language and the everyday.

Lefebvre's chapter on 'Linguistic Phenomena' in his *Everyday Life in the Modern World* is the crucial point of reference here, and also provides one way of locating Stein's texts in their historical context. Lefebvre begins with what he calls 'the significant *decline of referentials* at the beginning of the twentieth century', as a result of 'various pressures (science, technology, and social changes)' (*ELMW* 111, 112). Lefebvre describes how the unity of signifier and signified had, previous to the innovations of early twentieth-century art, guaranteed 'the referential of perceptible reality' (*ELMW* 113). A schism in art at this time put pressure on either side of this division, and gave rise to a split in this previously taken-for-granted unity; Lefebvre explicitly cites the cubists on the side of the signifier. Stein's 'cubist' texts, *Tender Buttons* in particular, are clearly also part of this emphasis on the signifier. However, as Jo-Anna Isaak insists, 'Stein's intention [. . .] is not just to reduce language to its surfaces':[45] *Tender Buttons* does not, or does not just, represent an emptying out of the content of words. Rather, by overturning language as it is conventionally used, Stein, in Isaak's words, 'enabl[es] the conventionally suppressed to come to the surface'.[46] Isaak does not describe what she thinks this 'conventionally suppressed' might constitute; I would offer 'everyday life', and for reasons put forward by Lefebvre.

Lefebvre describes the dialectical process of the replacement of relations of activity by linguistic relations, and the simultaneous devaluation of those relations:

Language endows a thing with value, but in the process it devalues itself. Simultaneously it makes everyday life, is everyday life, eludes it, disguises and conceals it, hiding it behind the ornaments of rhetoric and make-believe, so that, in the course of everyday life, language and linguistic relations become *denials* of everyday life. (*ELMW* 120–1)

Our paradoxical inability fully to experience the everyday life in which we most fully exist is a result of our attempts to express it, and the rapidity with which successful communication, precisely because it is successful, becomes shorthand, and therefore clichéd and meaningless – as we have already seen argued by Bergson and James. Lefebvre draws attention to the 'coupling [of signifier and signified] made anyhow, anywhere', indiscriminate and thus devaluing language. He also notes that 'it is in everyday life that the coupling of signifier and signified takes place' (*ELMW* 119). Lefebvre himself despairs of this indiscriminate coupling, citing the meaningless appropriation of certain disconnected signifiers by a system such as fashion. Despite the apparently liberating qualities of the everyday, as Lefebvre describes it, we are, he seems to be saying, doomed to create less and less meaning as we produce more and more signs; coupling takes place 'more or less successfully, and rather less than more' (*ELMW* 119). Yet it is precisely the improvisational, indiscriminate quality of the everyday that, I would argue, is displayed and critiqued in texts such as *Tender Buttons*. That is, the text explores and exploits the ongoing coupling and recoupling that the everyday allows, but it refuses to create more 'signs'. The text will not address everyday objects as objects of objective knowledge or truth, and thereby evades the pitfall of 'judging a society according to its own standards, because its categories [of objective knowledge, of the referential model of language] are part of its publicity' (*ELMW* 71).

Tender Buttons forms part of a contemporary European interest in the object, and what kind of an object a work of art might be – the *objet trouvé*, the surrealist object, and so on. Yet while the *objet trouvé* was generally an object found in the city street, falling under the indiscriminate gaze of the distracted *flâneur*, and the surrealist object a product of the unconscious, of dreams, the objects in *Tender Buttons* are thoroughly domestic. The text's sections, 'Objects', 'Food' and 'Rooms', indicate its setting within the home, among the domestic objects of everyday life – as Susan E. Hawkins says, 'at a very comprehensible level Stein reveals to us, in an extraordinary way, the house we live in every day'.[47] Yet the text also refers to the work done in the home, usually by women; a kind of work usually undervalued, one that involves a transformation without destruction, and more likely to pro-duce use-value than exchange value. Throughout the three sections, there is an emphasis on verbs of transformation, and of the transfer of energy: 'dirty diminishing [. . .] no rubbing'; 'Enthusiastically hurting'; 'The kind of show is made by squeezing' (*TB* 10, 11). Although the setting is com-fortable and domestic, there are numerous dramatic, even violent energies being exchanged. Further, Stein seems to be engaging quite explicitly with conventional bourgeois notions of work in phrases such as: 'What is bay labored what is all be section, what is no much. Sauce sam in' (37) and 'Then there is a way of earning a living. Who is a man' (45). These phrases include conventional associations of 'earning a living' with the masculine: 'Who is a man', 'sam'. Stein seems to be distancing herself from these notions of work: 'What is bay labored' is 'no much'; the 'way of earning a living' is 'a man', that separate, monosyllabic phrase emphasising the distancing of the speaking voice from the man.

Of course, Stein's own ambivalent gender identification always hovers over the question of perspectives on gender in her texts. While biograph-ical evidence certainly suggests that Stein personally took a highly con-ventional masculine role in a same-sex relationship, critics have warned against simplistic readings of Stein's gender identification. Although never explicitly aligning herself with what might be called the 'women's move-ment', the characteristics of Stein's texts are such that 'a growing consen-sus has arisen among many critics of Stein that her writing, particularly after about 1910, reveals a feminist concern with gender hierarchy, a sys-tem of domination allied with the dominance of certain narrative methods and linguistic forms over others',[48] and hence implicitly concerned with a female subject position. Nevertheless, private statements from Stein such as 'Pablo [Picasso] and Matisse have a maleness that belongs to genius. Moi aussi, perhaps',[49] serve to indicate the level of ambiguity, particularly as concerns the relationship between creativity and gender, within Stein's thought.

Conventionally valorised work – already associated with the masculine in being embodied in Jeff rather than Melanctha – seems to disengage from the everyday and everyday temporality. The vigorous, continuous movement of energies in *Tender Buttons*, however, suggests a different kind of work, one of constant engagement with the ongoing patterns and rhythms of the home and of course the body. The everyday, particularly as it appears in the domestic preoccupations of *Tender Buttons*, has always been associated with the feminine, as noted in my Introduction, while the valorisation of work as something outside of and superior to everyday activity is concomitant with its association with masculinity. Here, however, there is something that in its rigour and vigour might be associated with work, but incongruously appears in a domestic setting. Further, we might remember that Stein does not exclusively associate work with the masculine in *Three Lives*; although such a gender division is apparent in 'Melanctha', the female protagonists of the two other stories in *Three Lives* are explicitly described as hard-working. Once more, Stein will not allow traditional binary divisions to hold sway; while mustering gender stereotypes to distance herself from a certain kind of more or less alienated work – as 'a way of earning a living' – her evocation of the more immediate, sensual practices of domestic work nevertheless demands that the gender divide along work/non-work grounds be reconsidered. It reminds us once more that conventional definitions of work, which I have indeed made use of, are precisely conventional, and describe a restricted area of activity within the many and various activities and states of mind that might constitute 'work' – not least among which we might include, of course, reading and writing.

Tender Buttons, in its vocabulary and its syntax, is itself not averse to using some traditional notions of work. 'Build is all right' (38) the text concedes, and building is indeed what it does, building one term alongside another – although, and crucially, it is less the final construction than the process of construction toward which the texts direct us. In this spirit, then, I will initiate such a process of constructing meaning around one of Stein's objects, and leave aside the usual Stein critic's caveat on the anti-Steinianism of the work of interpretation; I will, to appropriate de Certeau's felicitous phrase describing the arts of the everyday, 'make do', *bricoler*.[50] De Certeau describes *bricolage* as 'artisan-like inventiveness';[51] it describes the variety of tricks, ruses and creative practices in which individuals, alone and in groups, take part in the interstices of large, regulated structures and systems. The intersection here of work ('artisan-like') and recreation ('inventiveness'), alongside the improvisatory connotations of 'making do', is precisely pertinent to a practice of reading that aims to be creative and inventive, but that also builds, makes, works.

To demonstrate my process of making, or recreating, meaning, I will focus on an example from the OBJECTS section of *Tender Buttons*; an example which will be, as examples necessarily are, both simply a random instance, and in some sense exemplary.

A TABLE.

A table means does it not my dear it means a whole steadiness. Is it likely that a change.

A table means more than a glass even a looking glass is tall. A table means necessary places and a revision a revision of a little thing it means it does mean that there has been a stand, a stand where it did shake. (15)

The very title of Ann Banfield's recent publication *The Phantom Table: Woolf, Fry, Russell and the Epistemology of Modernism* suggests that the table holds a kind of exemplary status in philosophical, and particularly modernist, discourse. Bertrand Russell's table in *The Problems of Philosophy* – which, Banfield argues, also appears as the object of the philosopher Mr Ramsay's epistemological anxiety in Virginia Woolf's *To the Lighthouse* – is similar to Stein's in that, in contemplating this everyday object, both Russell and Stein engage with the necessity of constantly representing, recreating, the object. Stein's standpoint, however, is emphatically one of user, while Russell's is one of contemplator, of the object in question. She attends to the table in order to explore and experience its everyday usefulness as well as everyday aesthetic value, while philosophers retain the distance required for their truth-seeking. Once more, we find that Stein's texts indicate a tension within modernism and between modernist thinkers; a distinction between a Russellian, positivist search for precision – the true, perfect, conceptually rigorous, that which can be clearly named – and interest in the real, useful and concrete, as evinced in Stein.

I begin my conversation with this example from Stein's text, then, by elaborating the sense in which I see it as everyday. Clearly the subject matter, insofar as it is signalled in the title, is of the most domestic and commonplace, as are the other objects referred to: 'a looking glass' and 'a stand'. Yet the ways in which 'A table means' – upon which the text itself insists through repetition of this opening phrase – also describe the everyday. 'A table means does it not my dear' is an example of the conversational register in which Stein often works, and as such signals the discourse of the everyday. Further, the use of the affectionate appellation 'my dear' as a part of an implied discussion around the capacity of a table to 'mean' grounds the text in a discourse of domestic negotiation, where meaning is not given but predicated on the interaction between individuals and the objects available for their use. The valorisation of making meaning rather than finding truth is further suggested through the syntactic parallelism of the phrase 'A table *means* more than [. . .] a looking glass *is* tall', where the verb 'to mean' is given precedence over the verb 'to be'.

The first 'meaning' offered is 'a whole steadiness'. These are practical, everyday characteristics we require from a table, that it is complete and steady. Their opposite is, however, invoked at the end of the piece; the familiar experience of finding a table that should be steady and yet shakes (and 'it *did* shake') is alluded to, distancing this object from the Platonic ideal of a table, and insisting on its materiality, its everyday deviation from the perfect. This materiality, however, is only perceptible through inter-action with a moving subject, for the shakiness or steadiness of the table can only be established by testing it. The physicality of the everyday, its human scale, is distributed throughout this fragment. The image of the looking glass as 'tall' involves the placing of a subject before the looking glass – otherwise who is doing the looking? – and thereby implies a literal reflection of the physical stature of the individual. 'Stand' could be read as a verb as well as a noun, and is placed exactly 'where it did shake'. The 'nec-essary places' in this text address the object through the epistemology of the everyday, where it matters where you are physically placed in relation to that object, rather than a truth-seeking epistemology, such as Russell's, where it does not – the philosophers, or indeed the scientists, take no 'necessary places'. This relationship is precisely that which Bergson shows where he contrasts a scientific, detached orientation to temporality with what might now be called the 'necessary time' one takes in everyday life, where 'I must, willy-nilly, wait until the sugar melts' (*CE* 10).

Lily Briscoe's (mis)interpretation of Mr Ramsay's Platonic table in *To the Lighthouse* translates the knowledge afforded by the philosopher's table into that offered by the table of everyday experience, by attaching the image of the table to the idea of 'Mr Ramsay's work', and thereafter seeing it wherever she happens to be whenever she thinks of this work (note the connection of the term 'work', not with practical, evidently useful activity, but with cognitive, logical, philosophical activity). The vividness with which Lily 'sees' the table, 'lodged now in the fork of a pear tree, for they had reached the orchard',[52] bears testimony to the particularly spontaneous, subjective, context-specific knowledge of what this table might mean.

Yet it is not only philosophers whose mode of attention to objects is in contrast to Stein's. The specificity of the quality of Stein's attention to objects in relation to her modernist literary contemporaries is helpfully elucidated through Peter Nicholls's comparison of Stein's aesthetic with

'[T. S.] Eliot's account of "naming"'. Eliot emphatically requires the poet to find 'the right name' for an object, in order that it not 'dissolve into sensations which are not objects'.[53] For Stein, as Nicholls remarks, 'the domain of writing is precisely that of "sensations which are not objects"';[54] there is no such anxiety around the imprecision of sensation. And indeed, it is precisely as 'sensations which are not objects' that we experience the everyday. It is not necessary for us to name a book, a train, the rain, for us to be able to make sense of them in relation to us; and the ways in which we will make sense of them will vary depending on our individual subjectivities, our environment, over time, and so on. The constant dialogue between these two aesthetic positions, implied by Stein and Eliot, and their connection to ways of knowing, might be described by returning to Lefebvre: 'The limitations of philosophy – truth without reality – always and ever counterbalance the limitations of everyday life – reality without truth' (*ELMW* 14). And this formulation returns us to 'Melanctha', where we saw the limitations of both Melanctha's 'wandering' recreation and Jeff's 'thinking' and working, and the counterbalancing of the one with the other, at the level of textual process as well as of character.

There are, then, at least three levels of everydayness involved in *Tender Buttons*. There is the everydayness of Stein's choice of object. There is the everydayness of her attention to an object: her response to it not as Platonic ideal, but as uniquely context-bound and in dialogue with the human subject. Finally, I want to suggest that the way in which this orientation is revealed – the processes gone through above to address the object in its everyday use-value – are themselves examples of everyday meaning-making, and specifically a re-creational meaning-making.

I referred in the introduction to this chapter to Stein's own use of the phrase 'recreation of the word'. Not only, I would argue, does Stein attempt a recreation *of* the word, but involves the reader in recreation *through* the word. Reading poems is itself a recreational activity, in the usual sense of the term; but Stein's texts also involve the reader in a re-creation of the objects to which attention is paid – never, for Stein, a creation from origins, for as critics have almost everywhere insisted, originary meanings are constantly undermined in Stein, by contrast with an Eliotic search for originary, or at least absolute, meaning in 'the name'. Such atavistic modernists as Eliot reach for new foundational structures, new beginnings, cores of humanity, with which to build their aesthetic of modernity; Stein's is a vocabulary of now and here, the sensual and the contingent. At the same time, in requiring the reader literally to experience the semantic re-couplings of her text, Stein's texts reawaken in us the awareness of the ongoing and always potentially valid production of meaning that goes on in everyday life. The quality of attention paid to these objects is indicated through Stein's vocabulary of the senses, which itself is deployed in a manner which simulates not just cognitive patterns, but the patterns of sensual knowledge; fluid, improvised, tangential, 'wandering', a dialogue between subject and object.

It is crucially Stein's agrammaticality that allows, indeed encourages, such a wandering, improvisatory reading. Stein is always directing the reader toward ways of creating those meanings that are to do with the visual, the tactile and the aural. For example, I have extricated the word 'looking' as verb from its location as adjective in the phrase 'looking glass' (note also the pun on 'glass is/glasses', so that what one looks at is imbricated with what one looks through); I have evoked the tactile through my discussion of standing and shaking; I have 'coupled' the signifier 'stand' with a cluster of signifieds around domestic stability and sensual contact, using both aural and visual effects (the alliteration of '*st*and' and '*st*eadiness', for example). I have, like every reader of Stein, re-created these meanings with her – not created them from scratch; 'stand', for example, has always conventionally had these associations, but the term has been put to the test under conditions of intense syntactic pressure, and found its capacity to recreate meaning.

The use of the term 're-creation' has been employed to enable an emphasis on the distinction between this kind of production of meaning, and that related to 'work', with its associations of coming to an end (having an 'object' in the way that these 'OBJECTS' do not), of using up time rather than experiencing it, and perhaps of producing surplus value – the idea of 'surplus' being simply incompatible with Stein's model of limitless meaning, for how can anything be seen as surplus, excessive, redundant, in a system where meaning is endless? Stein shows this very simply: as she puts it in 'The Transatlantic Interview' of 1946, 'I made innumerable efforts to make words write without sense and found it impossible. Any human being putting down words had to make sense of them.'[55] While a bare minimum of sense can and will, Stein argues, always be found, precisely what that sense might be cannot be defined in advance; it might, indeed will, be inflected through the difference of every moment, every reader, every place. To argue that a particular meaning is surplus to requirements (as implied by Eliot's search for the name) is effectively to invalidate that meaning, and implicitly to restrict the conditions under which valid meanings can be produced.

We can focus further on the importance of the processes involved in *Tender Buttons* (those processes of working *on*, modifying energetically without destroying or reaching an end) by considering B. F. Skinner's claim that *Tender Buttons* was an example of automatic writing, coming out of Stein's experimental work with James. Bridgman is representative of most Stein critics when he dismisses Skinner's assertions, stating that 'Although the results she achieved [in *Tender Buttons*] may not differ appreciably from those produced in automatic writing, the psychological distinction is a fundamental one.'[56] In other words, again we find that the product is less important than the process.

Tim Armstrong also makes this observation about Stein's writing in his discussion of the Stein/Skinner controversy, using an example from 'Miss Furr and Miss Skeene' to suggest that in Stein's writing of this kind 'at the level of the sentence there is process rather than a sense of destination'.[57] Yet Armstrong views the relationship between Stein's texts and automatic writing as less clear-cut than Bridgman seems to suggest. He argues that Skinner's assertions, though rejected by Stein herself, nevertheless point to automatic writing as a 'conceptual framework which validates Stein's textual production': a framework of distraction, a mode of attention with no connection to memory or even the unconscious.[58] Armstrong argues that, for Stein, automatic writing did not reveal internal, unconscious processes – unlike, for example, André Breton who saw automaticity as revelatory of the "true" self; rather, automatic writing was produced by 'a disconnection of the link between utterance and intention'.[59]

If we accept Armstrong's argument, then the mode of attention I have been describing in *Tender Buttons* bears similarities to automatic writing as Stein conceived it. As with automatic writing, the difficulty of the texts seems often to foreground their phatic function, as primarily examples of attempts at communication ('utterance'), regardless of content. Disruption of syntax means that the concept of 'intention' is undermined, as even less than in other texts can there be any way of assuming that the writer's supposed 'intention' is conveyed. Further, the idea of an 'everyday' mode of attention, where articulating the object's name is less important than locating those attributes of the object that are useful or important to you at that moment, reinforces the separation of 'intention' from 'utterance'. In the light of Armstrong's discussion, this everyday mode of 'attention' should perhaps more properly be called a mode of 'distraction'; once again the slippage between attention and distraction is particularly evident when we consider the concepts from the perspective of a critique of the everyday. To set Stein's writing within this conceptual framework of 'distraction', or perhaps better 'distracted attention', further distances Stein's mode of operating from one of conventional 'work', which implies 'attention', concentration, focus on an outcome, and so on. Finally, Armstrong's provocative statement that *The Waste Land*, that most learned, concentrated and highly 'worked on' modernist text (worked on by its author, its editor, and subsequent critics), is itself a 'distracted text', and that Stein is therefore 'making explicit the methods which others efface',[60] hints at the investment there might be, even in the most experimental and groundbreaking of modernist writing, in the ideas of attention, labour – 'work'.

I want to conclude by addressing more directly the question of the relationship between the practice of reading, and that of work. Other readers' experiences of Stein attest to a distinction between a conventional reading practice associated with work, and an alternative practice which Stein's texts encourage; this is the alternative practice or process which I have located as the third level of everydayness in Stein's work. Returning to Marianne DeKoven, for example, we find that her own vocabulary indicates ways in which her reading of *Tender Buttons* might be opened onto my investigation of the temporality of work and its alternatives. The term 'work' appears, as a noun, in DeKoven's phrase 'the coherent work' which reading *Tender Buttons* entails our giving up, immediately reminding us of the associations of completion and cognitive coherence aroused when a text is described as a 'work'.[61] Further, DeKoven opposes the kind of reading afforded by Stein's text to the injunction to 'plough through' that we might infer other texts involve. DeKoven's use of the vocabulary of affect – 'thrill', 'tantalizing pleasure', and so on – adds to the picture of a standard practice (of reading/working) that involves some sense of compulsion or unpleasant effort, in particular one which takes up time (we might here think back to Jeff's suspension in reading, thinking, working) and an alternative practice involving an immediacy, sensuality or intuition in which time is not 'taken up', as some commodity at a distance from the human subject, so much as lived through or experienced directly and in the present; a Melancthan recreational, even wandering, activity. Again, it is not necessarily that the latter model is being championed, either by Stein or by DeKoven, as a replacement for the former, but rather opened up as an alternative which is a crucial complement to it. Work and re-creation are in constant dialogue: the endless capacity of the human subject to *make* sense, to be caught up in a continuous present of ongoing meaning-making, is resisted by a, doubtless necessary, injunction to restrict sense, to learn from our experiences, as Jeff is able to do, and refine our expression of them – to search, as Eliot would have us do, for '*the name*'.

We make meaning in Stein's texts, then, not according to any ideal of comprehensive or precise understanding. Through the plotlessness and insistent, repetitive phrasing of 'Melanctha' and through the agrammatical proliferation of meaning of *Tender Buttons* each text in its particular way consistently resists what might be called the tyranny of completion, the readerly work, that hangs over most reading experience. What Susan E. Hawkins calls Stein's technique of 'dashed hopes' in *Tender Buttons* clearly plays on this kind of expectation: 'Syntactic habits create particular expectations in readers. Generally when we hear a question, we anticipate an answer. Stein definitely works with such expectations in order to derive certain results.'[62] Such results include 'reader unease' and an implied challenge to the whole structure of logical thought and deduction; if, as I am arguing, the experience of reading *Tender Buttons* approximates an everyday experience, then these 'dashed hopes' also reflect the disappointment, the unanswered questions, that everyday life genuinely entails. Thus, I have not set out to produce any closed or complete system of correspondences or relations between the terms 'work', 'recreation' and 'the everyday', nor to produce any closed definition of each; Stein's texts affirm to us that ambiguity is the gateway to the proliferation of useful, practical readings, available to be taken up, modified and tactically deployed, as Melanctha would put it, 'every moment when its needed'. Rather, I have attempted an approach which approximates Stein's own; like *Tender Buttons* in particular, it both resists an ends-driven mode of attention, and encourages it. That is, along with Stein, I want to resist a teleological reading, to a temporal or epistemological 'end', but at the same time focus the reader on practical 'ends', uses, values, since, as Stein says, 'always beginning and ending is as destructive to existing as never beginning and ending'[63] – you have to stop somewhere.

I have suggested that the kind of attention we pay to Stein's texts operates as a kind of conversation between object, text, writer and reader. I would like to finish by emphasising that this conversation is not restricted to the reader's experience of textuality. The attention we pay to Stein's texts mirrors that which we pay to real everyday objects, according to what we can or need derive from them at that moment; our relationship with them is, to return to the vocabulary suggested to us by de Certeau, tactical: fundamentally temporally inflected. We do not need to know every detail of how a kettle works in order to make use of it, and each time we use it we do so for a different purpose; we do not need to know what 'A TABLE' 'means' in order to know that, as the text insists, it does mean, just as we do not need to know what a table means – even that it is 'a table' – for it to have meaning for us. In other words, most of what we do in everyday life is not worked at, or worked through. The kind of dailiness explored in Stein's writing – Melanctha's wandering temporality, the improvisatory attentiveness of *Tender Buttons* – leads the reader himself or herself into a counter-form of attention; we are shown that attention as work, focusing externally, measuring time chronologically and quantitatively, is far from being adequate to yielding up the mysteries and the beauties of the everyday. Or, put another way, by drawing our attention to the everyday, Stein's writing makes us aware precisely of the quality and value of the attention that everyday life demands; attention that is not ends-driven but that both takes pleasure in and makes use of the ongoing, constantly shifting temporality in which our everyday life consists.

CHAPTER 4

War-days: H.D., time and the First World War

I have not painted the war [. . .]. But I have no doubt that the war is in these paintings I have done.[1]

INTRODUCTION: 'THE WAR', DAILINESS AND TRAUMA

H.D.'s autobiographical narratives *Her, Asphodel, Bid Me To Live* and *Paint It Today* form a palimpsest of texts covering the years from H.D.'s adolescence in Pennsylvania, through her establishment in London in the early years of the twentieth century, to the birth of her daughter in 1919. The dramatic changes which take place – both in the protagonist and in the world – through this period, can be gauged by examining the different responses to the day and dailiness in these texts, as an apparently stable temporal referent takes on a range of very different associations.

The narrative of H.D.'s early youth, *Her*, is characterised by a stifling sense of restriction, expressed through descriptions of the oppressive heat of the Pennsylvania summer, and of the limited and limiting social circle, the 'Anglo-saccharine backwash', of Pennsylvania society – associated with Bryn Mawr, the college at which H.D. (and hence her protagonist here, Hermione) was deeply unhappy. Hermione's attempt to explain and understand the disturbing currents in which she is caught up in this period of her life – her relationship with George Lowndes (the Ezra Pound figure), her engagement to him, and crucially her lesbian relationship with Fayne Rabb (Frances Gregg) – provides the strongest statement to be found in these texts of the day as, unexpectedly, aggressor. After a searing argument with Fayne, 'Days have done this, said Her Gart sitting upright on the hard floor. She noticed that the floor was hard. The floor didn't used to seem hard. Days are doing things to me' (*H* 165). Hermione's terrified sense of lack of control is expressed in this distressing reversal of everyday life. The background has come right up to the foreground; the day, which can usually be taken absolutely for granted, remaining the unquestioned backdrop to life, has become the agent of violent change, just as the floor which is usually simply there to support one suddenly becomes hard, painful. The reversal of the relation between foreground and background is cited by Ben Highmore as a 'necessary prerequisite for a [potentially progressive, humanising] theory of the everyday'.[2] However, H.D.'s texts demonstrate that, under some circumstances, such a reversal may not be without its risks, even its trauma.

By the time H.D.'s narratives have moved on to the happy early expatriate years in London, days have, fittingly, become much less oppressive; indeed, there is comfort rather than violence in the succession of days. This is clearly seen in the distinction between the oppressive tea-parties of Hermione's youth in *Her*, and the liberating, sheltering London teatime. In Nellie Thorpe's 'Anglo-shabby' drawing room, Hermione is burdened with questions about her future: 'They were always taking things up or why didn't you take things up, this up or this up or this up. Life was going on in circles' (*H* 59). This imperative to have some definite occupation is, as we have seen even in the Bohemian circles of the later chapter-novels of *Pilgrimage*, a pressure which pervades the texts under discussion, and it will become even more acute for H.D. in time of war. However, by contrast to these anxiety-inducing Pennsylvania teatimes, 'London at teatime when one is sheltered from the crowd, gives one, as no city in the world gives one, a background' (*PIT* 37). Here the background stays where it should be, unlike in the combative days of *Her*; London teatime represents stillness, stability. Hermione reflects 'this was London. A clock striking, that little church like a cheese-box George said. [. . .] Churches in London never moved an inch for all the traffic. That was the nice thing about them. That was the nice thing about London' (*A* 70) – the chiming of clocks for teatime, regularity, stillness. This is the London with which H.D. nostalgically connects during her psychoanalytic sessions with Freud some twenty-five years later: 'the Professor [Freud] had asked me why I was so happy to have the hour 5 P.M. for my sessions. I told him how I had associated my happiest memories of early London with the inevitable four o'clock or five o'clock tea' (*TTF* 165). The succession of days, comfortingly marked by teatime, does not 'do things' to the protagonists of these later narratives, nor does it put pressure on them to 'take things up'; rather it enables the protagonists to do things, providing a supportive background in which they become more themselves.

With the horrific disruption to dailiness effected by the advent of the First World War comes a return to the sense of days as oppressive, reified. '[F]or days after all were days', says Hermione in *Asphodel*, and in this war-world 'she felt days as days . . . heavy lead-winged days that had to be endured for at the end of days and days there were worse days . . . worse days . . . days of fire and slaughter' (*A* 176–7). While Hermione may seem to be attempting to confine days to themselves, 'days as days', they rapidly stretch out, via ellipses, into the eternity of violence that was the war; at the end of days there are only more days. This is a compelling expression of the contemporary belief that, as Paul Fussell has put it, 'the war would literally never end and would become the permanent condition of mankind'[3] – a belief hinted at in the opening pages of *Mrs Dalloway*, where the narrator reiterates, as if it is not quite to be believed, that 'the War was over [. . .] thank heaven – over' (*D* 4–5). The disintegration of days in the nocturnal existence of those fighting at the front, the sense of war as a series of discontinuous events, piling one on top of the other with no causal link or sense of chronology or duration – as expressed in a variety of narratives of the front, on both sides of the line, to which Fussell draws attention – is mirrored in a similar, though ultimately incomparable, temporal disruption felt by those at home.[4]

Frank Kermode provides a useful model for the kind of succession H.D.'s war-narratives describe. He takes the example of a ticking clock; asking us to agree that it says tick-tock, he then describes how in experiments, subjects are able to '"[. . .] reproduce the intervals within the structure accurately, but they cannot grasp spontaneously the interval between the rhythmic groups," that is, between tock and tick, even when this remains constant. The first interval is organized and limited, the second not.'[5] 'The interval between the two sounds, between *tick* and *tock* is now charged with significant duration', and Kermode takes this as 'a model of what we call plot', whereas 'the tock-tick gap is analogous to the role of the "ground" in spatial perception'. The tock-tick gap is 'negative space' or 'negative time', given shape or temporality only with reference to the objects or events located against it; it is a temporality of 'humanly uninteresting successiveness'.[6] H.D.'s war-time, like that of many other narratives of war, describes just such 'humanly uninteresting successiveness': it is 'men, men, men [. . .] guns, guns, guns', just as 'at the end of days and days there were worse days . . . worse days . . . days of fire and slaughter' (*A* 176–7). These are days going on and on, spiralling out of human time and becoming simply a succession of meaningless events, pure chronology – since as Paul Ricoeur has it, chronology stands as the true contrary of temporality.[7] This is the meaninglessness, the chaos which H.D.'s war-narratives describe.

'There was a war' (*PIT* 45). This absolutely minimal statement about the event, the crisis, which enveloped the Western world in the years 1914–18

says both nothing and everything about those years. Its deliberate inartic-
ulacy reminds us that there is not, in these texts or in general, a simple way
to describe the First World War. It was an event unprecedented in human
history – indeed, an 'event' which it is difficult to imagine as such, given its
vastness in time and space as well as the irreconcilably conflicting accounts
of how, why, even when and where its constituent parts occurred, and in
what these consist. It is, then, immediately something about which it is
difficult, even impossible, to speak. As Kermode has it 'the absolutely New
is simply unintelligible, even as novelty'.[8] H.D.'s narratives, as attempts to
articulate the 'simply unintelligible' war, reveal the radical rethinking of
temporality that such an apocalyptic experience necessitated. In this chapter, attention to the disruption of dailiness will open out onto the question
of temporal disruption in general in H.D.'s narratives of the First World
War.

The aspect of these texts to which most critical attention has thus far
been paid is as narratives of trauma. Analyses of the war trauma of H.D.'s
narratives have tended to emphasise a psychoanalytic reading which too
often results in a pathologisation of textual articulations of trauma, and
an attempt to diagnose either the author or the characters – or, even more
problematically, to conflate the two. The question of the legitimacy or
otherwise of psychoanalytic approaches to H.D.'s work is complexified by
the fact that H.D. was herself immersed in psychoanalytic theory from
the 1930s onwards, and underwent psychoanalysis by Freud himself during
1933 and 1934. Indeed, H.D.'s biographer Susan Stanford Friedman states
that 'the volume Freud wanted her to write became *Bid Me To Live*',[9]
suggesting a close relationship between this text and H.D.'s psychoanalytic
experiences. Psychoanalytic models are therefore both inside H.D.'s texts,
and have been brought to bear on them from the outside, mirroring the
kind of doubling that is central to the question of trauma itself.

Suzette Henke has recently suggested a diagnosis of the symptoms of
the protagonist of *Bid Me To Live*, saying 'At the beginning of *Bid Me To
Live*, Julia is apparently suffering from traumatic dysphoria, a symptom
of post-traumatic stress disorder characterized by "confusion, agitation,
emptiness, and utter aloneness. [. . .] Depersonalization, derealization, and
anesthesia are accompanied by a feeling of unbearable agitation."'[10] What
is striking on reading this passage is the way in which the list of terms
might describe not just a psychological state, as suggested here, but the
characteristics of this particular section of the text itself. The text is confused, agitated; it is often empty, depersonalised, derealised and anaesthetic.
Reading H.D.'s texts with detailed attention to rhetorical, structural and

grammatical features of the narrative itself is a strategy supported by H.D.'s most striking direct statement about the profound effect the First World War had on her. H.D. believed that the miscarriage she suffered in 1915 was brought about as a result of hearing the news that the passenger ship *Lusitania* had been sunk, with the death of 1,200 civilians. But, describing this event years later, she would put the emphasis on the role of form as well as content: she describes the miscarriage as having come about 'from shock and repercussions of war news broken to me *in a rather brutal fashion*' (*TTF* 40, my emphasis). As Trudi Tate puts it in her important essay on H.D. and the First World War, 'It was a story which did the damage.'[11] My emphasis, then, is on the 'fashion' in which H.D.'s texts communicate something of the experience of the woman at the home front during the First World War, how the story is told of what Henke has called 'the female world of vigilance, patience, emotional helplessness, isolation, impotence, and fear'.[12]

That it was precisely the symptoms of shell-shock in soldiers during the First World War that famously required Freud to revise his theories of trauma, and attempt to account for the phenomenon of the repetition of unpleasurable experiences, in his *Beyond the Pleasure Principle* of 1920, makes the relationship between narratives of the war and any reading of these narratives informed by Freud's own modernist text particularly fraught. As Friedman has put it, '*Beyond the Pleasure Principle* was Freud's answer to the challenge of the Great War.'[13] It is worth, therefore, making explicit the connections between Freud's description of trauma and the specific characteristics of H.D.'s texts that I will be paying attention to here. Freud's observations about the repetition of childhood distress in the psychoanalytic situation, together with his puzzlement at the recurring dreams of victims of what he calls 'traumatic neurosis', lead him into difficulties with regard to his hypotheses of the pleasure principle, and the concomitant 'wish-fulfilling tenor of dreams'.[14] In the course of the text, Freud develops the hypothesis of the 'death instinct', 'the most universal endeavour of all living substance – namely to return to the quiescence of the inorganic world', which, he concludes, the pleasure principle in its efforts to release and lower tension in mental life ultimately serves.[15] There are two crucial elements here. Firstly, the element of repetition: as we have seen, repetition is central to my understanding of the temporality of dailiness, as well as being a rhetorical structure particularly characteristic of modernist texts. Further, and relatedly, it is a temporal structure particularly characteristic of war-time experience. My discussion of the complex repetitions and recapitulations, disruption of firsts and lasts, in H.D.'s texts, will be opened by addressing their relationship to models of trauma. Secondly, there is a temporal ambiguity, at the level of Freud's terminology, regarding the 'death instinct' or, as I will prefer, death drive. How can the trajectory toward death, an event which commonsensically would always, as regards the individual subject, seem to be a moving forward in time, involve 'a *return*'? The temporality of death, then, is problematised, and this problematic temporality is suggestive for explorations of death as it is rewritten in these narratives of the First World War. Finally, discussion of the concepts of event and experience, problematised through H.D.'s refiguring of death, leads into the general question of how to define everyday life, and of that which justifies, or validates, everyday life in war-time.

WAR-TIME, REPETITION AND THE UNCURABILITY OF TRAUMA

Freud's explorations of the structure of trauma have, of course, been subject to subsequent revision and complexification. Freud describes the analytic situation as something of a compromise between getting the patient to remember their repressed experience, which is the most desirable outcome, and, if this is not possible, getting the patient to 're-experience' or repeat the repressed material, but crucially with a 'degree of aloofness' such that the patient is able to realise that what appears to be a contemporary experience is actually a repetition or 'reflection of a forgotten past'.[16] This cure hinges around the authenticity of the repetition or reflection, and crucially the analyst's ability to persuade the patient of this – to create a 'sense of conviction'. Yet, as Cathy Caruth comments, Freud's later work hints at a problematisation of this 'forgotten past'. Freud describes the 'latency' involved in the case of traumatic neurosis, where symptoms do not appear until some time after the event of shock. Yet, in paying attention to the effect the accident has on the victim at the time – or rather the lack of effect (the victim gets away 'apparently unharmed') – Caruth posits 'an inherent latency within the experience itself'.[17] Rather than being a case of repeating (in the guise of hysterical symptoms, dreams, transference, etc.) an event that is supposedly already safely lodged in the past, it is the repetition itself that brings the event into being, or more rigorously, 'since the traumatic event is not experienced as it occurs, it is fully evident only in connection with another place, and in another time'.[18] It is not that a traumatic event is accidentally, as it were, forgotten, but that the nature of the event itself involves its own forgetting; 'it is only in and through its inherent forgetting that it is first experienced at all'.[19]

This inherent latency, necessary repetition, is evidenced in the palimpsest scene which comprises Chapters 2 and 3 of *Bid Me To Live*. Early in the morning, Julia's husband Rafe leaves her in bed and goes to the war. Yet it is a repetition of a scene that has no origin, the first description of the leave-taking in Chapter 2 being already a repetition of a first leave-taking, left undescribed; it is as if the text itself has 'forgotten' the first traumatic instance of this event. It is both one scene and a palimpsest of the scene, containing within it the many leave-takings which have already occurred, which will occur; H.D.'s narrative represents the difficulty of lodging the event safely in the past. Indeed, repetition is already explicitly involved in the scene from the very opening of Chapter 2: 'He would come back, just as he had always done' (*BMTL* 15). As Laplanche has it, 'it always takes two traumas to make a trauma'.[20] Here there are already at least two experiences in play. One could draw a number of helpful analogies between the psychoanalytic situation sketched above and the structure of this narrative (revised, it is worth noting, well after H.D.'s own analysis with Freud). Julia both remembers and re-experiences the traumatic event of Rafe's departure, just as '[t]he ratio between what is remembered and what is reproduced varies from case to case'.[21] Indeed, this scene might constitute a further modification to Caruth's own sophistication of Freud's 'latency' model; the traumatic event of forgetting is itself caught up in a pattern of actual repetition – Rafe actually does leave again and again – so that experience, re-experience and remembering overlap, and the moment of completion or closure, whether as a 'release of tension', 'success' (Freud) or '*fully* evident' experience (Caruth, my emphasis), is constantly deferred.

Repetition, say Laplanche and Pontalis, 'reflects all the hesitations, the dead ends and even the contradictions of Freud's speculative hypotheses'.[22] Indeed, the palimpsest leave-taking scene contains within it many suggestive hesitations, dead ends and contradictions, in particular in terms of its presentation of temporality, that will resonate throughout H.D.'s narratives of war. My exploration of the narrative disruptions of H.D.'s texts, then, works alongside rather than after Freud, exploring precisely the hesitations, dead ends and contradictions thrown up by repetition, not to try to resolve them, but to indicate what they might imply for concepts of modernist, particularly post-First World War, time. Rather than suggesting that H.D.'s narratives express and find a resolution for a personal trauma, I want to explore how their repetitions and oscillations express the traumatic disruptions of war-time, and the extent to which these repetitions are grounded in a temporality of dailiness. This is not to suggest that the temporality of dailiness is itself necessarily traumatic. However, there is an 'inherent latency' in the temporality of dailiness, as there is in the initial traumatic event; the first day, whether of an individual life or of humanity in general, is not accessible to us – we cannot remember it, it is always already forgotten. The potential trauma inherent in the structure of dailiness (hinted at in the 'days are doing things to me' phrase from *Her*) is, then, exposed where this structure, with its sameness-and-difference, its oscillations, its ungrounded repetitions, is overlaid with the explicitly traumatic experience of the war.

'This is no ordinary thing, war time' (*A* 152); attempts to hold on to 'ordinary' time in H.D.'s narratives are, initially, associated precisely with the day. In *Bid Me To Live*, Julia clutches at the day in an attempt to retain some sense of temporal continuity:

But just now, it was as if she had reached some definite turning-point, or some point where, if she did not keep her balance, she would fall off. The last straw. Not yet. [. . .] Not to-day, anyway. To-day she would relate to yesterday and by a subtle and valiant trick of léger-de-main, to to-morrow. The thread binding past and present was not broken, would not yet break. (*BMTL* 42)

The effort to preserve continuity from day to day, in the rituals of smoking ('Every cigarette, if you came to think about it, was continuity', *BMTL* 17), and, crucially, drinking tea, is recorded repeatedly in H.D.'s work, and is heightened in *Bid Me To Live* in particular by being set against a war-time background of day-to-day instability. Yet, from the beginning, 'today' is not the right moment for Julia to work out her black, nebulous fears. 'Sufficient unto the day. This was not that day' (13); H.D. makes use of familiar phrases, only to unsettle us with unfamiliar treatment of them. There is a problem, then, with 'today', the day – not only this particular day, but the day in general. The disruptions of war-time are in part contingent on the instability already present in the structure of dailiness itself.

James Hafley's comment that in *Mrs Dalloway* Woolf 'used the single day [. . .] to show that there is no such thing as a single day' resonates with the effect of the palimpsest scene of *Bid Me To Live*.[23] Both Woolf's and H.D.'s texts create this effect primarily through the constantly mobile temporal orientation of the narrator. In *Bid Me To Live* as in *Mrs Dalloway* the narrative moves between memory, anticipation and intense experience of the present moment, switching between descriptions of the scene in the room and the conversation between Julia and Rafe, and Julia's internal thought processes. The apparent attention paid to the sequence of hours, 'It was five o'clock, it would soon be six, it was morning' (*BMTL* 21), is undermined by this meandering through time past and future; H.D., to pick up on Hafley's formulation, uses a single time, 'five o'clock', to show that there is no such thing as a single time. However, a notable distinction between H.D.'s text and Woolf's is not only the consistent first person narrative of *Bid Me To Live*, but the proximity, in this autobiographical text, between protagonist, narrator and author; as Friedman remarks, 'Instead of remembering the past – gaining control over it by making an orderly story about it – the writing self gets swallowed up by the narrated self and is compelled to repeat the past.'[24] Hence, perhaps, the temporal dislocations of *Bid Me To Live* appear that much more intense, indeed traumatic, than in *Mrs Dalloway*, focused as they are through the doubled narrated/writing self of Julia/H.D.

Any attempt casually to locate the palimpsest leave-taking scene of *Bid Me To Live* 'in' a certain time ('five o'clock') is further problematised as time itself becomes a player in the scene. Rafe's parting gift to Julia is, ironically for this narrative of temporal disruption, a watch, his wristwatch that has been identified with time itself: '"Look at it – I forgot it." "It?" [. . .] "Oh, the – time –"', where 'it' is, it seems, for Rafe the watch, for Julia the time or, by extension, time in general. Rafe forcefully, almost violently, straps the watch to her wrist, in a gesture intended to create a feeling of shared experience; the implication is that Julia will be able to look at the watch and feel close to him in time if not in space. Yet Rafe's inability to articulate what it is he means by the gift is characteristic of the hiatuses, interruptions, the inability to achieve communication or to resolve, which mark the scene in general: '"I don't want it, damn it," he said. "I'm leaving it with you, to give you some idea –" what was he saying?' (29). His words are obscured by the rough sensuality of his uniform pressing against Julia; the physical reality of war interrupts human communication.

The mistrust of words and anxiety around the failure of language in H.D.'s narratives relates once more to a reading of *Bid Me To Live* in particular as a narrative of trauma. Suzette Henke has made a persuasive case for viewing the writing of *Bid Me To Live* and *Asphodel* as part of the 'scriptotherapy' which Freud prescribed for H.D. as a cure for her writer's block in 1933 and 1934.[25] More profoundly, Henke argues that this 'veiled autobiographical narrative has, indeed, effected a therapeutic recovery from the haunting resonances of war time trauma'.[26] The extent to which H.D. herself, the historical individual Hilda Aldington, experienced a personal recovery from her trauma through writing these books is, however, less interesting here than the contraindications to the possibility of a narrative 'cure' for trauma which persist in the body of the text. For much of the text of *Bid Me To Live* is unpersuaded by its own narrative. 'And she would think (not thinking in these words)' (*BMTL* 15) – in a narrative such as this, firmly located in Julia's consciousness, who is thinking the words she is not thinking? Is this the narrative remembering what Julia does not? The examples themselves pile up, 'But she did not think that' (16), 'She did not think this' (23). There is an insistence on a level of thought that is 'present or existing, but not manifest, exhibited or developed', as the term 'latent' is defined in the Oxford English Dictionary. Yet the narrative's refusal to attach its corroborative voice to these glimpses of latent thought, exposing them only to snatch them away – like the just-withheld 'other vistas' behind closed doors, drawn curtains, that 'she did not think' (23) – holds back from the 'sense of conviction' required for the psychoanalytic cure. If *Bid Me To Live*'s early chapters are a narrative of trauma, then it is a trauma without a narrative cure; more profoundly, it may be that this narrative of trauma (and that narrative-making is the aim of the psychoanalytic cure makes this more than a simply analogous situation) draws out the particular 'uncurability' of a trauma. We can insist that the irreducibility of the trauma expressed within *Bid Me To Live* is not ultimately closed off by any apparent recovery from trauma achieved either by the end of the text, or by the author herself.

To return to the specific qualities of the temporal disruptions involved in the crucial leave-taking chapters of H.D.'s narrative, we can usefully draw on the appearance of a scene of waking, the prominence of which in modernist texts on time we have already seen. This banal and literally everyday act becomes for Julia a powerful, even painful, certainly not effortless, moment of rebirth. This is made explicit in the 'first' getting-up (the term 'first' should be seen as under erasure, undermined as such a concept is by the vertiginous repetitions of H.D.'s text, but serves here to indicate that this particular passage occurs first in the narrative):

Sheets, a bed, a tomb. But walking for the first time, taking the first steps in her life, upright on her feet for the first time alone, or for the first time standing after death (daughter, I say unto thee), she faced the author of this her momentary psychic being, her lover, her husband. (*BMTL* 19)

The commonplace birth/death opposition/identification is evident (as is the sleep/death equivalence or metonymy – 'a bed, a tomb'). Yet there are many more levels on which this fragment resists a linear chronology. The repetition of the term 'first' itself exposes a telling counter-logic at the simple level of the relationship between syntax and meaning: the word 'first' can be allowed to recur under the rules of syntax, and yet how can the 'first' be repeated? This generalised tension functions at many levels throughout H.D.'s fiction. It is both alluded to explicitly in the narrative, as here, but also played out at a structural level, as in this palimpsest narrative where a notional 'first scene' is continuously erased and rewritten. A similar structural disruption of firsts appears at the beginning of Part 2 of *Asphodel*, whose first two paragraphs begin with a repetition of the phrase 'Darrington came across the room' (*A* 107); whether this indicates two separate events or a repetition in the narrative of the same event is undecidable.

Bid Me To Live is particularly concerned with firsts and lasts, and other explicit uses of the terms in the narrative bear closer consideration. Early in Chapter 3, 'after' Rafe has left her, Julia links a memory of Florence, which has seamlessly entered the narrative at the same level of perception as the 'present' narration, back to Rafe's repeated leave-taking: 'He had given her something [in Florence as here], as if for the last time. It was always the last time. Well, let it be the last time' (*BMTL* 32). To say 'it was always the last time' is, of course, as counter-logical as to repeat the first – or to have a repetition without a first, as in the inherently latent structure of trauma. Equally problematic is the question 'For the last time or the first?' (69). How can one be unable to distinguish first from last? – since if one understands an event as having been experienced, it is evident that it cannot occur again for the first time, and if one understands an event as never having been experienced before, it is evident that it must be a first (although it may also be last, but not either/or as Julia puts it). The lacuna at the centre of traumatic experience is amply demonstrated in these temporal confusions, together with the 'hesitations, the dead ends and even the contradictions' aroused here by repetition. Further, while the instability of war-time renders these ambivalences more acute, the text raises the question of the extent to which it is possible to understand events as experienced in this way at all, as first or last. The sameness-and-difference temporality of dailiness itself mitigates against such an understanding of experience.

Explicit attempts to express temporality through dailiness, however, return H.D. to the problem of language. Being so ubiquitous, so taken-for-granted, dailiness appears in many of our most familiar idioms and expressions. For example: 'To-morrow and to-morrow and to-morrow. It was the same scene, the same picture, it was herself and Rafe Ashton, for the last time' (*BMTL* 69). The quasi-quotation from *Macbeth* (which also appears in *Her* 216) draws attention not only to the endless succession of days which mark war-time experience ('for at the end of days and days there were worse days . . . worse days' (*A* 177)), but also indicates the way in which the representation of temporality in language falls easily into cliché, into familiar patterns and turns of phrase, as Bergson, James and indeed Lefebvre have warned us. Further, the scene itself has been rendered all too familiar by its repetition in the text, of which the narrator is herself aware – 'it was the same scene, the same picture'. However, the clichéd phrase 'for the last time' is undermined by the first line of the next paragraph (set apart by the white space so important to the structure and rhythm of this text): 'For the last time or the first?' (69), emphasising the narrative's constant effort to break out of these familiar, automatic patterns of thought and expression. The returning to and re-turning of familiar phrases – idiomatically familiar to the English language or made familiar to this text through their repetition – forms part of a structure of inability to leave, more particularly an inability to leave alone, or compulsion to return, clearly resonant with Freud's model of the compulsion to repeat, manifest on many different levels in H.D.'s oeuvre: Rafe's repeated leave-taking, *Bid Me To Live*'s inability to leave the scene, H.D.'s own compulsion to return again and again to the story of her life, rewriting it in numerous different ways. The structure of *Bid Me To Live* in particular, where white space often precedes an elaboration of the previous paragraph, even a repetition of its last line, rather than the expected break from it, also reflects this general tendency. Instead of proceeding from one scene to the next, the next scene cannot leave the previous one alone.

The prevalence of this 'ungrounded' repetition in H.D.'s texts – to use Miller's terminology – resonates with Caruth's description of the dislocation of the event in trauma. For Caruth, '[n]ot having been fully integrated as it occurred, the event cannot become, as Janet says, a "narrative memory" that is integrated into a completed story of the past'.[27] So, we are unable as readers to reconstruct a 'completed story' of the leave-taking scene(s) in *Bid Me To Live*. The subtle epistemology of trauma is unfolded: the traumatic re-enactment (remembering, repeating, re-experiencing) conveys 'both *the truth of an event*, and *the truth of its incomprehensibility*'.[28] Indeed, the literal gap which many modernist texts make of the war as a whole reflects precisely the lack of integration of this paradigmatically traumatic event, its incommunicability in a narrative situation – we might think, for example, of Ford Madox Ford's *Parade's End*, Richardson's *Pilgrimage*, and Woolf's *Jacob's Room* and *To the Lighthouse*. The rupture of war marks H.D.'s texts in different ways. *Paint It Today* is stark: 'There was a war', and moves on from there. *Asphodel* is clearly divided by white space into two parts, pre- and post-'chasm'; this division around the war recalls the structure of *To the Lighthouse* where 'Time Passes' stands for the war years. *Bid Me To Live* is less clearly divided, but one could argue for a division at the point where Julia leaves London and goes to Cornwall with Vane, leaving that 'war-ridden city' (*BMTL* 40) for the 'new dimension' of 'not-war'

(115) – defined, nevertheless, only in opposition to 'war', never escaping it entirely. Yet there is a constant attempt in H.D.'s war-narratives to get over this 'chasm' of the war (*A* 108); convey it, cross it and recover from it. 'The past had been blasted to hell, you might say; already, in 1917, the past was gone' (*BMTL* 24); H.D.'s novels tell of an attempt to recuperate the past – not the comfortable 'pre-war', but both events in her past, and this temporality in general. The past is radically deracinated, as it were, 'blasted to hell' or severed from the present. The war was, with hindsight, a 'sudden poignant unmistakable dividing line between the past and the future' (*PIT* 65–6), marking a rupture in a human temporality that, from Augustine onward, has necessitated an understanding of the past as indissociable from the future; as part of a continuum of past, present and future (or, from Augustine, a 'threefold present'[29]) without which humans would be unable to imagine their existence in time.

This radical rupture in human time effected by the traumatic event represents a challenge to a scientistic epistemology, where a truth is guaranteed by its potential or actual comprehensibility. Thus the epistemological implications of trauma are placed alongside those of literature, one might argue modernist literature in particular, which itself insists upon a truth without comprehension – that is, risking tautology, without being comprehensively comprehended. There is an intensification of this epistemological situation in the case of texts grappling with the incommunicable in the form of the First World War. In particular, any epistemology which hopes to ground the concepts of 'event' and 'experience', whether psychically or temporally, will be radically undermined by the structures of trauma, by attempts to express these in narrative. Indeed, we see how the inextricability of the psychic from the temporal is made acutely apparent through the complex functioning of trauma. The disruption of event and experience in the temporality of H.D.'s narratives will now be explored through returning to the second aspect of Freud's revision of the pleasure principle referred to in my introduction to this chapter, namely, the question of the temporality of death.

DEATH, EVENTS AND THE PRESENT

'"I won't come back," he had said the last time but he came back' (*BMTL* 32). '[T]he last time' again, here with another turn, meaning both the last time he left, the most recent time, and also potentially the last time ever, the time which is never to be repeated. The event of Rafe's non-return, in other words his death, which he emphatically insists upon, is experienced by Julia as an event which does not actually occur. 'She had already faced the worst inwardly' (45); 'He was dead already, already he had died a half-dozen times, he was always dying' (32). To experience the death of a loved one, to feel as if it occurs simultaneously with their departure for the front (as, statistically, it was not unlikely to), only for this experience to be falsified, must have been a familiar pattern for millions of people during the war. For example, in a letter written in August 1915, Vera Brittain comments on 'an article on women & war in the "Times"', expressing empathy with the feeling that, for the woman at home, 'The moment in which she sends her dearest out to war is the very moment of death.'[30] The pain of having this pattern repeated, and of having one's experience continually falsified, is such that Julia separates Rafe into two different people, pre-war 'Rafe' and war-time 'not-Rafe': 'I love you, Rafe, but stay away, don't come back; don't, for God's sake, take that book now off the shelf, don't turn now and be Rafe; stay away, don't mangle my emotions any more' (46). The present tense of this whole passage heightens its intensity; the corporeal presence of the man is strongly evoked, reaching out to take a book off the shelf. The necessity, and yet impossibility, of living with this permanent contra-diction, the embodiment of Rafe and not-Rafe in one man, is metonymic of the general impossibility of living in the war, of its terrible impossible logic.

Just as events that have been experienced do not actually occur, such as Rafe's death, events that can logically only occur once are experienced as recurring. There are numerous last times, Rafe 'was always dying'. The black humour of the phrase 'he was always dying', mimicking the tone of a wife complaining about an irritating yet endearing habit of her husband, poignantly indicates the domesticity of war experience – death in battle is assimilated to the experience of married life. The terrible impossibility of war is again expressed at the level of syntax; in Chapter 2, Julia thinks of something to say to distract herself from the situation, 'For she couldn't do this again, she couldn't do this again, she couldn't do this again' (*BMTL* 19). The paradox is not only that the phrase itself is repeated, running counter to its 'not again' imperative, but of course that she does do it again, Rafe leaves again and again and again, dies again and again.

This ubiquity, constant occurrence, of death, is rejected by the pro-tagonist of *Paint It Today* thus: 'Why not live, said Midget to herself, it is so commonplace to die' (*PIT* 70). H.D. uses the terminology of the everyday – 'commonplace' – to evoke a class discourse here; yet the class prejudice evident in Midget's apparently flippant comment – par-ticularly shocking coming as it does in a chapter of 'Retrospect' over the war years when millions of people of all classes lost their lives – should not completely obscure a reading of the claims being made for life in this phrase. The relationship between the voice of the protagonist and the voice of the narrator is crucial here. Unlike in *Asphodel* and *Bid Me To Live*, in *Paint It Today* distance between the two voices is, sometimes violently, insisted upon – 'You might have called me Midget if you were very stupid, but I was not Midget' (*PIT* 25). Yet this insistence is deliberately undermined, for example where experiences attributed to Midget are reflected upon with the narratorial 'I' as subject. There is no clear-cut distinction between the narrator and Midget at the level of *énoncé*: their vocabularies, their access to and figuring of interiority, are often indistinguishable, making the sudden insistences on distance disorientating and ironic. Here, Midget's comment 'it is so commonplace to die' is followed by a paragraph of restrained narratorial comment, a moment of intimacy between narrator and reader which places Midget in perspective and in doing so, because of the underlying identification of the narrator with Midget, implies a humbling of the narrator herself: 'She seems, to you, a morbid child. I have said that she was the froth or the nothingness of the crest of the deceiving breakers' (70).

The narrator recapitulates an image employed earlier in the book to describe how Midget dealt with the war, described as a 'tidal wave'. 'A tidal wave does one of two things', she argues: either it 'swirls you about' and you are 'comfortably heroic and out of the dead run of the common level of usual sea' (the terms 'common', 'usual' still indicate a class-position); or it 'slashes you out, in the crest, as it were, high, high above the rest of itself and the rest of humanity', implying selection for some kind of elite (*PIT* 48). This second is Midget's experience, and although it is stated that one is chosen for this experience, it is also implied that Midget herself had some active role in choosing it. Perhaps in defence of Midget's stance, which it is acknowledged was 'not altogether a good trick', the narrator argues persuasively, 'You cannot argue about a tidal wave. You escape it if you can.' Although 'It is not an altogether healthy nor wholesome nor sane feeling to feel as Midget did, so thoroughly out of touch with all humanity', it is nevertheless 'a pleasant sensation to behold the great mass, and the flow and black lift of it, beneath you' (48). The elitism clearly indicated here is tempered to some extent by the narrator's argument: you would indeed escape the war if you could – you would choose life – though the discourse of war, of sacrifice, and of duty, might persuade some not to. The crest-of-a-wave image allows Midget to rise above the concrete reality of life and death, the stark poles of the war, such that they come to be seen as something like aesthetic choices – 'so commonplace to die'.

Midget places herself apart from life and death perhaps as the only way of dealing with the possibility of death, brought up close by the war. The seeds of this are sown in her desire to live only in the past and the future, leaving the 'commonplace' (we might infer) present to those masses who live in it – who might include, we note, her closest family and friends: 'A fear possessed her, a fear that if they [her family] did not let her go, something terrible and tragic would [. . .] beat her back, back into the present' (*PIT* 41). A similar position is presented where she asserts her communion with the classical world in a moment of revelation in a museum: contemplating a statue of Jason 'the present was swept away like the scum on a muddy river and she was looking into the past or into the future' (63). That this attitude of distance from, even disdain for, the present moment is made so explicit is again possible partly through the sporadic assumption of distance between narrator and character, where Midget's 'morbid' comments are glossed within the text. Expressions that would appear violent in the mouth of Julia or Hermione are given context and, though not excused, explained. *Paint It Today* tries to understand why and how individual reactions to the catastrophic horror of the war can be, indeed perhaps had to be, so detached, so flippant.

We begin to see, then, that the temporality of death itself, or what is called death, is understood in a complex way in these texts. Midget's somewhat adolescent attempts to place it outside the realm of her own possible experience require her to lift herself out of human temporality, the present, and rather assume the temporality of the forces of nature, or of the classical world, denying involvement with the everyday present in which 'it is so commonplace to die'. The implication is that the temporal location of death is excruciatingly present, now, here, confusing its status as never present, or that which constitutes the alterity of presence. In *Bid Me To Live* and *Asphodel*, attempts to negotiate one's own relationship with the temporality of death are found in part through the expression of a close proximity between death and birth. Near the beginning of *Bid Me To Live*, Julia describes receiving a minor injury in an air raid. While Rafe is attending to her wound, she 'realized or might have realized that if she had had the child in her arms at that moment, stumbling as she had stumbled, she might have . . . No. She did not think this. She had lost the child only a short time before' (*BMTL* 12). Trudi Tate notes that 'Like H.D., Julia has lost a newborn child during the war, and she has the peculiar sense that the war will kill the child for a second time.'[31] The dead child appears as a ghost which, in the strange temporality of the war-world, seems able to die a double-death, just as Rafe dies again and again. The miscarriage suffered by Julia in *Bid Me To Live* and Hermione in *Asphodel* is, more subtly in the former but quite explicitly in the latter, identified with the war – in *Asphodel* the 'chasm' in time, the other side of which Hermione strives to reach, stands for both the war and the miscarriage. It is not only that, as Tate explains, H.D. believed that her baby died as a result of the shock of hearing 'war news broken to me in rather a brutal fashion' (*TTF* 40), a view expressed in the blunt statement 'Khaki killed it' (*A* 108). There is in this narrative an alignment of the two events, of war and miscarriage, precisely in terms of their temporality. In the passage in which 'Khaki killed it' appears, Hermione is describing her experience in the nursing home while recovering from her miscarriage, and the grim co-incidence of birth with death is driven home by the emphatic use of the present continuous along with italicisation in the text: 'But would eau-de-cologne mean anything to anyone who was having a baby, *having I say a baby*, while her husband was *being killed* in Flanders?' (108, emphasis in original). The present continuous tense expresses absolute contemporaneity; duration is also lent to death, for rather than 'was killed' we have 'was being killed', drawing out both events to emphasise the pain and impropriety, both moral and aesthetic, of their exact co-incidence. That Hermione's miscarriage is precisely a death-in-birth heightens the grotesque and vertiginous condensation of each event in the other.

Indeed, the protagonists' sense that they themselves have in some way experienced death is explicitly articulated throughout the novels, associated in various ways with the war, miscarriage, marriage and loss of identity within marriage, and so on. We find just such an articulation in the getting-up scene from *Bid Me To Live* discussed above: 'for the first time standing after death (daughter, I say unto thee)' (19). The miscarriage is alluded to by the use of parentheses which bring the words 'death (daughter [. . .])' into juxtaposition. The 'death' is Julia's own death and, here, miraculous rebirth, but it is associated by this simple proximity, rather than syntactic connection, with the death of her child. Later in Chapter 2 we find 'her death, or rather the death of her child' (24); two events, which though potentially contemporaneous would still be understood as separate, are made into one by this 'or rather'. The 'or rather' implies a taken-for-grantedness of identification, the sense that the alignment does not need explaining, and indeed at this point there is no further explanation of why the description of her miscarriage is initially introduced as 'her death'. Much later still the alignment of the two deaths – experienced as one and the same event – is made more explicit:

Herself projected out in death, was that dead child *actually*. He [Rico] had been part of that, meeting him just as she was beginning to realise that it had happened. It happened *actually almost identically* with the breaking out of the war. Well, the war. (141, my emphases)

Here her own death, the death of her child and the war itself are explicitly drawn together: Julia 'begin[s] to realise' what the text has known for quite some time.

Again, H.D.'s ambivalent syntax allows for a number of suggestive readings, each serving further to problematise temporal categories. For example, Julia talks of 'herself projected out in death', which 'projecting' we understand as the 'it' which 'happened actually almost identically with the breaking out of the war'. Yet 'herself projected' indicates a continuous state, or possibly a movement, something having duration, rather than an event, an 'it' which might have 'happened'. Duration and instantaneousness, instead of being presented as two different temporal modes which disrupt each other, as an event erupts through the background of historical duration, are presented as equivalent. This alignment occurs at another level in this passage. The fragment 'Well, the war' could be taken simply as a wry, ruminative narratorial moment, conversational and with a shrug of the shoulders. But it could also be read as indicating that the death of the child had happened identically with 'the war' as a whole, rather than simply the breaking out of the war. An event having a shorter duration than the First World War, that is a miscarriage, is described as taking up exactly ('identically') the same temporal space: a death is extended to take up years of time; or equally those years of time are compressed into the moment of a death.

Yet both these 'events' have problematic temporalities. Death itself is not normally understood as having any duration at all, being an instantaneous transformation from one state to another. This event without duration is set against an event experienced in the text as endless: 'The war will never be over' appears as a refrain, repeated again and again (*BMTL* 12, 71, 87, 133). This passage from *Bid Me To Live* discussed above, including the difficult fragment 'Herself projected out in death' (141), can be considered, then, as another example, albeit a particularly dense one, of death reformulated as something with a more complex relation to the human individual than is generally understood. There is a tension at the level of syntax, where 'projected' implies a dynamic trajectory, activity, at odds with the passive nothingness, non-being, of death. '[D]eath' here seems to mean death in general rather than Julia's own death, implying the possibility of experiencing death which does not involve your own death. It is not just that with the miscarriage, some part of her died – there is a grotesque accuracy to the double meaning of the phrase in this context – but precisely that a part of her lived through this experience of death. Death is cheated, it is lived through before it arrives to the individual.

So, then, must death always be in the future? And if not, as H.D.'s texts seem to suggest, what can it mean to have experienced death, and still go on living? Gillian Rose posits the future as 'the supreme anachronism' thus: 'For the future is the time in which we may not be, and yet we must imagine we will have been.'[32] Rose's focus is on the 'not'; however, the other part of this proposition is elucidatory – what she describes as 'the curious ecstasies of verb-tenses transporting finite being around in time', that is, the future as 'the time in which [. . .] we must imagine we *will have been*' (my emphasis).[33] For the formulation implies both a future time in which we will be, and an immediate consignment of that presence to the past – 'will *have been*'. We can only, in a sense, imagine the future as a kind of past, anticipation of events which will have been. When one is in a war, the future becomes more or less unimaginable – both too horrific to imagine, and particularly for H.D., unpredictable. Further, the imminent possibility of death, of non-being, is most strongly felt, if not so much for oneself as for, say, one's husband. These intensifications combine to bring the 'will have been' of the future to such a pitch that this future death, this pastness which is in the future, needs to be experienced. To attempt to live *now*, H.D.'s protagonists must have imaginatively experienced their own death. And the question of what makes up now, the present, returns us to the concept of the day.

'How did she get through the *days* of the war' (*PIT* 69; my emphasis) draws attention to the dailiness through which the present reality of wartime is experienced. *Bid Me To Live* has Julia describe a 'war-Sunday'; days are inflected through their being-in-the-war. Everything, even the ineluctable pattern of day following day, is absorbed into the war: '[A]s the war crept closer, as it absorbed everything, the thing that bound body and soul together seemed threatened' (*BMTL* 68). The present, and specifically the continuous present, the comfortable mode of everyday existence is made repulsive or simply impossible: 'The present was dead. They were all dead', Midget mourns (*PIT* 46); 'this mire, this mud pond, this vast wash of débris and death and filth that is our present' (*A* 136) – the war absorbs everything such that the present is nothing but the war. 'Five years. This was the present' (*PIT* 45). Presentness in general, in both senses of presence to oneself ('the thing that bound body and soul together') and as a temporality ('The present was dead'), is radically polluted by the war.

It is signal, then, that the present continuous is a tense which H.D. frequently employs and problematises. For example, when, after her day out with Cyril Vane, Hermione is 'caught back into the body of Mrs. Darrington' and with it the awareness that she has acquiesced in the matter of her husband's affair, she protests 'How was she to know after it *happened*, after it *kept on happening*, [. . .] that she would so care?' (*A* 144, my emphases). This syntactical structure 'happened [. . .] kept on happening' also appears in the hiccupping beginning of Part 2 of *Asphodel*: 'Darrington called her darling, had always called her darling, had been calling her darling forever' (107); and in *Bid Me To Live*: 'he was dead already, already he had died a half-dozen times, he was always dying' (32). This constant sliding of a singular event ('it happened', 'called her darling', 'dead already') into a continuous tense ('kept on happening', 'had been calling her darling forever', 'was always dying') indicates an inability to keep events in their place. Events will not remain unproblematically situated in a past (which we know has been 'blasted to hell'); once something has happened it has entered into a present in which it seems trapped, endlessly repeating itself. The war *is* the continuous present, present continuous. This centripetal subsuming of everything into the present continuous of war is vividly expressed when Julia is caught in a bombing raid and the text launches mid-sentence into '. . . clinging to an iron rail, clinging to a dead branch' (*BMTL* 110) – into the middle of the present moment, of direct experience of war.

The problem of what it might mean to be 'in' the war, specifically understood as a temporal location, might be considered with reference to a distinction made by Geoffrey Bennington 'between the time that has come and the time *in* which it comes, between the moment as container and the moment as arrival',[34] a model of temporality we have already seen in Richardson's days as rooms. Or, as H.D. puts it, 'There was the war and things that happened in the war' (*BMTL* 97); there is the event, and there is experience of the event. There can of course be no complete distinction between the two kinds of time, or none that could be properly experienced as such. Hence H.D.'s 'and' (the conjunction is so often the pivot around which the complexity of meanings generated by H.D.'s prose develops) can be read as implying both a distinction and a connection – what might be called a non-oppositional difference, recalling (though not identical to) the structure of the non-oppositional binaries in Stein's work. However, the notion of two kinds of time is useful as a model for the disjunction, or 'out-of-jointness',[35] of temporality detected in H.D.'s war novels.

'This is no ordinary thing, war-time' (*A* 152); war-time is so out-of-the-ordinary that even the standard for naming the passage of time, in calendar years, is itself rendered strange. In Chapter 9 of *Asphodel*, Hermione looks out at the Cornish landscape and 'an odd sky that was not as other skies (it was 1918)' (160), as if the date itself is a self-explanatory marker of strangeness. Once again, signifiers come under interrogation; dates take on their own, unarticulated, significance, divorced from the period of time they are meant to denote – or rather, having become so unbearably significant with reference to that time, they no longer require explanation. Numbers are repeated like a mantra: 'they could dance 1918, they could dance. 8, 8, 8. It was nineteen eighteen. 1918. Let them dance' (120); 'the days long ago, 17, 17, 17. Seventeen was long ago [. . .]' (123). The familiar experience of a word becoming absurd simply through hearing it repeated is suggested, and overlaid with the specific absurdity of making sense of the war-world, of the passage of time, of the past and the present, through these slight marks.

These moments once more mark a point of tension, or oscillation, here between an ironic and a credulous position, between cynicism and optimism, each position undercutting the other – a tone common to much of H.D.'s narratives. Hermione mocks 'them' dancing to '8, 8, 8', and yet the repetition of dates, here as elsewhere, shows a desire, as if in spite of herself, to locate events in stable temporal units, to concretise past and present. This is strongly suggested in H.D.'s later short story 'Ear-ring'. The protagonist, Madelon, tries to forge a connection between herself and other guests at a dinner party by repeating the date to herself: 'Nineteen-twenty, Madelon repeated, like some abracadabra (1-9-2-0), a charm to make this snap into some proportion.'[36] Madelon knows it is superstition, a deliberate and forced attempt to make a connection, which 'jerked her into some feasible contact with these others'. She can find nothing more profound than the fact of them all being alive at a time called 1920 through which to connect with the other human beings around her. Yet, as she examines the figure in the detail of its annotation – 'Write it in a row, like a sum from the baby-arithmetic, or write it, with dashes in between, like a Morse-code signal', both infantile and militaristic (echoing the consistent parallel between the war and her miscarriage in H.D.'s narratives) – it becomes something that no longer simply signifies the present: 'already, in nineteen-twenty, pre-war'.[37]

This temporally disorientating formulation, 'already pre-war', can be found elsewhere in H.D.'s war narratives (see for example *BMTL* 9, 137). 'Already', implying something which has come too soon, before its time, is countered by 'pre-', indicating anteriority. Although difficult to unpack, one way of reading the phrase is as denoting a too-ready distinguishing of a time 'before' the war – an intempestive, indeed arrogant, anticipation of its past-ness to come; a past-ness of which H.D.'s protagonists are all too unsure, caught in an inescapable and permanent war-present. The implication is that the annotation '1920' harks back to pre-war certainties of temporal and spatial community, false certainties revealed as such by the war. '1920' works as a ploy, but Madelon knows it is no more than that: a collective hallucination. This is temporality revealed as container, the time 'in which' time comes: the dislocation between 'the moment as container and the moment as arrival'[38] is apparent where the phrase 'already pre-war' disengages past events from the past itself. That is to say, experience of the 'pre-war' is yet to be had, held in suspension as it is by being on the other side of the chasm of war. Once again, the inherent latency of trauma is apparent: as Caruth has it, 'since the traumatic event is not experienced as it occurs, it is fully evident only in connection with another place, and in another time';[39] yet even in 1920, H.D.'s protagonists are not yet ready to locate the 'pre-war', to place it in their experience.

H.D.'s quasi-autobiographies are all retrospective accounts, in a way which goes beyond the general necessity that any narrative come 'after' the events, fictional or otherwise, which it describes. Tate's description of *Bid Me To Live* as 'a *survivor's* account of the First World War [. . .] revised in the years surrounding the second'[40] would apply equally to *Asphodel* and *Paint It Today*. The very fact of the texts' existence bears witness to the survival of the writer. And yet the narrative will cease; as Kermode puts it, 'it is one of the great charms of books that they have to end'.[41] Again, there are claims about the structure of reading and writing in general which might be alluded to here – for example, Walter Benjamin's reading of the genre of the novel, described by Peter Brooks in terms which resonate with my discussion: 'It is the "meaning of life" that is at the center of any true novel. And since the meaning of a life is only revealed at the moment of death, one reads a novel in order to know death, that death that we will never know in our own lives, that which, through the figuration of a fictive life, gives us an image of what might constitute meaning.'[42] H.D.'s premature attempts to understand death, even to claim to have experienced it, can thus be seen as part of her attempt to understand the '"meaning of [her] life"'.

The positing of meanings, of 'what might constitute meaning', is, of course, necessary throughout any narrative as it is throughout any life. Yet H.D.'s novels draw attention to the provisionality of meaning through their continual returning to past (and future) scenes; their characteristic tension between opposing narratorial modes (irony/credulity); and their counter-logical statements and syntax, problematising the concepts of event and experience, of death and presence, and mitigating against a straight-forward resolution to trauma. Their internal counter-logic is grounded in a narrative where access to the protagonists' interiority is more or less universal, and hence one cannot read internal contradiction of this kind – 'No. She did not think this' (*BMTL* 12) – out of the text; one cannot resolve it. Since any end, any reaching of meaning is a fiction, and yet, 'the image of the end can never be *permanently* falsified',[43] H.D. 'ends' humanly, as Gillian Rose says of her work: 'positing and failing and positing again';[44] itself, perhaps, a useful model for the ongoing repetition, constant shifting, and enduring uniqueness, of dailiness.

THE EVERYDAY: BEING IN THE WAR

The preposition most commonly used, in H.D.'s texts as elsewhere, to describe how experience is located with reference to the historical event or crisis of war, is 'in'. However, there are many different ways in which this 'in' might be understood. The most inclusive, though Westernised, would be to argue that, by definition, everyone alive at any time between 1914 and 1918 was 'in' the First World War; at the other end of the spectrum, one could argue that only those who had seen actual physical combat could be said to have been 'in' the war. Between these two there are numerous more or less inclusive potential demarcations: those who were involved directly in the war effort, those living in the combatant nations, those whose person or property was damaged in the war, and so on. Anxiety over what it meant for an upper-middle class American civilian woman living in London to be 'in' the war pervades H.D.'s war novels, and similar concerns are to be found in other war-time narratives; this anxiety is part of the larger question of that in which 'everyday life' for a non-combatant in the war might consist. We will see how the problem of that in which a life consists, the use to which life should be put, becomes particularly pressing in the context of the disruptions of a war-world.

Asking what it might mean to be in the war, then, returns us to the problem of language, of what 'the war' means. H.D.'s narratives of the war are never sure what exactly they mean when they say 'the war'. As Suzanne Raitt and Trudi Tate point out, ignorance about the events of the war characterised most people's experience of it, both at the front and at home: 'No-one knew what was going on throughout the Great War.'[45] But this general inability to grasp what was going on, to make any sense of the war-world, is radicalised in H.D.'s novels through an undermining of the individual units of language themselves, before one even attempts to string them into coherent expressions about the world. H.D.'s interrogation of the minutiae of language is, to be sure, apparent in her oeuvre in general, explicitly articulated, for example, in her narrative of the pre-war years, *Her.* 'What was "now" and what was "doing" and what was "what" precisely?' (*H* 54). This sudden sensitivity to the use of specific words is heightened when it comes to consideration of what the word 'war' might mean: 'she must remember, try to remember, try to be things she had been before the war – no before *it* started' (*A* 114). Certainly, the replacement of 'the war' by 'it' serves partly to indicate that Hermione is referring to the whole series of private traumas that came at the same time as the war, around her miscarriage and her husband's infidelity; in everyday life, experiences cannot be clearly separated from each other, but coexist, the effect of war running alongside that of more specific individual disruptions. However, the long dash after the word 'war' suggests an abrupt breaking off, a sudden mistrust of articulating 'the war' as such, as if it would be inaccurate, misleading, to give it a name.

In *Asphodel*, a similar formulation to that found in *Her* draws attention to the inexpressibility of war in particular: '[. . .] no-one has been here since the – war. What is the war? There is a thing you mean when you say "since" and "the"' (*A* 149–50). Again, the long dash before 'war' marks a hesitancy to name it. Asking herself 'What is the war?', her initial response is not to question the meaning of that word, but that of the words which locate it – 'since' and 'the', words without external referents but only having meaning with reference to the other terms which they situate. Unable to address 'the war' directly, attention is deflected onto where and how it is located by these familiar, safe terms, which are then themselves necessarily problematised, since that which they purport to locate is so elusive. If we have agreed, thinking back to Bergson and James, that the everyday is characterised in the period as that which is taken for granted, then this questioning of the meaning of prepositions and pronouns can be seen as part of an implicit critique of the everyday running through H.D.'s narratives, one intensified dramatically by the advent of war.

The suggestion of this critique of everyday life in the war-world is supported by what follows in the text. The question is immediately repeated: 'What is the war? People, faces that don't matter' (*A* 150), and Hermione goes on to describe these, elements in her own daily drama: the woman her husband is having an affair with; a casualty on the front whose story she has heard. However, the indignation which Hermione expresses at the casual, illogical way in which this last piece of news was reported – 'they said it that way as if the whole column being swept out was the reason for him being swept out and that explained it' (*A* 150) – indicates that, just as her husband's lover must 'matter' to Hermione, much as she may try to make her irrelevant, the death of this boy matters also. Hermione has already agreed, in the pre-war section of *Asphodel*, that: 'little things mattered, not the great things. Things that wracked and tore you were forgotten.' This principle, of the primary importance of 'A clean towel [. . .] Hot water. Hot tea' (74–5), of the stuff of everyday life, will come under particular pressure with the advent of that which 'wracked and tore' beyond anything that had happened before – that is, the war. This tension pervades H.D.'s war-novels: a tension between protestations that the war does not matter, can be pushed away, made to belong to other people, while one's own daily life goes on; and on the other hand the war's inescapability, its pervasion of the protagonists' daily lives, language and sense of time.

'She was in the middle of something. They all were. That war' (*BMTL* 10). The uneasiness of Julia's relation to the war is, from this early stage, expressed in the tension between being 'in the middle of something', hence one might suppose experiencing it directly, and 'That war', where the 'that' points outwards, at something exterior to her own sphere of experience. Being 'in the middle' precisely is important, implying as it does a point of extreme submersion, equidistant from both beginning and end. And yet this extreme point also, paradoxically, involves calm, stasis, balance. Frank Kermode's repeated deployment of his catchphrase for the modern condition, 'men in the middest', draws attention to the strength of that term; it does not simply describe a contingent position but a necessary condition: 'to live is to live *in* crisis' (my emphasis).[46] In H.D.'s war-writings the violent subsumption of the necessary human condition 'in the middest' into the middle of a global crisis intensifies the experience of life itself as crisis, in a structure of *mise-en-abyme* or indeed palimpsest.

The violence of this all-encompassing crisis is indicated by the imagery H.D. employs to describe the war. In *Bid Me To Live* as in *Paint It Today*, the war is figured as a natural, meteorological disaster (contrasting with the imagery of machinery used elsewhere, particularly in *Asphodel*); here, during an air raid, it is not a tidal wave but a cyclone that strikes:

But now, everything was different. At least, everything was exactly the same, but so much worse, like the centre of a cyclone. The centre of a cyclone is still. So she was. But there was the table, the book-case, her constant inventory. But looking at table, at book-case, taking inventory, she gauged, as it were, the strength of the storm without, by the behaviour of the objects within, like watching small articles in a state-room in a ship in a storm. (*BMTL* 106)

This passage is dense with the broad themes of my discussion: sameness-in-difference, repetition, everyday objects. It crystallises a moment of stasis ('The centre of a cyclone is still. So she was') which is yet almost unbearably pregnant with possibility, with change – for, following through the simile, after the eye of the cyclone must inevitably follow more destruction. And indeed, though finding a moment of calm through this dramatic experience ('she herself had been centralised, had found a focus', *BMTL* 106), this calm is broken into by Cyril Vane, who literally and metaphorically takes her out into the storm, and forces her to confront both The War and her own private war.

The relation between the everyday objects in the room and the events 'without' indicates the tension in H.D.'s narratives between the desire to keep the war as '*that* war', to place it at a distance, and the inability to do so, indeed the conflicting desire to find a connection with others' experience of war. This is further apparent as Julia's afternoon with Vane progresses. Julia appears to have established a sense of her self, of what is connected with herself and what is not: 'What was going on outside, was going on outside. It had nothing to do with her' (*BMTL* 122). Julia's assertion has the familiar ring of someone telling herself something they want to believe – a tone which strikes one strongly at various moments in H.D.'s narratives. Julia attempts to abject 'outside', for which we must surely read 'the war', particularly since she is literally inside at this point, inside a cinema hiding from the bombing raids. Yet this scene contains a rare sense of community with the rest of the cinema audience, made up primarily of soldiers: 'She was part of this. She swerved and veered with a thousand men in khaki' (123). What was going on outside is going on inside, the two are not so easily separable. Ordinary, private, everyday practices such as going to the cinema are inescapably mortgaged to 'outside', to the war which is never just going on 'out there'.

Other texts of the period evoke more readily the intersection of daily life and the war. Gertrude Stein, for example, though expressing very different war-time experiences from H.D., takes her insistence on 'mixing the outside with the inside'[47] through her war-time poetry: Elizabeth Gregory describes Stein's war-time poetry as 'snippets of the war as Stein saw it, as it intersects with the dailiness of life in the towns and villages around Perpignan and Nîmes'.[48] As Gregory comments of the poem 'Won' of 1917, the elements in the poem, 'the arrival of US soldiers, the winning of the war, good food, and the operation of Stein's car', are all put 'on a par'; 'the trivial concerns and pleasures of everyday life are precisely the point'.[49] Gregory draws attention specifically to Stein's 'emphasis on daily pleasures and the ordinary lives of people in extraordinary circumstances',[50] and indeed, this emphasis is much in evidence in, for example, the war years chapter of *The Autobiography of Alice B Toklas*: the battle of the Marne is described in terms of Alice's schoolfriend Nellie's inability to get a taxi to Boulogne; Stein and Toklas are given souvenirs, *objets*, made out of bits of artillery – the war literally comes into their home.[51] Stein's sense of her active engagement with military aspects of the war – not least because she was living in an occupied country – enables her to see it as more fully integrated with an everyday life going on before and after it; running below or alongside it.

However, for many of those left at home, and hence women in particular, during the war, the war and everyday life would have seemed much harder to integrate: 'But now, everything was different. At least, everything was exactly the same, but so much worse' (*BMTL* 106). That life seems both different and exactly the same creates a particular tension for noncombatants. Men going to the front were being launched into a totally alien environment, whereas those left at home might have had the paradoxical experience of life continuing 'as normal', carrying on familiar routines in familiar environments; although of course many women were sent to work in munitions factories or on the land, Julia, Hermione and Midget have no such duties. The terrible uncanniness of everything being 'exactly the same' and yet the world different beyond measure is indicated, heightening the stakes involved in the anxiety-inducing imperative to act, do, work, found elsewhere in H.D.'s narratives; Hermione, for example, is plagued with the question 'Why haven't I ever *done* anything?' (*H* 109).

Stein records the conscious decision to 'get into the war';[52] H.D.'s wartime protagonists respond differently to the dilemma posed by the question of what to do *in* the war: 'What was her duty?' (*PIT* 46). In *Asphodel*, where the imagery connecting war and childbirth is strongest, Hermione casts her second pregnancy as her war effort: 'God had given her the choice even now, it was a mangy sort of choice for she couldn't help it. It was like "yes I joined the army as a volunteer"' (*A* 164). This 'choice' to have the child, albeit a 'mangy' choice, is nevertheless much more real as an engagement with the war than the activities arranged, one supposes, for upper-class ladies: 'one couldn't believe that Delia's, that Lady Prescott's red cross section represented the whole of life. Being good, being good, rolling, unrolling lint until her fingers ached and she knew she would go mad but anything was excused when one's husband came back' (*A* 119) (the repetition of Delia as 'Lady Prescott' emphasising the association of this activity with a particular class and national identity).

Chapter 9 of *Asphodel* traces Hermione's discovery that she is pregnant through various phases of responses, up to her determination to have the child regardless of the vacillations of the men around her. That this determination is apparently based on a pseudo-mystical moment when a swallow enters her room, as if in answer to her question, further enmeshes her resistance to the war in the structures and vocabularies of myth (as in *Paint It Today*). Hermione is aware of her own interpellation by these structures – 'Classic images here blend with images of Christian beauty' (*A* 154) – yet the power of this occurrence remains; again, self-awareness coexists with a leap of faith. The power lent to her body by the new life inside it resists any obstacle: 'Men could do nothing to her for a butterfly, a frog, a soft and luminous moth larva was keeping her safe. She was stronger than men, men, men – she was stronger than guns, guns, guns' (162). The masculine, technologised war-world is graphically resisted by the essentially female, and here ultra-feminised, natural process of reproduction, and yet the pregnancy is figured as like volunteering for the army. As Raitt and Tate have it, in a formulation which seems particularly apt for the ways in which H.D.'s protagonists figure their war-identity: 'Women become soldiers, soldiers become mothers, and mothers become children.'[53] Motherhood, they argue, is both 'part of what is threatened by war, which goes against the biological and moral instincts of the women on whose behalf it is fought', and yet 'war can remake the world in terms of maternity [. . .] In writing by both men and women, maternity is oddly displaced from gender and re-emerges as a fantasy of tenderness and power.'[54]

The depiction of Hermione's pregnancy in *Asphodel* does not, however, conform to this observation on the unshackling of maternity from gender. Chapter 9 places Hermione very definitely in an oppositional position with regard to the men around her; her maternity is thoroughly grounded in her gender, though tenderness and power are indeed precisely what it arouses in her. Maternity, and in particular the suffering it involves, allows Hermione to feel she is doing her duty, just as the soldiers do theirs; the chapter, though taking place in Cornwall far from the fighting and bombing, is nevertheless inescapably *in* the war, as men, guns, boats, are repeated again and again in different combinations. Yet her war-time duty is one of resisting precisely the structures of war and machine which make that 'duty' part of such a powerful discourse at the time, that of, in Jay Winter's coinage, 'Big Words'.[55] Here is an example, perhaps, to back up Winter's argument going 'beyond the cultural history of the Great War as a phase in the onward ascent of modernism', suggesting that 'the overlap of languages and approaches between the old and the new, the "traditional" and the "modern", the conservative and the iconoclastic, was apparent both during and after the war'.[56] Just as Woolf, rather than rejecting outright her Victorian heritage, needs to engage with that past in order to break with it,[57] so H.D. uses the traditional imagery and vocabulary of war in order to intensify her resistance to it.

Paint It Today shows a less concrete, and more problematic, resistance to war. From the chapter 'Snow and Ash', in which the war happens:

All about her, people cried of nobility, of sacrifice; all the world was led to its devotion to sacred duty. All the world was splendid and heroic. Every soul she knew. All had some song of duty or distinction. Someone they knew, someone had proved high servant, arch-priest or sacred offering to duty. What was her duty? (46)

The proliferation in this passage of 'Big Words' – duty, sacred duty, devotion, distinction, nobility, sacrifice – together with the repetition of 'all', describes Midget inescapably surrounded by these imperatives. Her motto '*Cras amet qui numquam amavit*' has been undermined: 'There was no love, save love of duty, love of sacrifice.' Midget's answer, or 'trick', is that of the tidal wave discussed above, where Midget raises herself, or is raised, above the 'common' experience of war. This apparently dismissive, elitist move is, however, to some extent recuperated in the chapter 'Retrospect', which looks back over the war. Here we find a careful narratorial exploration of Midget's place 'in' the war:

How did she get through the days of the war, this Midget, you may ask, if she took no part, if she did nothing at all to help, one way or the other? It is all very well to talk, during a war. People can talk. Who dare ask us in our ordinary years what we do with ourselves, how we pass the time?

There was impertinence in the air. Midget was often asked, but what are you *doing*?

What, when it comes to that, does anyone ever do?

Midget did very little. [. . .] Midget thought much.

[. . .] But I never pretended greatness for Midget. I said that she was the froth or the nothingness of the crest of the black wave. (69)

The question raised by this extract is, broadly, the extent to which public life should intrude onto private life. Midget resents the interrogation of her daily existence by forces – ideologies, if you like – in whose logic she does not participate. In response to the question 'what are you doing?', Midget, or the narrator, responds 'What, when it comes to that, does anyone ever do?' As Frank Kermode has it in his discussion of Macbeth: 'Nothing in time can, in that sense be *done*, freed of consequence or equivocal aspects.'[58] 'Doing' is not a simple, unequivocal activity; as the parallel syntax hints to us ('Midget did very little. [. . .] Midget thought much') there is a relation between doing and thinking which does not necessitate a mutual exclusivity, nor an inherent hierarchisation of the former over the latter, upon which the ideology of war will insist. As Midget has asserted, 'There is nothing to be done or said. But there is a great deal to be thought' (*PIT* 63). Thus the text raises the question of the validity of mental activity, the question of the kind of 'doing' that 'thinking' might constitute, evading rigid categories of work or duty.

My reading of Midget might be set alongside Trudi Tate's of Woolf's Clarissa Dalloway: 'It would be all too easy to construct a purely satiric view of her, a ruling-class woman who lives in Westminster and thinks "it was very, very dangerous to live even one day"',[59] just as it would be easy to construct a purely satiric view of Midget as an upper-class young woman who excuses her apathy in the face of worldwide death and destruction by pleading private contemplation as an equally legitimate response. However, a number of factors would have to be considered in the assertion of this satiric view. There are historical factors, such as the question of what activities were actually available to an upper-class woman during the war (lint-rolling is the only directly practical one offered, in *Asphodel*, and 'one couldn't believe' that this activity 'represented the whole of life'), as well as that of H.D.'s protagonists' position as Americans in England. There are also issues internal to the narrative, particularly to an autobiographical narrative such as this. In particular, there is the question of the scope of the plea being made for Midget's position. It is of course specifically Midget's story which is being written to be read, and to have any communicable significance must be seen as making some claims beyond the uniqueness of this individual story. An autobiographical narrative, more urgently perhaps than narrative in general, asks to be read both as simply an example and as exemplary, as a text, as Laura Marcus puts it, 'whose exemplariness, paradoxically, lies in its representation of the uniqueness and singularity of the individual life'.[60] However, 'I never pretended greatness for Midget,' says the narrator, attempting to refuse any implication that Midget is representative or indeed important. Thus, while this 'purely satiric view' of Midget as a spoiled young lady may retain some purchase, the narrator may be seen as already acknowledging this view by creating distance between herself and Midget. While Midget might be dismissed as irrecoverably snobbish and elitist, it is harder thus to dismiss *Paint It Today*.

As Moretti has suggested, 'we must specify that what characterizes every-day life [. . .] is not the nature or the number of its pursuits but their "treatment". [. . .] We may thus speak of everyday life whenever the indi-vidual subordinates any activity whatsoever to the construction of "his own world".'[61] The compulsive attention to, repeated attempts to, render the 'uniqueness and singularity of the individual life' constituting H.D.'s palimpsest of war narratives is consistent precisely with just such a subor-dination of activities to the construction of her, or better her protagonists', own world. Her challenges to conventional linguistic and syntactic struc-tures, as well as the narrative disruptions of her texts, perform the attempt to address 'the absolutely New', the unique and unprecedented trauma of the First World War. And yet this attempt to articulate the 'uniqueness and singularity of the individual life' involves precisely raising the question of that in which this individual life consists, should consist, how it is validated. H.D.'s texts demonstrate how the experience of the woman at home dur-ing war radically challenges assumptions about that in which the everyday consists, of what is to be 'done', as well as indicating how the temporality of dailiness, far from necessarily constituting a comforting background, can be cognate with a temporality of trauma. These challenges, while arising out of the context of this acute historical moment, and the position of women in particular, continue to be suggestive for the more general ques-tion of how we understand the grounding of our lives in the everyday and a temporality of dailiness.

CHAPTER 5

Reading, writing and thinking: a Woolfian daily life

INTRODUCTION: 'WHAT IS LIFE?' – OSCILLATION AND DAILINESS

'[T]o find a literary form for the representation of daily life, or to put the whole of "life" into a single day (*Mrs Dalloway, Between the Acts*) is exactly what Woolf attempts to achieve in her novels'.[1] Rachel Bowlby puts forward this critical assessment of Virginia Woolf's literary aims in her important collection of essays, *Feminist Destinations*. But appearing, as it does, only parenthetically (within a chapter on 'Orlando's Undoing'), this statement reflects the heretofore parenthesised, inadequately theorised, question of the daily in modernist writing.[2] My intention in this chapter is to take seriously this proposition – remove it from its parentheses. Exploration of these two approaches to dailiness in Woolf, the 'representation of daily life', and the idea of putting 'the whole of "life" into a single day', will form the two main sections of this chapter. In particular, I will suggest how the processes of thinking, writing, and in particular reading – both as they are explicitly addressed in Woolf's work, and in terms of how her work modifies and expands upon our understanding of these processes as part of the production of the text itself – form part of a particularly Woolfian understanding of that in which 'daily life' consists. As Hermione Lee says, 'Reading, quite as much as writing, is [Woolf's] life's pleasure and her life's work. It is separated from the rest of her activities by its solitude and withdrawal, but she is always comparing it to other forms of behaviour and existence – relationships, walking, travelling, dreaming; desire, memory, illness. When she writes about reading she makes it overlap with these things.'[3]

In the first section of this chapter I will address the idea of putting 'the whole of "life" into a single day', asking how the various temporalities of everyday life are framed and evoked by the structure of the one-day novel. Through a discussion of *Mrs Dalloway* as an exemplary text, I will challenge some of the distinctions between different daily temporalities implicit in critical work on this novel. I will go on to show how the complex functioning of memory and repetition in Woolf's texts draws the structure and temporality of reading into the matrix of dailiness suggested by the one-day novel and its concerns. In the second section of the chapter, I will return to the first part of Bowlby's phrase to look more closely at the question of 'the representation of daily life'. My primary texts here will be *Orlando* and *The Waves*, the pair of texts which, Gillian Beer suggests, are 'at the centre of Woolf's career'.[4] I regard these texts as a pair not only because documentary evidence shows us their parallel gestation,[5] but because in both these texts, as Beer puts it, 'How to write lives became for Woolf a more inclusive question: how to write life.'[6] Broadly speaking, my understanding of the relationship between these two texts is that, while *Orlando* explicitly and compulsively raises the question 'what is life?', *The Waves* explores it implicitly by eliminating much of that which might normally be considered 'life', and in doing so, radically undermines assumptions about how to answer this question. *The Waves* will be revisited under the genre-breaking definition of 'poetic play'; thus, I will argue that while *Orlando* asks, even describes, what life is, *The Waves* performs it. As I explore the 'daily life' which Woolf is writing in these texts, the question of the status of the activities of reading, writing and thinking will emerge, amplified through discussion of Woolf's essay 'Reading', and of scenes of reading in *Between the Acts* and *To the Lighthouse*. The chapter will conclude with some final remarks on the shape of the day in Woolf, its function as chronotope, and the way in which viewing the day thus reveals the firm grounding of a Woolfian daily life in its socio-economic and cultural context.

Before beginning my section on life in a single day, I want to draw attention to a crucial feature related to the dailiness of Woolf's texts: that of oscillation. Throughout Woolf's writing, and writing about her writing, there is a tension, or, as Gillian Beer suggests, 'oscillation',[7] between chaos and order, the random and the structured, movement and stasis, the transitory and the enduring. Nowhere is this more evident than in Woolf's essay 'Modern Fiction', cited so often as a gloss on her own writing practices that it has come to be viewed as a Woolfian manifesto.[8] Indeed, and interestingly for my discussion, Hermione Lee states that 'though this essay [. . .] is always cited as her manifesto for the "new" kind of novel she is now going to write, it is as much about reading as writing'.[9] In this essay, Woolf suggests we:

Examine for a moment an ordinary mind on an ordinary day. The mind receives a myriad impressions – trivial, fantastic, evanescent, or engraved with the sharpness of steel. From all sides they come, an incessant shower of innumerable atoms; and as they fall, they shape themselves into the life of Monday or Tuesday, the accent falls differently from of old; the moment of importance came not here but there. [. . .] Let us record the atoms as they fall upon the mind in the order in which they fall, let us trace the pattern.[10]

While usually quoted to emphasise the difference between the rigidity of the Edwardian novelist and the fluidity of the modern writer, this passage in fact is evenly balanced in its emphasis on randomness – 'myriad impressions', 'trivial, fantastic, evanescent', 'from all sides', the repeated verb 'fall'; and structure – 'they shape themselves', 'the accent falls', 'the moment of importance', 'the pattern'. Days, given the illusion of unity by their separate names, 'Monday or Tuesday', participate in an ongoing oscillation between fluidity and order, difference and sameness. Ann Banfield suggests that in both of Woolf's ways of figuring her atomised universe, the 'window-room' and the 'mirror-pool', we find that 'a momentary order is imposed on the unordered units'.[11] Beer gives another example of the oscillation which she identifies in Woolf's work where she argues that '[Woolf] is drawn most to that which is perpetually changing, and I give equal force here to both elements';[12] both to change and to perpetuity. In a different context, Bowlby proposes that just such a structure of counterbalancing is paradigmatic of Woolf's response to modern life – from pleasurable and unclassified sensations, to 'judgement, or order, or permanence, or depth'.[13]

The structure Bowlby suggests here can be detected in what is often read as an exemplarily intuitive, random, sensual response: the 'moment of being' as described in Woolf's autobiographical text 'A Sketch of the Past'. Woolf's 'moment of being', an intense and only partly articulable experience which remains with Woolf in memory and has a strong influence on her sense of self – indeed, which for Woolf would form part of the answer to the question 'what is life?' – arises without warning, unexpectedly, in a chaotic fashion. Crucially, however, such a 'shock is at once in my case followed by the desire to explain it'.[14] Woolf's 'moment of being', far from being a unified, self-sufficient, self-explanatory temporal unit, participates in what might be called a structure of supplementarity; namely, it is defined precisely by that which it demands in order to supplement it, the 'desire to explain it' which follows it 'at once'.[15] The moment of being, like Orlando's manuscript, 'want[s] to be read' (*O* 190), reflected upon, explained. Specifically, Woolf says, she 'make[s] it real by putting it into words'.[16] We see, then, that for Woolf the practices of reading and writing are not an abstraction of experience, as rendering in language might conventionally be regarded – indeed, as both Bergson and James might contend – but centrally a part of it; experience is impossible without such a rendering: 'I *make it real* by putting it into words.' To make use of Bergsonian terminology, intuition is not enough for Woolf, it must be counterbalanced by intellect; and this counterbalancing, or indeed oscillation, finds expression specifically in the practices of reading, writing, 'putting it into words'.

This pattern of oscillation feeds directly into the dual thread of my enquiry, on daily time and on the everyday. Firstly, a temporality of dailiness itself evidently participates in an oscillatory pattern, between stasis and movement, sameness and difference. Secondly, this oscillatory movement is explicitly related to the question of what constitutes life – what is important and what is not. Thus, it leads us back to the question of the definition, the value or otherwise, of the 'everyday'. Throughout Woolf and Woolf criticism, there is an oscillation between the everyday as the unmarked, banal background activity and experience of life which has little or no effect on the individual, and on the other hand the sense that what usually goes unmarked is in fact that which we should recognise as fundamental in making up our lives. The first definition of the everyday given here informs the model of life-writing found in nineteenth-century biography, where events which society will recognise and affirm as important are plucked out of everyday existence and emphasised as those which define the life of the subject. It is analogous to the model of 'cotton wool' surrounding 'moments of being' in 'A Sketch of the Past'. However, Woolf's model modifies its Victorian forbears in that its exemplary events are not, to quote from *Orlando*, 'articles by Nick Greene on John Donne nor eight-hour bills nor covenants nor factory acts that matter' – not, in other words, public or institutional events, the stuff of nineteenth-century biography, but 'something useless, sudden, violent; something that costs a life; red, blue, purple; a spirt; a splash' (*O* 199). The accent may still fall, there may still be 'moment[s] of importance', but 'the accent falls differently from of old'. Woolf's 'moments of being' are thoroughly 'everyday' in the conventional sense – they arise during a childhood fight with her brother, while examining a flower, when coming across a puddle on a tedious family walk. And in noting how the accent thus falls differently, falls on that which would normally, in life-writing, have been passed over, attention is drawn to of all those otherwise unmarked moments, all that unmarked time, all those disregarded activities, in which most of daily life is spent.

'LIFE' IN A SINGLE DAY: REPETITION AND READING

I begin this section with a consideration of how Woolf might, as Bowlby suggests, 'put "life" into a single day'. Most critics agree that the structure of the one-day novel, both in Woolf and in general terms, tends to suggest a reading of the text as representing 'a life in the day'. Indeed, all literary texts are to some extent an attempt to represent the whole through the part, to say more about a life, or life in general, than can really be encompassed by a single narrative.[17] Yet the naturally framed day provides a particularly convenient structure through which to express a life – both being periods of consciousness between unconsciousness, of light between darkness. Of all Woolf's texts that might be described as one-day, *Mrs Dalloway* is the one which has received the most attention in this regard. *Between the Acts* in fact covers more strictly a period of twenty-four hours; while *Mrs Dalloway* takes place entirely in the light (the evening itself, arguably, lit up by Clarissa's party), *Between the Acts*, perhaps appropriately for so dark a novel, also encompasses night-time (although this goes unnarrated, falling into the first of the white spaces dispersed throughout the text). *The Waves*, while narrating lives in their entirety, is firmly structured by the natural rhythm of a single day described in the interludes. *To the Lighthouse* also makes use of a one-day structure; the first and last section each cover a period of no more than a day, and the novel's overall structure encourages a reading of 'The Window' and 'The Lighthouse' as two days separated by the night of 'Time Passes' – the diagram which Woolf drew in a draft of the novel to express the form she meant *To the Lighthouse* to have further emphasises this point.[18] Even *Orlando* has been read as a kind of one-day novel; in an explicitly Bergsonian reading of the text, James Hafley suggests that '*Orlando* occupies only the one day in 1928, and from it are projected back into space the three hundred years of its first five chapters'.[19]

Although, then, the one-day novel appears in a surprising variety of forms in Woolf's work, it should be possible to make some general comments about the effects of this structure. As suggested above, there is a strong critical tendency to read the structure as signifying a larger temporality than the one day which it explicitly encompasses, as an attempt to 'put the whole of "life" into a single day'. Jean Guiguet's words are perhaps representative of the critical consensus where he says that the 'slight framework', the plot of *Mrs Dalloway* he outlines, 'is only a pretext. What is actually revealed to us is the whole of Clarissa Dalloway's life, and that of Septimus Smith.'[20] Or, as J. Hillis Miller puts it, 'the "story" of *Mrs Dalloway* [. . .] is something which happened long before the single day in the novel's present'.[21] Such a reading tends, however, to efface the specificity of the choice of a single day. In particular, it neglects to address the ambiguous structure of dailiness where the day is both supposed to represent a life, from outside, and is also always already a part of that life. Both metaphor and metonymy, the day is already a repetition or a doubling, since it appears both as the singular, exemplary day, and as one day within in the broader temporality it is describing.

Paul Ricoeur's treatment of *Mrs Dalloway* in his classic work *Time and Narrative* draws attention to the variety of differing, even competing, temporalities in the novel, making a particular distinction between clock time – or, after Nietzsche, 'monumental time' – associated with history and authority; and internal, subjective, personal time. However, Ricoeur warns against a 'simplistic opposition between clock time and internal time',[22] and, in his analysis of the effect of the 'tunnelling' techniques of the narrative, explores how the various intersecting temporalities of the novel allow for a communion and communication, whether direct or indirect, between characters. Monumental time, for example, is signified in the slow progress of the royal car, or the tolling of Big Ben; but the simultaneous perception of this object, recognition of this chime, by a variety of otherwise unconnected individuals, provides the mobile narrator with a bridge between these individuals' various interior worlds. The tolling of Big Ben, which makes a connection between daily time and monumental time as the latter is marked out by the hours of the day, also links dailiness with wider temporal structures. The sounding of the hour exactly repeats just such soundings in previous days, making it cyclical as well as linear, the same as well as different, but also it affords the narrator the opportunity to express the many and various psychic temporalities at play in the everyday life of the individual, the tolling of the hours marking these Londoners' shared experience of time. As Susan Dick has it in her careful reading of clock time in *Mrs Dalloway*, 'Her design involved moving the characters through the streets of London while also timing their movements in a way that will create the impression of disparate events occurring simultaneously.'[23] *Mrs Dalloway*, Ricoeur concludes, presents both many temporalities, in the various characters' excursions into the past and experiences of the present, and one experience of temporality, that of the underlying psychic connection explored by the tunnelling narrative technique. Or, using terminology suggested to us by Stein in *Composition as Explanation*, there are many times *in* the composition, but one time *of* the composition.[24]

Any 'simplistic opposition between clock time and internal time', Ricoeur admirably explains, is, then, held at bay through the novel's fluid narrative technique. Yet this technique is made possible, I would argue, by exploring the possibilities given to the narrator through the structure of dailiness. *Mrs Dalloway* explores precisely how daily life, everyday experience, is not simply divided – between clock time and internal time, between public and private time, between the present and the past, between work and recreation. Indeed, one might say that this is what makes *Mrs Dalloway* possible.

The extent to which the everyday remains undertheorised in critical discussions of Woolf, as of modernist writing more generally, is indicated in Ricoeur's own writing where he suggests that in *Mrs Dalloway* the art of fiction 'consists [. . .] of mixing together the sense of everydayness and that of the inner self'.[25] That Ricoeur is able to describe a 'mixing together' suggests that these two elements, 'the sense of everydayness' and 'the inner self', are conceivable, indeed generally conceived, as separate. We find a similar assumption in Karen Schiff's essay 'Moments of Reading and Woolf's Literary Criticism'. Schiff reads an identification between certain experiences of reading in Woolf, and the 'moments of being' described in Woolf's autobiographical writings; she suggests that these '[m]oments of being or reading connect us to a wholeness that is not so accessible in daily life'.[26] Schiff maintains this distinction as her argument progresses, and yet at one point states that 'the "flash" [of the moment of being/reading] always occurs in the context of daily life'.[27] By this Schiff means to emphasise that these moments do not occur as part of events which would normally be marked or considered important – rites of passage, public events, and so on. And yet how is it possible that these moments could do anything other than occur as part of 'daily life'? Daily life, or everydayness, is not a thing apart from life in general, it is the dailiness of life which enables us to structure and organise public events, moments of being, our inner self and the chiming of Big Ben. In my chapter on Stein, I challenged any separation of 'work' from 'everyday life', suggesting that both work and recreation find their place in the everyday and that the complex relationship between these two concepts is more readily explored from this perspective. Here I would continue that gesture by challenging Woolf critics to examine more carefully the divisions which are set up when 'the inner self' is separated from 'daily life'. By structuring a narrative around the day, as Woolf does in many of her texts, the question with which this study began is foregrounded; 'What *is* a "day," and what multitudes does "it" contain?'[28]

This is not to say, of course, that Woolf's 'moments of being' are not marked out from other experiences. What the structure of dailiness precisely enables us to do is to compare, juxtapose and organise our experiences, giving us as it does a background of repetition, of the same coming around again and again, against which striking events stand out the more strongly. In 'A Sketch of the Past', Woolf remembers one particular fight with Thoby, out of the many she may have had over many days in her childhood, for a reason she is unable fully to understand; but this does not mean this event was any less part of her everyday life.[29] It does mean that this event also now participates in the repetitive temporality of memory; it recurs psychically for Woolf in a way that other events may not, requires her reading of it, her 'putting it into words', prompted by that 'desire to explain it', and thus appears in her text, to be read and repeated again and again.

I now want to explore how the relationship between repetition and daili-ness might be elucidated through, and in some senses bound up with, the temporality and attentive quality of the activity of reading. It is through memory, and the repetition that memory constitutes, that the single day, like the moment of being, comes to signify more than its apparently singu-lar temporal unity. Indeed, it is through 'memory as a form of repetition', as J. Hillis Miller puts it, that the narrative of the one day of *Mrs Dalloway* opens that day out into its many other temporalities. Miller states that 'the day of *Mrs Dalloway* may be described as a general day of recollection'[30] – although one might ask what day is not 'a general day of recollection', since one need not be a fully paid up Bergsonian to agree that consciousness func-tions through a constant drawing on memory to reconstruct and synthesise our experiences. However, Miller goes on to explicate how *Mrs Dalloway* constitutes a particularly intense engagement with the processes and strata of memory as repetition. This not only indicates the importance of certain privileged memories, and the centrality of memory in the construction of the subject, but also, by magnifying these processes, reveals to us the pro-cess of remembering and memorialisation through which human subjects operate every day.

'Narration itself is repetition in *Mrs Dalloway*', argues Miller;[31] this narra-tive relies upon the narrator's 'repeating' the characters' thoughts, sensations etc., so the characters do not exist without the narrator, but the narrator only exists as just such a repetition of the characters: 'In *Mrs Dalloway* nothing exists for the narrator which does not first exist in the mind of one of the characters.'[32] The anteriority and intrinsic repetition gestured to here – the idea that there must be something before the narrative for the narrative to describe – is central not only to this text, but to the con-cept of narrative in general. But I want to look in detail at a particular instance of 'memory as a form of repetition', a literally repeated memory, in

Mrs Dalloway, in order to locate the specific quality of repetition here and the way in which it might relate to the structure of dailiness.

The remembering that takes place in *Mrs Dalloway* is far from exact, precise, reliable; it is, to make use of vocabulary suggested by de Certeau, 'tactical', improvisatory, contingent, and in a sense pragmatic. This is evident in, for example, the shellshocked memories of Septimus Smith, where the traumatic appearance of the past in the present (when, for example, Septimus hallucinates Evans appearing in the park) forms part of the psyche's attempt to deal with trauma. But it is also apparent through the minute modifications of memory that take place throughout the text. For instance, during Clarissa's first reminiscence about her life at Bourton, we hear how the compelling Sally Seton began to be attractive to Clarissa's father 'rather against his will (he never got over lending her one of his books and finding it soaked on the terrace)' (*D* 38). Later, however, when Sally has appeared in person at her party, Clarissa remembers how 'she left a priceless book in the punt' (*D* 199). We, of course, have no way of knowing whether there were in fact two different occasions on which Sally left a book outside and it was ruined, or whether this is an example of the unreliability of memory, Clarissa remembering the same event in two different ways – and deciding between these alternatives is not the point. What we must consider, rather, is the effect of this repetition with modification.

We see, then, how for Woolf, as for Stein, 'to allow exact repetitions would be to falsify the small mutations of consciousness'.[33] Memory is inexact, and particularly when rendered in language, likely to yield different configurations of words and images each time it is drawn upon; we recall Bergson's model of our constant plundering of the resources of memory to fit the need of the present moment. We might even speculate on why Clarissa remembers this book-ruining differently on each occasion. The first time, it is remembered in parentheses, as if Clarissa would rather not remember it, as part of what inflected Sally's relationship with Clarissa's father. However, the mention of the terrace seems directly linked to what follows in Clarissa's memory; that is, Sally's spurring them on to go 'out onto the terrace' and walk up and down, which general memory leads to perhaps the single most important of Clarissa's memories, that of Sally's kiss. It is almost as if this is the memory towards which, consciously or otherwise, Clarissa has been reaching, and the appearance of the 'terrace' in the remembered book-ruining incident, which would otherwise be rather unpleasant, helps to lead Clarissa to the cherished memory. On the second occasion of remembering, however, Sally is actually in Clarissa's presence, and direct memory of the kiss might be disturbing, disruptive. The book-ruining appears simply in a list of Sally's various rebellious escapades, the alliterative phrase trips along more easily than that earlier awkward parenthesis, as befits the sparkling party mood. Indeed, it is not specified here that the book was ruined – although the reader's memory might lead him or her to assume that it was. The reader's memory might be further drawn on if they are familiar with *To the Lighthouse*, where the radiant, Sally-esque Minta is anxious that Mr Ramsay will not quiz her about her reading since she 'had left the third volume of *Middlemarch* in the train and she never knew what happened in the end' (107). This repetition of a situation consisting of anxiety surrounding a book, experienced with regard to the relationship between a vibrant young woman and a father figure, is an example of the broadest level of repetition Miller describes in his introduction: 'an author may repeat in one novel motifs, themes, characters, or events from his other novels'.[34] It also suggests the importance of reading itself as a theme in Woolf's writing. Woolf's texts repeat both intra- and inter-textually, implicating the reader as much as possible in the construction of meaning through repetition.

The proliferating meaning of this book-ruining memory is drawn out, then, by the fact of its being repeated. Each occurrence of the memory resonates with the other; significations oscillate between them. Further, our attention is drawn both to the importance of the specific language or imagery we use, but also, perhaps paradoxically, to the insufficiency or even irrelevance of that language. That this memory is repeated in a different form suggests that what is truly significant is that which lies beyond Clarissa's ability to describe it; 'the thing that lies beneath the semblance of the thing' (*W* 123). A memory, like a book, is 'not form which you see, but emotion which you feel';[35] the forms we find for rendering these emotions are contingent, inexact – but nonetheless suggestive. For of course, *per* Bergson, memory has gone through a further abstraction in being rendered in language in the first place. And yet we know that, for Woolf, language makes real, or can make real – 'I make it real by putting it into words.' Further, the rendering in language of this memory in two different ways on a particular day is just one example of how the everyday and ongoing act of remembrance explores the resonance of one day, any one day, far beyond its temporal boundaries. As Roy Pascal puts it, 'A single day's experience is limitless in its radiation backwards and forwards.'[36] This day maps itself onto other days, to expose both its similarity to and difference from them (how similar and/or different, for example, is this party, where Clarissa, Peter and Sally are all together, from those sociable evenings at Bourton?); it also frames the tunnelling process of memory which Woolf describes in this novel.

As James Hafley notes, in *Mrs Dalloway* Woolf 'used the single day [. . .] to show that there is no such thing as a single day'.[37] Or, as the narrator of *Orlando* reassures the reader in a characteristically faux-naive idiom, after the pastoral parody preceding Orlando's giving birth, 'nothing of the sort is going to happen to-day, which is not, by any means, the same day' (*O* 205). Reassurance is needed that today is not 'by any means' the same day as one gone before, suggesting that there might be means by which it were; in this particular fantastical novel, anything is possible, yet the general implication remains of the impossibility of living one day as if it were one day, and by no means, in no way, the same as any other.

My final remarks on repetition will touch on the convergence of temporality and attention in the practice of reading. We have already seen, in my chapter on Stein, that there are at least two temporalities involved in narrative. Reading participates in the temporality that the book proposes; hence in an hour's reading the reader may 'experience' many years, or a few minutes. 'The narrative text', says Genette, 'like any other text, has no other temporality than what it borrows, metonymically, from its own reading',[38] and yet, just as the specific language used to describe memory may be contingent but is still significant, the temporality the text describes does signify – it matters to the experience of reading. In addition to this 'time *in* the composition', as Stein puts it, we have already seen in my discussion of Ricoeur's reading of *Mrs Dalloway* that there is another kind of textual temporality. This 'time *of* the composition' is the temporality proposed by the text itself as the means by which the experience the text describes is understood: the tunnelling temporality of remembrance found in *Mrs Dalloway*; the prehistoric, universal temporality lying beneath and alongside the surface of *The Waves*; the consistency of the human subject throughout chronological, historical time proposed in *Orlando*.

However, there is a third temporality of narrative revealed where attention is paid to the process of reading. As argued above, reading is always a kind of doubling. But not only must it come after a text having been written; it also always repeats another person's activity of having read the text – since even the writer of a text must also at the same time be reading it. Physiologically, neurologically, the activity is a precise copy of someone else's; each reader looks over precisely the same words in precisely the same order (conventionally at least; the reader is, of course, at liberty to read the text in whatever order he or she desires). And yet, every occurrence of reading is completely unique to the individual concerned, and it still takes up time. Indeed, the completely unique yet precisely repetitive experience of reading once more maps on to the sameness and difference structure of dailiness; any given day is completely unique and has its own duration, yet is in another sense precisely the same as every other. To the time in the composition and the time of the composition, we should then add a third time, the time *of the reading of* the composition, the clock time taken to read the text.

I would argue, then, that the relative emphasis laid on each of these three kinds of temporality in any given instance of reading is what gives that instance of reading its particular attentive quality. Remaining aware of clock time, of the time taken up in the practice of reading, the reader's attention will be only partially engaged with the text, and will still be fully aware of external objects and pressures. At the other end of the spectrum, losing the sense of clock time, being immersed in the time the text describes, will be a kind of all-embracing attentiveness, perhaps even involving a loss of sense of self. By contrast with the kind of normative attentiveness Crary argues is in place during the late nineteenth and early twentieth centuries, here the subject loses even a sense of their own embodiedness, their corporeality. Between the two, reading which attends to the temporality of the text, the 'time of the composition', will require the reader to attend to the variety of temporalities to which the human subject has access. Being made aware through the narrative strategies of the text of the way in which the characters in the novel receive and understand their experiences, the reader will therefore be made aware of the ways in which he or she not only experiences the text as a reader, but experiences his or her own life. Woolf's texts, with their particularly innovative and challenging varieties of 'time of the composition', encourage this kind of attentiveness, this kind of temporal experience, for the reader.

Gillian Beer makes a suggestive comment about the status of fiction when she writes that '[f]iction blurs the distinction between recall and reading. It creates a form of immediate memory for the reader'.[39] Beer goes on to pursue this proposition insofar as it sheds light on the ontology of Woolf's novel and its influences, rather than in terms of what it says about the temporality of reading; 'memory' for Beer in this context signifies consciousness of something that is absent, more than of something that is past. Memory, however, has both an ontological and a temporal aspect, since one cannot be said to remember something which is actually present – one rather perceives it – but remembering also necessarily implies an engagement with the past. This duality itself speaks to the imbrication of attention and temporality. Beer's statement does, indeed, allude to the specific double temporality of the reading of fiction, where what is 'remembered' comes into being only at the moment of its being read (since, as Beer puts it, in fiction 'nothing can be physically there'). Reading fiction both effects the eclipsing of temporalities into each other, as here the past comes into being only in the present moment; and opens them out, in the layering of temporalities it involves, from the vast historical sweep of a text such as *Orlando* to the brief span of *Mrs Dalloway*, via the various subjective temporalities through which the texts operate, to the reader's own precious time, from which the text, ultimately, is borrowing. Placing this complex of temporalities within a narrative fundamentally structured, in various ways, by the most familiar of all temporal units, that of the single day, facilitates the reader's apprehension of these various temporalities, and their own participation in them. Flux is expressed through order, the 'myriad impressions [. . .] shape themselves'. The value of the reader's time – the value of the time spent in reading, as well as in writing and thinking – is thus implicitly acknowledged in Woolf's work; it is also, I will go on to argue, explicitly recognised. This use of time in reading, so easily dismissed as unproductive, solipsistic, useless – then as now – is here given its proper attention in Woolf's work. Not only this, but reading, along with its concomitant activities of writing and thinking, is explicitly described as a privileged activity in Woolf's novels, or at least is an activity whose status on the boundary – whose oscillation – between direct and mediated experience, between unicity and community, is used in particularly suggestive ways.

THE WAVES, ORLANDO AND 'READING': THE REPRESENTATION OF DAILY LIFE

I suggested in my introduction to this chapter that, while *Orlando* compulsively asks, and attempts to describe, what life is, *The Waves* performs it, and performs a specifically Woolfian understanding of it. To explain more fully what I mean by this, I will begin by surveying a critical debate over the content of *The Waves*. Alex Zwerdling quotes Woolf's remark about her novel, that 'there's no quite solid table on which to put it', in order apparently to indicate that Woolf is distancing herself from this text; thus Zwerdling associates her with those of her critics who see *The Waves* as inexcusably opaque and divorced from the substantial, the material.[40] However, where Gillian Beer explicitly engages with Zwerdling's position, she refers back to the scientific discourses with which Woolf was engaging at the time of writing *The Waves* to remind us that 'doubting substance and solidity does not make work insubstantial'.[41] This position is backed up by Banfield's work on the interaction between contemporary science and philosophy and

Woolf's writing, showing that precisely the 'substance and solidity' of the table itself is in question.[42] Further, shrouded with doubt though the characters in *The Waves* may be, Beer asks us to note their 'preoccupation with the humdrum detail and the winning incongruities of daily life',[43] again, in explicit disagreement with Zwerdling's argument that in *The Waves* we do not know how the characters 'filled their days'.[44] Certainly, there are enough references to material details to build up some sense of the everyday lives of these characters, although some are more filled out than others; Susan's country life, for example, is clearly illustrated with flour and sons, grass and cows and bread, while the details of Rhoda's life are much less tangible, as befits the relative contentment in the physical world of these characters.

However, while Beer argues that there is important material detail in *The Waves*, the point of her argument is not to reverse Zwerdling's and argue that *The Waves* is 'really' a depiction of everyday life as fully materially and politically founded. While arguing for the importance of these material details, Beer finds that *The Waves* '*brings into question* the established hierarchies of what matters, what constitutes an event, how to write life – including knives and tables, and the presence of many people in a single street on a particular day' (my emphasis).[45] Everyday life, in Beer's reading, is not made up solely of the material detail of the external world available to our senses, but this material detail necessarily forms part of it. However, Woolf uses the substance of everyday life to challenge the way in which this materiality is conventionally depicted in fiction.

A more profound ambivalence regarding everyday life can be found in Guiguet who, in his reading of *The Waves*, equates 'the life of Monday, Tuesday and every day' with 'the life that can be told by one's biographer', and hence the life that Woolf wants to challenge, to get beyond – 'a convenient lie' or 'tempting illusion'.[46] Yet Woolf does include even in *The Waves* some of this 'life of Monday, Tuesday and every day', some of these details that biographers would use. Guiguet goes on to suggest that in *Between the Acts* 'the interval which was brought to an end by the rising of the curtain, and which the book has just shown us, is none other than everyday life, the life of Monday or Tuesday'.[47] If Woolf has gone to the trouble of showing us in her novels some of the 'everyday life' of 'Monday or Tuesday', we are inclined to feel that she has done so for a more complex reason than simply to expose it as 'a convenient lie', a 'tempting illusion'. This everyday life, with its gossip, incongruities, frivolity, bathos, is not mere surface, entirely meretricious. Woolf's attempts 'to find a literary form for the representation of daily life' include such aspects, but are not restricted to them. For Woolf neither the events of biography, nor the surface detail of material life, are necessarily irrelevant; rather, she suggests, even states, that the value they should be given, the role they play in all of 'everyday life', needs to be reconsidered, and re-presented in new literary forms.

However, it is possible to argue, following Woolf herself, that even a narrative in which such material details of everyday life were entirely absent would not necessarily fail to describe how its characters 'filled their days'. When Woolf attempts to envisage 'the greatest book in the world', it would be 'that was made entirely solely and with integrity of one's thoughts'.[48] Indeed, as Beer puts it, 'Woolf did not set thinking apart from ordinary experience',[49] since what are our days filled with if not, first, foremost and always, with thinking? Thinking, like reading, is not something we do when we are not living, or having experiences; both these processes are part of everyday life. Literature is, then, a space where the thinking that we are always doing can be thought about, can be represented; *The Waves*, perhaps, is representing what it is like to think about what we are thinking about.

Clearly there are problems with this tentative definition of *The Waves*. The novel is not, nor does it attempt to be, a stream-of-consciousness narrative. The language used is highly wrought and complex, not the kind we would associate with everyday thought; this is particularly noticeable in the early episodes when the characters are still children. In addition, the use of the 'dramatic monologue' form, presented through the repeated 'he/she said' phrase, abstracts the text further from thought, in which an interlocutor is not normally considered to participate. However, the challenge to genre presented in *The Waves* complicates these initial objections. Woolf conceived of *The Waves* as a poetic play – a genre that she argued in the essay 'The Narrow Bridge of Art' (written in 1927 during the gestation of *The Waves*) had been particularly lacking in recent literature. In this essay, which unsurprisingly reads rather like a proposal for *The Waves*, Woolf argues that as literature moves more emphatically in the direction of prose, and as the novel therefore cannibalises more and more other 'forms of art':

We shall be forced to invent new names for the different books which masquerade under this one heading. And it is possible that there will be among the so-called novels one which we shall scarcely know how to christen. It will be written in prose, but in prose which has many of the characteristics of poetry. It will have something of the exaltation of poetry, but much of the ordinariness of prose. It will be dramatic, and yet not a play. It will be read, not acted.[50]

In the same paragraph, and therefore presumably as part of this project, Woolf says 'we forget that we spend much time sleeping, dreaming, thinking, reading, alone; we are not entirely occupied in personal relations; all our energies are not absorbed in making our livings'.[51] Life is not entirely taken up with the traditional topics of fiction, or indeed of biography; while, as Lefebvre suggests, work ('making our livings'), leisure, and private life ('personal relations') all make up everyday life, there is yet something beyond these categories, the aspects of life defined as interstitial which precisely constitute the inexpressible and overlooked everyday. And it is precisely because these aspects of our lives, regarded as the most humdrum, the most banal – the time spent alone, in contemplation, daydreaming – have been so neglected, that 'we long for ideas, for dreams, for imaginations, for poetry',[52] for the highly-wrought language Woolf gives us. Woolf's most poetic, esoteric text is an attempt precisely to give us back an awareness of the value and the beauty, the profundity, the humanity, of these, our most everyday, unmarked, unremarkable activities.

The question of how to represent 'a mind thinking' thoroughly frustrates the narrator of *Orlando*. Finding Orlando apparently doing nothing but thinking, and forced to concur with 'the authorities' that, while life is 'the only fit subject for novelist or biographer', 'thought and life are as the poles asunder' (*O* 184), the narrator thus finds him or herself with nothing to say about their subject: 'The only resource now left us is to look out of the window', in a vain search for the elusive 'Life' (*O* 188). The very idea of 'the life that can be told by one's biographer' is here clearly being undermined. Indeed, Orlando poses the narrator a particular problem in spending so much time thinking, reading and also writing. These activities, which fall outside the remit of the biographer, nevertheless need to be acknowledged in an account of this life.

We are given a hint of the problems that arise in the representation of thinking in biography during what we might call the 'Time Passes' section of *Orlando* (184–9). Explicitly ironising her own earlier novel, Woolf attempts, here in a very different mode, to convey the passing of time, her narrator musing on the difficulty of so doing – especially when much of this time is spent in 'thinking'. Indeed, the biographer notes, 'when a man has reached the age of thirty, as Orlando now had, time when he is thinking becomes inordinately long; time when he is doing becomes inordinately short' (*O* 68). Difficult indeed for the biographer, whose task is first and foremost to record doings. Yet the narrator recognises that the time spent in thinking is not merely neutral, nothing, a blank; during a day spent thinking, 'It would be no exaggeration to say that he [Orlando] would go out after breakfast a man of thirty and come home to dinner a man of fifty-five at least' (*O* 68). This thinking is precisely and directly equivalent to a great deal of experience – twenty-five years' worth. One might go further and say that it is not just that certain kinds of particularly intense thinking, as implied here, can yield experiences of greater magnitude than could be encompassed by the clock time of the period of thought, but that thinking is always a kind of experience in itself, a part of experience, worthy of consideration. The narrator's own uncertainty as to how to name this process or activity – 'thinking (or by whatever name it should be called)' (60) – indicates that conventional definitions will not suffice; 'thinking' is not the simple, insignificant backdrop to our lives, serving only practical aims, but belongs to a whole spectrum of activity and experience having complex and dramatic relationships both with other activities and with time itself.

The question of what is meant by 'thinking' is further complicated as we explore the relationship between thinking, reading and writing in *Orlando*. For example, in the passage referred to above, where the narrator despairs of describing Orlando's apparent inertia, we are informed of the problem thus: 'sitting in a chair and thinking is precisely what Orlando is doing now' (*O* 184). And yet, the narrator's exasperated expedition out into nature in pursuit of 'Life' is halted ('just in time to save the book from extinction') by Orlando's exclamation 'Done!'; while the narrator has been distracted in his or her vain pursuit, Orlando has, in fact, been writing (189). 'Life' has been going on inside, as well as outside, the window. The elision in the narrative of the shift from thinking to writing encourages our sense of the two pro-cesses as cognate. Conventionally speaking, writing is clearly productive in a way that thinking is not – hence the convention-bound narrator's relief when something has happened in the form of the production of a piece of writing. Yet the way in which these processes are presented as inextricable, the change from one to the other being literally invisible in this text, implies equivalence, and equality, between the two. Complementing the narrator's drift into pastoral, then, we might imagine a parallel text to this section of *Orlando* in the style of *The Waves*, 'a mind thinking', Orlando's mind. This is just what is meant by the argument that while *Orlando* poses ques-tions about life, *The Waves* performs it. And yet we remember in Woolf's description of her new kind of novel that 'It will be read, not acted';[53] this imagined text of Orlando's 'mind thinking' would be a performance of the thinking mind which is located precisely in the arena between text and reader – it arises only out of this crucial relationship. It could not be a description, or it would be in the same register as the narrator's attempt to describe life.

Neither of these texts then, one actual and descriptive (the narrator's faux pastoral) and one imagined and performative (Orlando's mind thinking), is more important, more real, closer to answering the question 'what is life?', than the other. Orlando's own realisation on completing her writing, that 'The world was going on as usual. All the time she was writing the world had continued' (*O* 189), produces a genuine sense of futility, one which might speak for many writers and certainly, periodically, for Woolf herself. One might pursue this comment in terms of a material analysis of the effect of Woolf's own writing in the world (*per* Zwerdling). Here, however, I want to take a different approach, and examine more closely the relationship between the processes of writing and reading generally, and the outside world – specifically nature – as presented in Woolf's texts.

Although Orlando is initially so struck by the irrelevance of her writing that 'she could even imagine that she had suffered dissolution' (*O* 190), she almost immediately comes to view her manuscript in a different light: 'The manuscript which reposed above her heart began shuffling and beating as if it were a living thing [. . .] It wanted to be read' (*O* 190). The artefact asserts its value alongside that of the natural world which Orlando, in her despair, had observed going on around her, indifferent to her existence. Neither Orlando nor her narrator, nor Woolf herself, need come down on the side of nature or of art; even the pastoral passage, whose structural function is further to satirise the futile pursuit of life, nevertheless contains elegant phrasing and evocative imagery which partially undercut its ironic function. Thus the idea of asking nature 'what life is' is presented in a way which, while on one level absurd, yields both meaning – partial, infinitesimal meaning, but meaning nonetheless – and also, perhaps more importantly, beauty and therefore pleasure. Indeed, the pleasure of reading is as important an aspect of this practice to Woolf as any other, as suggested when she writes to Ethel Smyth that 'Sometimes I think heaven must be one continuous unexhausted reading.'[54] As Lee says, 'Reading, quite as much as writing, is [Woolf's] life's pleasure and her life's work.'[55] The affective power of Woolf's writing here is by no means entirely eclipsed by its irony, the aesthetic value of searching for 'life' only in the external world remains, even while the epistemological assumptions of this pursuit are being dismantled.

The interaction between nature, and the processes of reading and writing, are particularly close to the surface in *Orlando*; on numerous occasions Orlando experiences the two as somehow mutually exclusive, as if he/she must pledge allegiance to one or the other. Doubtless, this dual attraction is partly a reflection of the life of Woolf's subject, Vita Sackville-West, who divided her attention between her literary career and the activities of gardening, parenting and maintaining her family estate. But we see elsewhere in Woolf's writing an interplay between reading and the outside world, especially the natural world, which suggests a less oppositional, more mutually supportive relationship. Nowhere is this clearer than in Woolf's 1919 essay, 'Reading' – written well before *Orlando* was conceived and three years before Woolf met Sackville-West – a somewhat hallucinatory text describing the experience of reading while staying in a country house, and including readings of various different texts (and hence different kinds of reading) suitable to different times of day.[56] As Mary Jacobus notes, it is 'an essay unobtrusively structured by the passage from one day to the next, like *The Waves*'.[57] The hallucinatory quality of the text emerges early:

> [. . .] somehow or another, the windows being open, and the book held so that it rested upon a background of escallonia hedges and distant blue, instead of being a book it seemed as if what I read was laid upon the landscape not printed, bound or sewn up, but somehow the product of trees and fields and the hot summer sky, like the air which swam, on fine mornings, round the outlines of things.[58]

Here, the book as artefact in the possession of someone in the process of reading appears to blend physically with its background. There is an absolute continuity between book and world in this flattening of the visual field (as, perhaps, on a cinema screen); Woolf's imagery here skips the unpicking of the relationship between the content of the text and its source in the material world, simply referring to a physiological experience: 'even the gardener leading his pony was part of the book, and, straying from the actual page, the eye rested upon his face, as if one reached it through a great depth of time'.[59] Woolf does not state that the book actually includes a description of a person such as the gardener, which would more normally make him 'part of the book', but indicates that in the process of reading the outside world is itself modified. It is not just that the world permeates the book, but the book extends into the world; not just that the material is revealed through reading, but that reading takes place in the material.

The image of the world seen over the top of the pages of a book recurs throughout Woolf. Lee notes that 'often her female character [. . .] will look up over the edge of the pages of a book or a newspaper as the beginning of their train of thought',[60] although in fact this gesture is not restricted to female characters. For example, in *To the Lighthouse* Mr Ramsay stops to look at his wife and son and finds fortification in this undifferentiated sight 'as one raises one's eyes from a page in an express train and sees a farm, a tree, a cluster of cottages as an illustration, a confirmation of something on the printed page to which one returns, fortified, and satisfied' (38). We are not to assume from this that what is viewed over the top of the book is necessarily directly related to the content of 'the printed page', but that the processes of looking at the world and of reading are contiguous, related. Again, writing does not only affirm or reflect the material, but the material world also confirms that which might be supposed to come after it, literary representation; the relationship is mutual. We even find echoes of this permeable boundary in one of the first images presented in *The Waves*: '"I see a slab of pale yellow," said Susan, "spreading away until it meets a purple stripe"' (*W* 5), this image resonating with the 'broad yellow-tinged pages of Hakluyt's book' described in 'Reading'.[61] Even in our first utterances as a child, our first attempts to make sense of the world, the book appears, not as a subsequent, contingent modification of the world, but emphatically as already part of it. The liminality of the state of reading is drawn attention to; we are blurring the boundary between book and world, that purple stripe, 'like the air which swam, on fine mornings, round the outlines of things'.[62]

In the introduction to her *Psychoanalysis and the Scene of Reading*, Mary Jacobus sets out a series of relationships between a painting by Matisse, the reflections on painting of the artist Marion Milner, and the theories of D. W. Winnicott, in terms of their engagement with the effect of the line, the boundary, and its contiguity with 'the perpetual human task of keeping inner and outer reality separate yet inter-related'.[63] Jacobus describes a state which she calls 'inhabited solitude', defined as 'the capacity to be alone in the presence of an object, whether the mother, the analyst, or the book', and concludes her discussion of the relationship between her chosen texts thus: 'Matisse's painting can be understood as an attempt to render just such an inhabited solitude at the moment of contiguity-continuity. Because an open book provides its focal image, it identifies this moment with reading.'[64] Jacobus then goes on in the course of her book to describe in what ways this relationship between the open book (and hence reading), and the liminal, continuity-contiguity moment, is not purely contingent, arguing that the process of reading is revelatory of a particular kind of liminal consciousness. The approach taken by Jacobus in her elucidation of the peculiar qualities of reading, specifically in her discussion of Woolf's 'Reading', forms a useful point of comparison with my own.

Jacobus's commentary on the part of 'Reading' I have just been discussing correlates directly with my observations on the importance of oscillation in Woolf's work: 'The mutual dissolving and resolidifying of book and landscape, like the movement into the past and back to the imaginary time present of reading, structures Woolf's essay so insistently that it becomes an inescapable aspect of its meaning as well as its principal technique of evocation.'[65] Our approaches differ, however, as regards the 'aspect of [the essay's] meaning' we wish to emphasise. Jacobus focuses on 'dissolving and resolidifying', tropes of transparency, layering and visualisation in 'Reading' to produce a reading of this text as, in her words, 'giving conscious literary form to unconscious phantasies that delineate the boundaries between psychic reality and reading'.[66] While 'dissolving and resolidifying' are indeed crucial to my concept of reading, I want to attend to the rhythm effected by these movements, to the structure they produce. Broadly, I want to place the psychic transformations and oscillations of Woolfian reading, elucidated by Jacobus's attention to tropes of the visual in Woolf's essay, into their temporal context. The temporally liminal, ambiguous status of the practice of reading, particularly as it is here directly related to daily rhythms, opens out questions of the use and value of everyday time, returning us once again to the issue of that in which everyday life consists. Cognate with this return to the temporal is an exploration of the attentive quality of the process of reading here, and its imbrication with the processes of writing and thinking.

Woolf's 'Reading' begins with a brief description of the country house and its history, moving in to focus on the narrator's habitual experience of reading 'in those days' – the outside world is not a distraction, but a seamless part of the book itself. The reader then does look out at the landscape, seeing the gardener's face 'as if one reached it through a great depth of time'; having penetrated through this great depth, the reader-narrator is now able to 'see, with equal clearness, the more splendid figures of knights and ladies'.[67] Via these descriptions, the narrator comes to muse on the lives of these figures, quoting from their own writing, and considering the balance struck by them between their writing and 'the small shot of daily life'. The narrator derives from them this lesson, that 'the pen [. . .] must curb itself to walk slowly, not to run'.[68] The narrator then goes on to suggest that increased comfort, privacy, facility of travel, and leisure, contributed to, indeed effected, 'the death of English prose'; it was these improvements that '[broke] up the splendid sentences'.[69] But this line of thought is abruptly cut off by the first words of the next paragraph: 'It's a hot summer morning.' We are suddenly brought back out of these literary-historical musings into the present of the narrator, the here and now of the text. Then, once more, the narrator gradually winds her way into and around her reading, moves in and out of her immediate physical surroundings. And, once again, just when the narrator seems lost in her reverie of the literary and material world, present time and memory, fiction and history, we are brought firmly back to an awareness of a human individual and their physicality: 'So that, if at last I shut the book [. . .]'.[70]

The essay, then, oscillates between these moments of physical, present clarity, and the meandering, exploratory musings which come between them. Further, the activity – the kind of attention – being described in these exploratory passages vibrates at a liminal position between thinking, reading and writing. For example, in what we might call the first section of the essay, the narrator has stated that her eyes are 'straying from the actual page', she is not reading, merely thinking. However, not only is there a 'reading' of a history of England being performed here, presumably drawing on other texts which have been or are being read, but the direct quotation from Lady Fanshawe indicates that a particular text must have been read. Further, this explicit quotation, together with the image of 'the pen' that 'must curb itself', reminds us that part of what is going on here is writing – or we could not be reading it. Although emphasis falls at various points on one or another of these activities, these attentive states, it is impossible definitively to extricate each from the other. This essay, though entitled 'Reading', in fact evokes the various attentive states which arise out of the inevitable interrelation of writing with reading, and of both with thinking.

The structure of the essay constantly reminds us, however, that this activity, thinking/reading/writing, takes up a specific amount of clock time. As Ann Banfield reminds us, 'In Woolf, time really passes.'[71] First 'It's a hot summer morning', then 'it was, I supposed, nearly time to go into the woods'. The specific time of day, and the type of reading appropriate to that time, is addressed. Dawn, for example, when 'order has been imposed upon tumult; form upon chaos [. . .] is not the time for foraging and rummaging, for half-closed eyes and gliding voyages. We want something that has been shaped and clarified, cut to catch the light'[72] – we want poetry. Not only does reading take up time, then, forming part of our experience of daily life, but in turn the patterns of daily life inflect the kind of reading we do.

Woolf's awareness of the value of time is, then, reflected in her desire to match the activity to the moment, not to waste this precious time; to do what will suit, read what will suit, the moment best. In 'On Re-reading Novels', she acknowledges, albeit with a hint of irony, the specific demand that reading makes: 'one has enough life on one's hands without living it all over again between dinner and bedtime in prose'.[73] This draws attention precisely to reading as a kind of living, with the value and intensity of any other experience. 'Reading,' she confirms elsewhere, 'is a longer and more complex process than seeing',[74] as we have indeed seen in the reading of 'Reading' above, where apparently simple visual phenomena – of seeing a book against the background of an escallonia hedge, for example – are in fact only part of a complex mode of attentiveness comprising reading and thinking. And, as Rachel Bowlby notes in her discussion of Woolf's 'On Re-reading Novels', reading is not here presented as a respite from work, as elsewhere in Woolf's writing. Rather, it moves 'from distracted passivity to work';[75] as Woolf herself insists, 'To read a novel is a difficult and complex art.'[76] Bowlby's observations in this essay once again show how the oscillation between reverie, direct quotation, memory, present perception, free association, close reading, and so forth – reflecting an oscillating attentive state of the kind that we have observed in 'Reading' – is present at the level of Woolf's oeuvre as a whole, neither insisting on reading as always and necessarily requiring hard work to be valid, nor suggesting that reading is a process entirely void of effort or value. It is thus revealed as precisely one of those liminal processes, between 'personal relations' and 'making our livings', between work and leisure, and yet in some senses structuring our understanding of the world as a whole; an activity which both constitutes and critiques everyday life.

To amplify my discussion of the attentive quality of reading, and the cognate question of its temporality, I want to explore the place of reading in Woolf's construction of daily life with reference to two of Woolf's other novels in which reading plays a crucial role. Firstly, the end of the day comprising the first section of *To the Lighthouse* is marked by a scene of Mr and Mrs Ramsay in almost silent reading. Secondly, particular moments – including the end – of the day of *Between the Acts* find the inhabitants of Pointz Hall collected in one room to read. That people join together in order to read, to indulge in that highly intimate, private activity, is one of the paradoxes of this activity on which Woolf plays; it is both communal, and intensely personal.

The intimacy between Mr and Mrs Ramsay is shown during their scene of reading, the kind of 'inhabited solitude' described by Jacobus. Few words are spoken, but the complexity and subtlety, as well as the profound affection between husband and wife, is most evident here. Reading, Mrs Ramsay knows, is a particularly highly charged activity for Mr Ramsay not only because, as a philosopher, it is a central aspect of his job, but because of his personal anxiety that people go on reading his work; if they do not, he feels, he will have failed. Mrs Ramsay's sensitivity to this is evident when during the earlier dinner party somebody asks a general question about longevity, and immediately her 'antennae [. . .] scented danger for her husband. A question like that would lead, almost certainly, to something being said which reminded him of his own failure. How long would he be read – he would think at once' (*TTL* 116). To be read, then, ensures a kind of immortality – not a unique suggestion, to be sure, but one to which Mr Ramsay is particularly attached. Mrs Ramsay understands that Mr Ramsay is reading Scott precisely because it has been suggested that 'people don't read Scott any more' (128); this act of reading is, then, as much a gesture of solidarity and self-affirmation as a leisure activity.

Nevertheless, we see Mr Ramsay go through various kinds of reading during the reading scene. When he first picks up the book, it is with the initial desire to fortify his own position by affirming that of Scott as a response to the 'dangerous' dinner party question. Reading is not an activity involving a loss of the self, but rather one which reflects directly on the reader's own position, career, identity – the reader remains aware of externals, or at least external considerations inflect his act of reading. However, as Mr Ramsay progresses in his reading he shifts into an experience which is more immersed in the content of the text, which moves him, and in which he 'forgot himself completely (but not one or two reflections about morality and French novels and English novels and Scott's hands being tied but his view perhaps being as true as the other view)' (130). Woolf's parenthesis here is another caveat against imagining that there is any such thing as the purely internal, the purely external. Even in a reading so fully emotionally engaged that the reader is, as here, moved to tears, he still thinks about, and provides a commentary on, its context. Finally, on concluding a chapter, Mr Ramsay returns to viewing the novel as part of the intellectual combat which prompted him to pick it up in the first place: 'He felt that he had been arguing with somebody, and had got the better of him', although the lingering doubt remains 'if young men did not care for this, naturally they did not care for him either' (130–1). Mr Ramsay's reading oscillates between an attentiveness associated with here, now, the present time and external concerns, and the almost all-embracing attentiveness arising from the forgetting of clock time in favour of affective engagement with the time in the novel, the historical period favoured by Scott, 'the poor old crazed creature in Mucklebackit's cottage' (130). To return to the terminology which I developed from Stein's phrase in an earlier part of this chapter, he moves between the time of the reading of the composition, and the time in the composition.

For Mrs Ramsay, the practice of reading is less obviously loaded and hence, perhaps, more fluid. For her, thinking flows effortlessly into reading; rather than thinking about what she is reading, as Mr Ramsay seems to be doing, she thinks, or perhaps pre-thinks, what she reads. Murmuring lines from a poem in the moment between reaching for a book and opening its pages, her memory of these lines forms the bridge between her private reflections as she knits, and the words on the page. Further, rather than reading with an aim in view, as Mr Ramsay does, Mrs Ramsay, prefiguring the title of Woolf's last and unfinished work, 'began reading here and there at random, and as she did so she felt that she was climbing backwards, upwards, shoving her way up under petals that curved over her [. . .] she read and turned the page, zigzagging this way and that, from one line to another as from one branch to another' (129). Doubtless, this different rhythm of reading is partly because Mrs Ramsay is reading poetry, Mr Ramsay prose, and Woolf was highly attuned to the different experiences that reading these different genres yielded. Nevertheless, Mrs Ramsay's attentive state is markedly different from her husband's; rather than being in combative pursuit, in active emotional engagement, partaking of fortification, Mrs Ramsay is 'like a person in a light sleep', loath to be woken (131). Mrs Ramsay seems to follow more evidently the time of the composition, the rhythms and patterns suggested by the text, and this places her in a liminal temporality herself, suspended somewhere between consciousness and unconsciousness.

Indeed, Mr Ramsay senses something of her contented suspension in this particular attentive state, as he gazes at her, thinking 'Go on reading. You don't look sad now' (131), just as Mrs Ramsay has sensed her husband saying 'Don't interrupt me [. . .] don't say anything; just sit there' when their eyes met earlier in the scene (129). These fleeting moments of connection are the points at which, I would suggest, the otherness, the individuality, of each is recognised most fully by the other, and yet it is at these points that the communion between the two is clearest, at its most open, although no words are spoken. Each can recognise and respect the other's pleasure in reading, investment in reading, yet does not presume to intrude on their experience. It is the particular qualities of the practice of reading, an experience personal to each individual as well as accessible, theoretically, to all, that make the scene of reading a uniquely poised context for intimate everyday human interaction.

The intimacy involved in the practices of reading and of writing are implied in *Between the Acts* through Isa's unwillingness to let anyone else see the content of the bound book in which she composes her novel, or her poetry. As with Mrs Ramsay's bridging memory of the lines of poetry, it is often impossible to decide whether Isa is thinking, reading (whether directly or by remembering), or writing, composing new texts in her head. These three practices are for her inextricable, and also often threaten to spill out into speech; there are numerous occasions in *Between the Acts* where Isa's thoughts, quotations, murmurings to herself, are interwoven with conventional everyday speech, such as ordering fish over the telephone (*BA* 12). Thus writing does not appear in this novel solely in the overtly public writing of Miss La Trobe – although the transformation of this writing into a public spectacle does not suggest any less personal emotional engagement with it on the part of the author, as Miss La Trobe's sensitivity to the reception of her play indicates. However, while the pageant is a finished piece (notwithstanding the modifications that inevitably occur in performance), Isa's experience of this day represents to us the ongoing processes involved in writing, its inextricability from reading and thinking, and the inflection of all these through memory.

Inspiration for Isa's writing comes, indeed, from unlikely sources; the salacious plots of the newspaper are more seductive than the 'mirrors of the soul' provided by the Pointz Hall library. Isa reflects on how reading habits differ throughout history: 'book-shy she was, like the rest of her generation [. . .] For her generation the newspaper was a book' (*BA* 14, 15). The ritual of reading the morning newspaper – which Hegel suggested already in the previous century had replaced morning prayers – links this kind of reading very directly to daily rhythms. But it is not only as a structuring element of daily time that the newspaper appears in this text; it appears as a material object in play, or attempted play. Bart Oliver tries to amuse his grandson by forming his newspaper into a beak over his nose and springing out before him in the garden, but the boy is alarmed rather than entertained. The newspaper, which should be a vehicle for communication in the civilised world, has not only changed an old man into something resembling the prehistoric monsters of which Lucy Swithin dreams, inspired by her 'favourite reading – an Outline of History' (8), but it has become a tool of barbarism, frightening small children. And yet, with a characteristically Woolfian oscillation rather than transformation, the newspaper is returned to its original purpose; Bart wanders away from the child 'smoothing out the crumpled paper and muttering, as he tried to find his line in the column, "A cry-baby – a cry-baby"' (10). Reading material is not always and necessarily civilising, as Isa's compulsive dwelling on the grotesque rape story from the newspaper also attests – although it can quickly return to its disguise in an innocuous state, as the crumpled paper is smoothed out again. Even Mr Ramsay takes up Scott as a weapon in, precisely, intellectual combat. Particularly in the threatening pre-war moment of *Between the Acts*, there is danger lurking in the apparently harmless – indeed, supposedly edifying – practice of reading.

Karin Stephen, Woolf's sister-in-law, was one of the most important explicators of Bergson for the English-speaking world. While Leonard Woolf apparently doubted whether Woolf had ever read Stephen's book, nevertheless the resonance between some of Stephen's articulations in her Bergsonian text *The Misuse of Mind*, and Woolf's evocation of the imbrication of various psychic states, and various temporalities, in the activities of reading, writing, and thinking, is striking. Here describing the process of description itself, and cognition through description, Stephen states that 'in order to gather what a description of a fact means the hearer must take the general terms which are employed not as being distinct and mutually exclusive but as modifying one another and interpenetrating in the way in which the "parts" of a process of creative duration interpenetrate'.[77] Stephen's articulation of, indeed prescription for, a successful understanding of factual description could equally be read as an articulation of the kind of reading which Woolf's texts not only describe and prescribe internally, but which they encourage in the reader. Woolf, like any writer, is constrained by the 'general terms' which constitute language itself; however, the modification and interpenetration of these general terms, their constant inflection through each other, is foregrounded by Woolf's use of the many and various repetitive structures suggested to us by the temporality of daily life. Crucially, the process of reading Woolf's texts not only involves an understanding of the text as an ongoing 'process of creative duration', but also of our own experience of reading, and therefore the daily life of which this experience is a part, as itself just such a creative process.

Drawing once more on Stephen raises the question of influence, and the relationship between anxiety of influence and concepts of reading. Some Woolf critics are keen to distance her from certain individuals in her intellectual context; for example, Guiguet constantly insists that Woolf had not read Bergson; psychoanalytic critics (and indeed those who would critique them) always need to note that, as Elizabeth Abel states, '[Woolf] claims to have avoided reading Freud until 1939'.[78] Such anxieties often imply an assumption that reading somehow constitutes a subtraction; that, say, could it be proven that Woolf in fact read *Matter and Memory* before she wrote *Mrs Dalloway*, the achievement which this latter text constitutes would be diminished, rather than enriched. The 'strange sum' suggested by the structure of dailiness, posited in my chapter on Richardson, appears in this paradox: that by adding to one's experience through reading, one's subsequent achievements are thereby reduced. This suggestion relies on particular assumptions about the individual in time: that anteriority and posteriority are always and easily distinguishable; that individuals are separate, separable, and clearly definable as such; that reading is a process involving the clear and direct transmission of facts, thoughts, concepts, theories, which are again distinguishable and unified. Woolf's own texts, as well as those discussed in previous chapters, precisely involve a challenge to such assumptions, not simply to discard them, but to explore the extent of their validity. These assumptions are seductive, to be sure, as Bernard describes: 'the illusion is upon me that something adheres for a moment, has roundness, weight, depth, is completed' (*W* 183). Not only seductive, indeed, but important; an illusion without which communication, reading and writing, the interactions of daily life, would be impossible. And yet Woolf's own depiction of the complexity of the process of reading, and the experience of reading that her texts encourage, have insisted that we read, indeed that we live – to use her sister-in-law's terms without fear of suggesting a diminution of either writer's achievement – as a modifying and interpenetrating 'process of creative duration'.

The recurrence of the 'strange sum' of dailiness in my discussion here brings me to my final comments, on the shape of the day in Woolf, addressing the day as chronotope as in my chapter on Richardson. I noted that the day appears in Richardson's *Pilgrimage* in various spatial guises: as a room, as clothing, as a small handheld object, or as a counter in arithmetic. The arithmetic of dailiness also appears particularly suggestively in Woolf's novels. The model of days as something like counters being moved from one pile, in the future, or in the past (found at various points in *Pilgrimage*), resonates with Jinny's joyful experience of dailiness in *The Waves* – her sense of 'a new day to break open. I have fifty years, I have sixty years to spend. I have not yet broken into my hoard. This is the beginning' (*W* 40). Jinny's relationship to the temporal units of her life repeats that of one of her analogues, Clarissa Dalloway: 'She had just broken into her fifty-second year. Months and months of it were still untouched' (*D* 40). For women such as Clarissa and Jinny, privileged to be people at home in the world (for the most part), days are like coins, valuable, sparkling objects reserved for them and them alone, which they have no doubt (again, for the most part) they can continue to draw upon. Their daily life is inevitably a subtraction from this hoard, certainly, but the hoard itself represents the passing of days as a process drawing on an accumulation. Susan too sees the days counted out in front of her, in the strictly regulated institutional world of school, but for her they are oppressive; she wishes to destroy them, rather than break into them and revel in them: "'I have torn off the whole of May and June," said Susan, "and twenty days of July. I have torn them off and screwed them up so that they no longer exist, save as a weight in my side"' (*W* 38). Susan wants to subtract these days, to remove them, annihilate them, and yet traces of them remain 'as a weight in my side', added to her experience.

Yet despite the differences in the arithmetic of dailiness, the counting of days always involves ambivalence as to whether days add, or subtract; is there increase, stasis, or diminution? As we have seen, Richardson's answer is to create a geological paradigm for dailiness where addition takes place, but does not add to, does not enlarge, the whole; there is increased profundity rather than increased extensity, the compass of life stays more or less static. Elsewhere in Woolf, the diminution of our lives in the succession of days appears in 'the death we die daily' which Orlando associates with Bonthrop (*O* 213). Certainly, this is not meant simply to suggest that life is nothing but a protracted dying; rather, perhaps, that life includes the idea of escape from human temporality either in the periodic desire for 'separation and isolation', or indeed in the 'little death' of sexual ecstasy. Nevertheless, the deployment of this phrase connotes an arithmetic of life as diminution rather than increase, of a running out of time rather than an accumulation of time and experience. And yet, as we have seen, alternative arithmetics of dailiness are just as evident in Woolf. Even where subtraction appears to be the primary process, as with Susan, a residual sense of movement through time, of gaining more experience simply through having lived more days, cannot be completely negated. We recall Miriam's soap, which stores days safely within it even as it diminishes with every passing day; a suitably everyday instance of the paradox, the tension, within the temporal arithmetic of dailiness.

These various 'strange sums' of dailiness show how the characters' different relationships with their cultural context are reflected in their experience of daily life. Those who are content with institutional structures that maintain the status quo, who are married to Members of Parliament, who enjoy socialite parties, revel in the idea of days as commodities to be consumed. Those who feel alienated from such structures, who crave a return to unmediated nature, as in Susan's case, resent the days which have been reified to serve the purpose of ruling structures. Rhoda is particularly aware of what is at stake in the day: 'There are hours and hours [. . .] before I can let the day drop down, before I can let my tree grow, quivering in green pavilions above my head. Here I cannot let it grow. Somebody knocks it through' (*W* 41). This day is fragile because it is Rhoda's own; making the day one's own is a threat to the quantifiable, standardising demands of the institution, and must hence be done in secret, be protected from the wrecking intrusion of other institutional beings. Finally, there is a gendered dimension to the experience of days, especially noticeable while the characters of *The Waves* are at school; while the boys' days tend to be sundrenched, worthy of preservation, for the girls days are to be got through, to be endured rather than to make enduring. Even for Jinny, life is in the future, rather than in the present 'moment' which Louis tries to fix – it is yet to come. A concept as abstract as the arithmetic of dailiness cannot, then, be properly understood without being viewed in its cultural context. *The Waves* continues to be criticised for failing to display sufficient engagement with its material and social milieu; but attention to its manifestations of dailiness, that most universal of experiences, shows how profoundly such considerations inflect Woolf's text.

Afterword

Nothing happens; this is the everyday. But what is the meaning of this
stationary movement? At what level is this 'nothing happens' situated?
For whom does 'nothing happen' if, for me, something is necessarily
always happening? In other words, what corresponds to the 'Who?' of
the everyday? And why in this 'nothing happens' is there at the same
time the affirmation that something essential would be allowed to go
on?[1]

Blanchot's question 'what corresponds to the "Who?" of the everyday?'
has been, implicitly, central to this exploration of dailiness in modernist
literature. The rhetorical force of Blanchot's question is revealed when
we recall how the texts addressed have exposed notions of the everyday
as unmarked, unremarkable, where 'nothing happens', as deeply flawed.
Such notions risk, to use Woolf's observation about the traditional memoir
in terms precisely resonant with Blanchot's, 'leav[ing] out the person to
whom things happened'.[2] To return to the different strands of thought
on the everyday adumbrated in my Introduction, the phenomenological
attempt to parenthesise the everyday as a region in which 'nothing happens', and thus, by definition, I, you, we do not participate, 'leaves out
the person to whom things happened'. This construction of the everyday
hollows it out into an empty category, uninhabited, uninhabitable and
inhuman. These modernist texts have shown emphatically that there is
indeed no-one for whom nothing happens, and what happens to everyone is the everyday. However, this apparently straightforward answer to
Blanchot's question brings home that the subject is indeed central to the
everyday, and demands that we pay attention to what we mean when we
say 'me', or use any other such pronoun. During the early years of the
twentieth century, interest in the instability, constructedness and complexity of the human subject is at a zenith, to the extent that modernist
aesthetics are sometimes defined as being primarily concerned with the
question of subjectivity. What attention to dailiness in these texts turns out

to reveal is the particular instability of the ideology of the subject during this period.

The socio-economic forces having an impact on the construction of the subject in the late nineteenth century are nowhere more directly addressed than in *Capital*. As Ben Fine puts it, 'In *Capital*, after extensive economic study, Marx is able to make explicit the social coercive forces exerted by capitalist society on the individual. These can be the compulsions of wage-slavery or the more subtle distortions by which these forces are ideologically justified: abstinence, the work ethic, freedom of exchange, and commodity fetishism.'[3] In a similar way after extensive literary endeavour Richardson, Stein, H.D. and Woolf, and indeed to an extent Bergson and James, are also able to make these forces apparent, although less explicitly than in Marx. As we have seen, the work ethic is of particular concern to these writers, manifested in various ways. Richardson's Miriam is directly oppressed not only by the material necessity of work but by its class-ridden and socially reinforced ideology; Stein's Jeff is emotionally restricted through his attachment to psychic processes associated with 'working'. In my readings of H.D. and Woolf the question of 'work' is less directly apparent, yet a pervasive work ethic is detectable in H.D.'s protagonists' sense of the pressure to be 'taking something up', using time in a socially sanctioned way, and Woolf's texts display a general concern with challenging conventionally valorised activities – 'articles by Nick Greene on John Donne [. . .] eight-hour bills [. . .] covenants [. . .] factory acts' (*O* 199) – associated with, as Stein put it, 'what is known as work'. The 'subtle distortions' of the ideology of the work ethic – the way in which it excludes certain kinds of activity and devalues others; shackles activities to certain gender, class or race positions; or attempts to govern not only the time belonging to the individual but also the functioning of the individual psyche – are revealed through attention in these texts to the way in which life is lived in a daily way, from day to day; attention to the 'multitudes' contained in a single day. Thus while Marx's critique of established ideologies provides us with a framework through which to approach these texts' relationship to, for example, models of labour, their particular perspective on these ideologies is uniquely inflected through their position as, and depiction of, women, and intellectual labourers – positions which fall into, or rather reveal, the lacunae in a traditional Marxist model.

Exploration of the dailiness of other texts, or an alternative perspective on the dailiness of the texts discussed, would, no doubt, speak eloquently of the effect of the other ideological concepts Marx lists – abstinence, freedom of exchange, and commodity fetishism – suggesting several further directions which work on dailiness in twentieth-century literature could take. Some of the most interesting further lines of enquiry are suggested by viewing Marx's list alongside Lefebvre's description of the three elements which make up everyday life: work, leisure and the family. The extent to which all three of these concepts form part of the ideological matrix supporting the 'social coercive forces exerted by capitalist society on the individual' is a crucial question to bear in mind in any approach aiming at a critique of everyday life; the elements which make up that everyday life are already ideologically loaded. Indeed, Lefebvre's own use of the term 'family', together with his evident gender bias discussed earlier, implies certain assumptions within Lefebvre's own text about the centrality and stability of the concept, which might not be borne out by the everyday experience of individuals.

Attention to dailiness thus reveals dissident positions relative to the work ethic from the perspective of particular individuals. However, the demands of the work ethic themselves opens up a fissure in the very idea of the individual, specifically in their intersection with the concept of 'personality'. Indeed, the concept of personality could itself be added to Marx's list of 'subtle distortions'. Modern life, specifically commodity capitalism, relies on the concept of personality, of the sovereign human individual, to maintain its structures of exchange. An ideology emphasising the individual's right, indeed duty, to make optimum use of his or her individual capacities and characteristics arises alongside this economic need, and finds its ultimate expression in the concept of celebrity, which has continued to rise throughout the twentieth and into the twenty-first century. But this kind of 'personality' is, of course, an alienated, commodified version of what Franco Moretti describes as that 'multilateral and prismatic' concept which 'remains a constantly unsatisfied idol'.[4]

Personality, says Moretti, 'would prefer never to have to bend for anything, never to be the means toward an end, whatever that end might be'.[5] The 'most pliable realm' for what Moretti calls this 'centripetal and narcissistic manipulation of external reality'[6] is, he argues, that of everyday life. Moretti's argument that 'We may thus speak of everyday life whenever the individual subordinates any activity whatsoever to the construction of "his own world"'[7] has been cited at various points in my discussion, to describe, for example, Miriam's subversive re-appropriation of her employer's time in *Pilgrimage*, or H.D.'s attempts to represent the uniqueness of her experience of war-time. As Moretti points out and, more importantly, as these texts demonstrate, modern personality, the modern individual, cannot be fulfilled in a single activity, for example that of work. Through close attention to the dailiness, the everyday life, represented in these texts, we find a refusal to 'entrust [. . .] the definition of one's personality to any *one* activity'.[8] There appears in the texts under discussion a tension between the full expression of personality, encouraged by attention to the complexity and variety experienced in and offered by the continuous present of dailiness, and the compulsion to express that personality in work, in, as Miriam puts it, 'the part of life you do and are paid for' which takes up so much of that daily life. The conflict between these two pressures, both ideologies shackled to the structures of an early twentieth-century capitalist economy, is revealed.

The question, then, of whether the representation of dailiness in these texts evinces a fundamentally individualistic, narcissistic attitude to existence remains open. Certainly, texts such as *Pilgrimage* and *Bid Me To Live* lobby forcefully for the recognition of the validity of this particular protagonist's experience, this particular unique individual. Joyce's Stephen Dedalus expresses the link between the succession of days and a centripetal perspective of the individual in a manner reminiscent of William James where he says that, 'Every life is many days, day after day. We walk through ourselves meeting robbers, ghosts, giants, old men, young men, wives, widows, brothers-in-love. But always meeting ourselves.'[9] Viewing this as a possible answer to the question with which I began this project: 'What *is* a "day," and what multitudes does "it" contain?',[10] we find that the multitudes it contains ultimately are to be found within the individual that is always with us – namely, ourselves. This insight forms part of the modernist acknowledgement of subjectivity, of the understanding of all experience is filtered through the individual subject. It resonates with Bergson's description of the individual dissolving sugar in water: 'I must, willy-nilly, wait until the sugar melts' (*CE* 10), there can be no-one else who can do this waiting for me; as well as with James's comfortable recognition of 'the same old Me again [. . .] the same old bed, the same old room, the same old world' (*Psy* 215). The sameness of each day, which always offsets its difference, is in large part a result of it always being ourselves who experience it, whom we meet. 'Always meeting ourselves' – we are, indeed, the 'who' of the everyday.

What is particularly enabling about the concept of dailiness is, however, precisely that it happens to everyone; it is an inclusive rather than exclusive critical tool. As Miriam states in *Pilgrimage*, Beethoven washed his hands just as she does; everyone's life is everyday for them. There can be no hierarchy of dailiness, nothing and no-one is intrinsically more everyday than another; it is rather that, as Ben Highmore puts it, 'Perhaps [. . .] the everyday is the name that cultural theory might give to a form of attention that attempts to animate the heterogeneity of social life, the name for an activity of finding meaning in an impossible diversity'.[11] Finally, although it is inclusive and levelling, this is not to say that the concept of dailiness as a literary critical tool is blunt or homogenising. I have found those texts which challenge everyday language most strongly reveal most dramatically the multiple layers of experience comprising the 'everyday life' as it is articulated by theorists such as Lefebvre and de Certeau. We remember Lefebvre's articulation of the suspicion with which normative models must be viewed in a critique of the everyday: 'What we want to demonstrate is the fallacy of judging a society according to its own standards, because its categories are part of its publicity' (*ELMW* 71); not least, I would argue, normative models of language. This is not, however, to preclude extension of my readings to texts seen as 'naturalistic' or 'realist', particularly given the tendency in current criticism to revisit texts previously categorised as such and thus, by implication, as less sophisticated or complex than overtly experimental texts. I find an analogy for my own privileging of 'difficult' experimental texts in Woolf's discussion of Arnold Bennett's *Hilda Lessways* in 'Mr Bennett and Mrs Brown'. While the point of Woolf's essay is to expose the failings, as she sees them, of such a text, this is not to claim that she always and everywhere views Bennett as a failure; indeed, some admiration for his work is expressed in the essay itself.[12] Thus my assertion of a privileged status for experimental literature is made in this Woolfian spirit of polemic, without wishing to be seen as the last word on dailiness in writing of the early twentieth century.

My opening quotation from Blanchot draws attention not only to the problem of the status of the subject in the everyday – 'what corresponds to the "Who?" of the everyday?' – but also to the question of temporality: 'Nothing happens; this is the everyday. But what is the meaning of this stationary movement? [. . .] And why in this "nothing happens" is there at the same time the affirmation that something essential would be allowed to go on?' This oscillation, 'stationary movement', we have found to be central to daily time, in the constant counterbalancing of transience and endurance, sameness and difference, foreground and background, endless-ness and endings. Richardson's ambivalent relationship with the project of writing *Pilgrimage*, the constant counterbalancing of her desire to finish it with her endless deferral of its completion, is a manifestation in a bio-graphical context of this oscillatory structure. Or, at a textual level, Woolf's texts oscillate between the desire to find shape, structure and patterns, and to preserve of the fluidity and randomness of everyday life. Once again, Stephen Dedalus speaks to this counterbalancing in the ambiguous phrase

'Life is many days. This will end',[13] which reads rather like an inversion of H.D.'s 'Eternity was not this come-and-go; the war will never be over' (*BMTL* 87). The oscillatory movement remains in both phrases; there is constant dialogue between time in its inexorable forward progress, and the inevitability of endings.

In this elaboration of the temporal and political implications of dailiness, it is easy to overlook the importance of ends as well as of movement. As Kermode has it, 'it is one of the great charms of books that they have to end';[14] precisely the same could be said of days. The yearning for an end is at its clearest in H.D.'s narratives; not only is there a desire, of course, for an end to the war, but a desire for an end to the traumatic repetitions the war brings about, whether physical or psychic. More happily, Richardson's sense of the day as complete unit, counter, room, and so on, resonating with the figuring of days by Clarissa Dalloway and Jinny of *The Waves*, expresses the comfort to be found in the day which ends, which is clearly bounded. Yet it is not just temporal ends which are of concern here; as discussed most directly in my chapter on Stein, there is a constant negotiation, suggested by the structure of dailiness as well as the practices of everyday life, between the resistance to ends implied in a dissident social or intellectual position, and the sense of the need for an end, a purpose.

Pamela L. Caughie's unpicking of the rhetorical manoeuvres at work in Woolf's writing yields a particularly useful insight here. Caughie contrasts Woolf's perspective with that of Thomas De Quincey, stating that Woolf 'demonstrates that playfulness and laughter are frivolous [as De Quincey contends] only within the context of a purposive theory of motive and a referential theory of meaning'.[15] We are reminded of Stein's demonstration that 'wandering' is frivolous only within just such a context, and that alternative epistemologies will allow its potential to be revealed. However, Caughie reminds us that Woolf was engaged in a debate regarding 'playful versus purposive writing', both explicitly in her diaries and implicitly in her rhetorical manoeuvres. Just as working is not rejected outright by Stein in favour of wandering, playful writing does not entirely supplant purposive writing; each informs the other. Purposes, ends, play a part in playful, 'frivolous' writing as much as writing which purports to have a transparent relationship to an external reality, and it is important that Woolf's texts, like the others discussed here, play with a purpose. Their rhetoric is not just for itself but has 'its point',[16] and it is precisely the point, or points, it makes about dailiness, that I have been considering here.

It is not purposiveness in general which Woolf rejects, then, but 'a purposive *theory* of motive' (my emphasis), the imposition of an epistemological structure anterior to any given situation, rather than an exploration of the purpose, the end, that that particular situation might serve. A purposive theory fits with a world where 'human values and desires are seen to be eternal';[17] the texts I have discussed evince a challenge to precisely such an assumption, challenging the hierarchies which attempt to assign value in advance, to impose an ends-driven epistemology. On the contrary, in the tactical manoeuvres of everyday life ends unfold, indeed can only unfold, out of means, be they economic, cultural, or linguistic. While the experience of daily life is frequently eclipsed by the imposition of an end in advance, negating its temporal extensity or indeed intensity (to draw once more on Bergsonian terminology) by making it significant only in terms of its relation to this end, these texts draw our attention to the constant production of ends, uses, values, in the ongoing experience of everyday life, as Stein would have it, 'every moment when its needed' (*TL* 128).

The question of what might be at stake in a discussion of dailiness, and the principle toward which this book has gravitated, is succinctly summarised by Carol Greenhouse in her study of the politics of time: 'I view time as being primarily "about" accountability, legitimacy and criteria of social relevance.'[18] Time is not a neutral category; the ways in which time is marked, divided up, and valued, radically influence the ways in which we are able to experience, use, or enjoy time. In the words of Gillian Beer, these texts' various ways of attending to the ongoing rhythm of dailiness 'allow the writer to record changes in how it feels to be alive',[19] at a period when, as we have seen, 'the question of living is crucial'.[20] The particular intersection of the factors noted in my Introduction – technological change and the rise of capitalism, the effect of the First World War, the rise of feminism, and the development of the discipline of psychology, asking profound questions about what defines a human subject – means that questions of 'accountability, legitimacy and criteria of social relevance' are required to draw on an increasingly wide variety of experience and thought throughout the period we call modernist. That is to say, historical events and cultural changes meant that dominant ideologies regarding the relative value of different kinds of experience, or more generally what constituted a valuable life, were radically undermined. This is clearly manifested where the writers I address engage with discourses around everyday life; where, as I have argued, their critique of everyday life, which includes a critique of its language, expresses just such challenges to these dominant ideologies. But if time is primarily '"about" accountability, legitimacy and criteria of social relevance', then what is at stake in the exploration of temporality also becomes clear. These writers all, in one way or another, grapple with a dominant ideology that knows the power of manipulating time, of making individuals 'isolated, separated, and *inhabit time* as disempowered'.[21] Their literary experiments not only constituted attempts to articulate an empowered relationship to time, to 'restore time as the supreme gift (life time)' (*ELMW* 202), within their own socio-cultural context, but continue to present a challenge to us in our understanding of the ways in which we value, recognise and experience our own life time.

Notes

INTRODUCTION

1. Gertrude Stein, *Narration: Four Lectures*, ed. Thornton Wilder (1935; Chicago: University of Chicago Press, 1969), 10.

2. Martin Heidegger, *Being and Time*, trans. John Macquarrie and Edward Robinson (1967; London: Blackwell, 1988), 466.

3. Stephen Kern, *The Culture of Time and Space 1880–1918* (1983; Cambridge, MA: Harvard University Press, 2003), 29.

4. Barbara Will, *Gertrude Stein, Modernism and the Problem of Genius* (Edinburgh: Edinburgh University Press, 2000), 92.

5. Michael Levenson, ed., *The Cambridge Companion to Modernism* (Cambridge: Cambridge University Press, 1999), 4.

6. Paul Fussell, *The Great War and Modern Memory* (Oxford: Oxford University Press, 1975), 71–4, 71.

7. Richard Aldington, *Death of a Hero* (London: Chatto & Windus, 1929), 376.

8. Ford Madox Ford, *Parade's End* (1924–28; Harmondsworth: Penguin, 1982), 519, 569.

9. Virginia Woolf, *A Room of One's Own* (1928; London: Penguin, 1945), 68.

10. Morag Shiach dates this shift around the 1920s; see Morag Shiach, *Modernism, Labour and Selfhood in British Literature and Culture, 1890–1930* (Cambridge: Cambridge University Press, 2004), 117. See also the recent collection of essays in Leah Price and Pamela Thurschwell, eds., *Literary Secretaries/Secretarial Culture* (Aldershot: Ashgate, 2005).

11. Sara Blair, 'Modernism and the Politics of Culture', *The Cambridge Companion to Modernism*, ed. Michael Levenson (Cambridge: Cambridge University Press, 1999), 157–73: 164.

12. Karl Marx, *Capital Volume 1*, trans. Ben Fowkes (Harmondsworth: Penguin, 1976), 353–416.

13. Michael Bell, 'The Metaphysics of Modernism', *The Cambridge Companion to Modernism*, ed. Michael Levenson (Cambridge: Cambridge University Press, 1999), 9–32: 10.

14. Leo Charney and Vanessa K. Schwartz, eds., *Cinema and the Invention of Modern Life* (Berkeley, CA: University of California Press, 1995), 279–85.

15. Ben Highmore, *Everyday Life and Cultural Theory: An Introduction* (London: Routledge, 2002), 115.
16. Charney and Schwartz, *Cinema and the Invention of Modern Life*, 293.
17. Michael Sheringham, 'Attending to the Everyday: Blanchot, Lefebvre, Certeau, Perec', *French Studies* (2000), 54:2, 187–99: 188.
18. T. S. Eliot, *Selected Prose*, ed. Frank Kermode (London: Faber and Faber, 1975), 177.
19. The variety of analogues with and influences on Joyce's temporal model are surveyed in Margaret Church, 'Time as an Organizing Principle in the Fiction of James Joyce', *Work in Progress: Joyce Centenary Essays*, eds. Richard F. Peterson, Alan M. Cohn and Edmund L. Epstein (Carbondale and Edwardsville, IL: Southern Illinois University Press, 1983), 70–81.
20. *Ibid.*, 71.
21. *Ibid.*, 72.
22. *Ibid.*, 73.
23. Michel de Certeau, *The Practice of Everyday Life*, trans. Steven Rendall (Berkeley, CA: University of California Press, 1984), xxii.
24. Highmore, *Everyday Life and Cultural Theory*, 25.
25. Maurice Blanchot, *The Infinite Conversation*, trans. Susan Hanson (Minneapolis, MN: Minnesota University Press, 1993), 238.
26. *Ibid.*, 239.
27. See Sheringham, 'Attending to the Everyday', 187–99.
28. There has not been space here for a full consideration of the contribution of Simmel and Benjamin to the theory of the everyday; for an overview, see Highmore Chapters 3 and 5.
29. Highmore, *Everyday Life and Cultural Theory*, 18.
30. *Ibid.*, 163, 175.
31. Martin Jay, *Adorno* (London: Fontana, 1984), 67.
32. Jay, *Adorno*, 80.
33. Anthony Brewer, *A Guide to Marx's Capital* (Cambridge: Cambridge University Press, 1984), 37.
34. Ben Fine, *Marx's Capital* (1975; London: Macmillan, 1989), 10.
35. Brewer, *A Guide to Marx's Capital*, 45.
36. Marx, *Capital Volume I*, 341.
37. Peter Osborne, *The Politics of Time: Modernity and Avant-Garde* (London: Verso, 1995), 194.
38. Highmore, *Everyday Life and Cultural Theory*, 113.
39. Laurie Langbauer, 'Cultural Studies and the Politics of the Everyday', *Diacritics* 22:1 (1992), 47–65: 51.
40. *Ibid.*
41. Highmore, *Everyday Life and Cultural Theory*, 12.
42. Bettina Aptheker, *Tapestries of Life: Women's Work, Women's Consciousness and the Meaning of Daily Experience* (Amherst, MA: University of Massachusetts Press, 1989), 12.
43. *Ibid.*

44. *Ibid.*, 39.
45. *Ibid.*, 44.
46. *Ibid.*, 253.
47. Christopher Isherwood, *A Single Man* (London: Methuen, 1964).
48. Blanchot, *The Infinite Conversation*, 242.
49. *Ibid.*, 33.
50. Franco Moretti, *The Way of the World: The Bildungsroman in European Culture*, trans. Albert Sbragia (London: Verso, 1987), 33–4.
51. *Ibid.*, 40.
52. *Ibid.*, 41.
53. de Certeau, *The Practice of Everyday Life*, xxii.
54. Highmore, *Everyday Life and Cultural Theory*, 128.
55. Gertrude Stein, *Geography and Plays* (1922; New York: Something Else Press, 1968), 18.
56. Blanchot, *The Infinite Conversation*, 240.
57. For further discussion of the significations of the term 'gay' at the time, see Lillian Faderman, *Surpassing the Love of Men: Romantic Friendship and Love between Women from the Renaissance to the Present* (1981; London: The Women's Press, 1991), 308.
58. J. Hillis Miller, *Fiction and Repetition: Seven English Novels* (Oxford: Basil Blackwell, 1982), 6.
59. *Ibid.*, 16.
60. Osborne, *The Politics of Time*, 67.
61. Bell, 'The Metaphysics of Modernism', 15.
62. Julia Kristeva, *The Kristeva Reader*, ed. Toril Moi (Oxford: Blackwell, 1986), 187.
63. *Ibid.*, 190.
64. *Ibid.*, 191.
65. *Ibid.*, 187.
66. Sandra Kemp, '"But how describe a world seen without a self?" Feminism, fiction and modernism', *Critical Quarterly* 32: 1 (1990), 99–118: 100.
67. Kristeva, *The Kristeva Reader*, 191.
68. Kemp, '"But how describe a world seen without a self?"', 105.
69. Ann Banfield, *The Phantom Table: Woolf, Fry, Russell and the Epistemology of Modernism* (Cambridge: Cambridge University Press, 2000), x.
70. Jane Marcus, ed., *New Feminist Essays on Virginia Woolf* (London: Macmillan, 1982), 6.
71. M. M. Bakhtin, *The Dialogic Imagination*, trans. Caryl Emerson and Michael Holquist (Austin, TA: University of Texas Press, 1981), 84.
72. *Ibid.*, 250.
73. *Ibid.*
74. Jean Radford, *Dorothy Richardson* (Hemel Hempstead: Harvester Wheatsheaf, 1991), 46.
75. Bakhtin, *The Dialogic Imagination*, 84.
76. Highmore, *Everyday Life and Cultural Theory*, 175.

77. *Ibid.*, 23.
78. *Ibid.*, 21.

CHAPTER 1

1. Paul Douglass, *Bergson, Eliot and American Literature* (Lexington, KN: University Press of Kentucky, 1986), 2.
2. See *TFW* as a whole, and especially chapter II, for Bergson's elaboration of his concept of 'duration'.
3. Jonathan Crary, *Suspensions of Perception: Attention, Spectacle, and Modern Culture* (Cambridge, MA: MIT, 1999), 12–13.
4. Kern, *The Culture of Time and Space*, 8.
5. Wolfgang Iser, *Walter Pater: The Aesthetic Moment*, trans. David Henry Wilson (Cambridge: Cambridge University Press, 1987), 138.
6. *Ibid.*
7. Walter Pater, *The Renaissance* (1873; Oxford: Oxford University Press, 1998), 152.
8. *Ibid.*, 151.
9. Osborne, *The Politics of Time*, xii.
10. Mark Antliff, *Inventing Bergson: Cultural Politics and the Parisian Avant-Garde* (Princeton, NJ: Princeton University Press, 1993), 3, 4.
11. Shiv K. Kumar, *Bergson and the Stream of Consciousness Novel* (London and Glasgow: Blackie & Son Ltd, 1962), 7.
12. Crary, *Suspensions of Perception*, 60.
13. *Ibid.*, 302.
14. The English language does not make the distinction available in French between '*jour*' and '*journée*', both of which may be translated as 'day'. The latter term implies duration in the way that the former does not, as in '*toute la journée*': 'all day long'. Thus the concept of duration, *durée*, was available to Bergson in the very forms offered by his language: French invites consideration of duration by offering a word which specifically describes the extent of a period of time, as well as one which describes this period of time as discrete, measurable unit.
15. Crary, *Suspensions of Perception*, 3, 3–14.
16. *Ibid.*, 3.
17. *Ibid.*, 42.
18. *Ibid.*, 3.
19. *Ibid.*, 16.
20. T. S. Eliot, *Four Quartets* (London: Faber and Faber, 1994), 10.
21. *Ibid.*
22. Crary, *Suspensions of Perception*, 288.
23. *Ibid.*, 77.
24. Josef Breuer, 'Fräulein Anna O.', *Studies on Hysteria: Pelican Freud Library Vol. III*, ed. Angela Richards (London: Penguin, 1991), 73–102.

25. Mary Jacobus, *First Things: The Maternal Imaginary in Literature, Art, and Psychoanalysis* (New York and London: Routledge, 1995), 269–90.
26. *Ibid.*, 288.
27. Crary, *Suspensions of Perception*, 3.
28. Blanchot, *The Infinite Conversation*, 242.
29. Siegfried Kracauer, *The Mass Ornament: Weimar Essays*, trans. and ed. Thomas Y. Levin (Cambridge, MA: Harvard University Press, 1995), 331.
30. *Ibid.*, 334.
31. *Ibid.*, 331–2.
32. *Ibid.*, 323–8.
33. Sigmund Freud, 'Project for a Scientific Psychology', *The Standard Edition of the Complete Psychological Works Vol. I*, ed. James Strachey (London: Hogarth, 1966).
34. Georg Simmel, 'The Metropolis and Mental Life', trans. Kurt H. Wolff, *Simmel on Culture*, eds. David Frisby and Mike Featherstone (London: Sage, 1997), 174–85: 177.
35. James's use of the term 'duration', although suggestive for the reader of James alongside Bergson, should not be confused with the latter's specific use of the term.
36. Crary, *Suspensions of Perception*, 300.
37. *Ibid.*, 299.
38. John Mullarkey has discussed the importance of Bergson's self-avowed incoherence in '*La Philosophie nouvelle*, or Change in philosophy', *The New Bergson* (Manchester and New York: Manchester University Press, 1999), 4–5.
39. Max Weber, *The Protestant Ethic and the Spirit of Capitalism*, trans. Talcott Parsons (1904–05; London and New York: Routledge, 2001), 104.
40. Crary, *Suspensions of Perception*, 327.
41. *Ibid.*, 317.
42. This debate is comprehensively mapped in Peter Bürger, *Theory of the Avant-Garde*, trans. Michael Shaw (Manchester: Manchester University Press, 1984).
43. Lyndsey Stonebridge, *The Destructive Element: British Psychoanalysis and Modernism* (Basingstoke: Macmillan, 1998), 81.
44. *Ibid.*, 82.
45. Josephine Donovan, 'Everyday Use and Moments of Being', *Aesthetics in Feminist Perspective*, eds. Hilde Hein and Carolyn Korsmeyer (Bloomington, IN: Indiana University Press, 1993), 57.
46. *Ibid.*, 56.
47. *Ibid.*, 63.
48. *Ibid.*, 64.
49. Woolf, *A Room of One's Own*, 108.
50. Frank Kermode, *The Sense of an Ending: Studies in the Theory of Fiction* (Oxford: Oxford University Press, 1967), 177.
51. *Ibid.*, 179.
52. *Ibid.*, 178.

CHAPTER 2

1. Rachel Blau DuPlessis, *Writing Beyond the Ending: Narrative Strategies of Twentieth Century Women Writers* (Bloomington, IN: Indiana University Press, 1985), 145.

2. Elaine Showalter, *A Literature of Their Own: From Charlotte Brontë to Doris Lessing* (1977; London: Virago, 1999), 261.

3. Gillian E. Hanscombe, 'Dorothy Richardson Versus the Novvle', *Breaking the Sequence: Women's Experimental Fiction*, eds. Ellen G. Friedman and Miriam Fuchs (Princeton, NJ: Princeton University Press, 1989), 85–98.

4. Kumar, *Bergson and the Stream of Consciousness Novel*, 36–7.

5. Douglass, *Bergson, Eliot and American Literature*, 2.

6. *Ibid.*, 11.

7. References to *Pilgrimage* will appear in the text thus, indicating volume and page number.

8. Elisabeth Bronfen, *Dorothy Richardson's Art of Memory: Space, Identity, Text*, trans. Victoria Appelbe (Manchester: Manchester University Press, 1999), 192.

9. *Ibid.*

10. Sydney Janet Kaplan, *Feminine Consciousness in the Modern British Novel* (Urbana, IL: University of Illinois Press, 1975), 10.

11. Shirley Rose, 'Dorothy Richardson's Focus on Time', *English Literature in Transition* (1974), 17, 163–72: 170.

12. *Ibid.*

13. Dorothy Richardson, 'Comments by a Layman', *Dental Record* (1918), XXXVIII, 351.

14. Evelyn Underhill, *Mysticism* (1911; London: Methuen, 1960), 28, 380.

15. See the chapter entitled '"The Girl beside Me": V. Sackville-West and the Mystics', Suzanne Raitt, *Vita and Virginia: The Work and Friendship of V. Sackville-West and Virginia Woolf* (Oxford: Clarendon Press, 1993).

16. Gloria Fromm, *Dorothy Richardson: A Biography* (1977; Athens and London: University of Georgia Press, 1994), 286.

17. Jean Radford, *Dorothy Richardson* (Hemel Hempstead: Harvester Wheatsheaf, 1991), 39–40.

18. Bronfen, *Dorothy Richardson's Art of Memory*, 133.

19. Radford, *Dorothy Richardson*, 39; see also Kaplan, *Feminine Consciousness in the Modern British Novel*, 35–6, 42.

20. Dorothy Richardson, *The Quakers Past and Present* (London: Constable & Company Limited, 1914), v.

21. *Ibid.*, 72.

22. Fromm, *Dorothy Richardson*, 288.

23. Kristeva, *The Kristeva Reader*, 193.

24. Bronfen, *Dorothy Richardson's Art of Memory*, 31–46. See also where Bronfen suggests that 'the novel's central subject appears to be Miriam's assumption of creative activity in a movement towards an empty room' (200). It is also interesting to note here that Lefebvre quotes a description of going into a

room from Woolf's *A Room of One's Own* as exemplary of 'the subtle richness of the everyday' (*CEL* 28), reinforcing the connection between rooms and dailiness.

25. Bakhtin, *The Dialogic Imagination*, 250.
26. See Radford on this distrust of metaphor, citing *Pilgrimage* and Miriam's sense of oppression by a 'Metaphorocracy', and also a draft essay entitled 'The rampant metaphor' (Radford, *Dorothy Richardson*, 122).
27. Kermode, *The Sense of an Ending*, 179.
28. Gilles Deleuze, *Bergsonism*, trans. Hugh Tomlinson and Barbara Habberjam (New York: Zone Books, 1988), 41.
29. *Ibid.*, 31.
30. See also Richardson's short story 'Sunday', *Journey to Paradise: Short Stories and Autobiographical Sketches*, ed. Trudi Tate (London: Virago, 1989). The story describes a Sunday 'so perfect that I had forgotten there was anything in the world but its moments and they were going on for ever' (25); Sunday here too participates in an eternal temporality which is yet experienced moment by moment. Unlike Pater's one moment which stands out from all the others, here it is the very fact of moment following moment in a constant stream which constitutes the fulfilment and pleasure provided by this Sunday.
31. Crary, *Suspensions of Perception*, 1–2.
32. Richardson, *Journey to Paradise*, 132.
33. Bakhtin, *The Dialogic Imagination*, 249.
34. *Ibid.*, 248.
35. *Ibid.*, 249.
36. See also Carol Watts, *Dorothy Richardson* (Plymouth: Northcote House, 1995), 40–3, on women and work, and this exchange with Hancock in particular.
37. Shiach, *Modernism, Labour and Selfhood*, 71.
38. Crary, *Suspensions of Perception*, 51.
39. *Ibid.*, 42.
40. *Ibid.*, 3.
41. Quoted in Shiach, *Modernism, Labour and Selfhood*, 63.
42. Crary, *Suspensions of Perception*, 1–2.
43. See for example Crary, *Suspensions of Perception*, 77–8.
44. Kaplan, *Feminine Consciousness in the Modern British Novel*, 25.
45. Moretti, *The Way of the World*, 40.
46. *Ibid.*
47. *Ibid.*, 41.
48. *Ibid.*, 42.
49. Quoted in Fromm, *Dorothy Richardson*, 124.
50. Richardson, *The Quakers Past and Present*, 22.
51. Fromm, *Dorothy Richardson*, 246.
52. Sean Latham, *'Am I a Snob?': Modernism and the Novel* (Ithaca: Cornell University Press, 2003), 3.
53. Paul Ricoeur, *Time and Narrative*, trans. Kathleen McLaughlin and David Pellauer, 3 vols. (Chicago: University of Chicago Press, 1984–88), 2:86.

54. Fromm, *Dorothy Richardson*, 153, 180.
55. *Ibid.*, 153.

CHAPTER 3

 1. Quoted in Janet Hobhouse, *Everybody who was Anybody: A Biography of Gertrude Stein* (London: Weidenfeld & Nicholson, 1975), 95.
 2. Highmore, *Everyday Life and Cultural Theory*, 154.
 3. Sheringham, 'Attending to the Everyday', 190.
 4. de Certeau, *The Practice of Everyday Life*, 66.
 5. Henry James, *The Ambassadors* (1903; Harmondsworth: Penguin, 1986), 96, 236.
 6. *Ibid.*, 96.
 7. Faderman, *Surpassing the Love of Men*, 190–230 and *passim*.
 8. Gertrude Stein, *Composition as Explanation* (London: Hogarth Press, 1926), 12.
 9. Quoted in Sheringham, 'Attending to the Everyday', 190.
10. Crary, *Suspensions of Perception*, 10.
11. John Shotter's social constructionist model of 'knowing of the third kind' or 'knowing from within', with its emphasis on dialogue as a model as well as exemplary instance of this kind of constantly negotiated knowledge, always incorporating an element of chaos, luck or guesswork, draws attention to the importance of the notion of dialogue as revelatory of alternative forms of knowledge, as, within Stein criticism itself, does Harriet Scott Chessman's model of Stein's 'Creation as Dialogue'. See John Shotter, *Cultural Politics of Everyday Life: Social Constructionism, Rhetoric and Knowing of the Third Kind* (Buckingham: Open University Press, 1993); Harriet Scott Chessman, *The Public is Invited to Dance: Representation, the Body, and Dialogue in Gertrude Stein* (Stanford: Stanford University Press, 1989).
12. See for example this definition of recreation given in the 1928 compact edition of the Oxford English Dictionary: '3. a. The action of recreating (oneself or another), or fact of being recreated, by some pleasant occupation, pastime or amusement.'
13. Tim Armstrong, *Modernism, Technology and the Body: A Cultural Study* (Cambridge: Cambridge University Press, 1998), 209; see also Lisa Ruddick, *Reading Gertrude Stein: Body, Text, Gnosis* (Ithaca and London: Cornell University Press, 1990), 13.
14. Ruddick, *Reading Gertrude Stein*, 30, 15.
15. *Ibid.*, 30.
16. Richard Bridgman, *Gertrude Stein in Pieces* (New York: Oxford University Press, 1970), 49.
17. Chessman, *The Public is Invited to Dance*, 22–4.
18. Kenan Malik, *The Meaning of Race: Race, History and Culture in Western Society* (Basingstoke: Macmillan, 1996), 82.

19. Interest in 'primitivism' in the visual arts was at this time coming to the fore; Stein had certainly seen and admired that central artefact of modernist primitivism Les Demoiselles d'Avignon, and indeed owned several of the paintings that preceded and followed it out of Picasso's studio; see James R. Mellow, *Charmed Circle: Gertrude Stein & Company* (New York: Avon Books, 1974), 140–2.

20. Bridgman, *Gertrude Stein in Pieces*, 23, 33.

21. Malik, *The Meaning of Race*, 73.

22. *Ibid.*, 106.

23. Michael Bell, *Primitivism* (London: Methuen & Co. Ltd., 1972), 16.

24. I am using Genette's definition of the singulative and iterative narrative event; see Gérard Genette, *Narrative Discourse*, trans. Jane E. Levin (Oxford: Basil Blackwell, 1980), 114–16.

25. Ruddick, *Reading Gertrude Stein*, 38.

26. Marianne DeKoven, *A Different Language: Gertrude Stein's Experimental Writing* (Wisconsin: University of Wisconsin Press, 1983), 32.

27. Bell, *Primitivism*, 16.

28. See Chessman, *The Public is Invited to Dance*, 48; DeKoven, *A Different Language*, 27; Ruddick, *Reading Gertrude Stein*, 86.

29. Gertrude Stein, *Geography and Plays* (1922; New York: Something Else Press, 1968), 17, 21, 22.

30. *Ibid.*, 18.

31. Stein, *Composition as Explanation*, 18.

32. Stein, *Narration*, 10.

33. de Certeau, *The Practice of Everyday Life*, 38.

34. Moretti, *The Way of the World*, 42.

35. *Ibid.*, 40.

36. Ruddick, *Reading Gertrude Stein*, 38.

37. *Ibid.*

38. *Ibid.*

39. DeKoven, *A Different Language*, 31.

40. *Ibid.*, 75, 81.

41. *Ibid.*, 82.

42. Ruddick, *Reading Gertrude Stein*, 7.

43. Jo-Anna Isaak, 'The Revolutionary Power of a Woman's Laughter', Richard Kostelanetz, ed., *Gertrude Stein Advanced: An Anthology of Criticism* (Jefferson: McFarland & Company Inc., 2000), 29, 41.

44. *Ibid.*, 40.

45. *Ibid.*, 26.

46. *Ibid.*

47. Susan E. Hawkins, 'Sneak Previews: Gertrude Stein's Syntax in *Tender Buttons*', *Gertrude Stein and the Making of Literature*, eds. Shirley Neuman and Ira B. Nadel (Basingstoke: Macmillan, 1988), 123.

48. Chessman, *The Public is Invited to Dance*, 8.

49. Quoted in DeKoven, *A Different Language*, 36.

50. de Certeau, *The Practice of Everyday Life*, 66.
51. *Ibid.*, xviii.
52. Virginia Woolf, *To the Lighthouse* (1927; Harmondsworth: Penguin, 1992), 28.
53. Quoted in Peter Nicholls, *Modernisms: A Literary Guide* (Basingstoke: Macmillan, 1995), 208.
54. *Ibid.*, 209.
55. Quoted in Bonnie Kime Scott, *The Gender of Modernism: A Critical Anthology* (Bloomington & Indianapolis: Indiana University Press, 1990), 504.
56. Bridgman, *Gertrude Stein in Pieces*, 136.
57. Armstrong, *Modernism, Technology and the Body*, 200.
58. *Ibid.*
59. *Ibid.*, 200, 198.
60. *Ibid.*, 204.
61. DeKoven, *A Different Language*, 82.
62. Hawkins, 'Sneak Previews', 121.
63. Stein, *Narration*, 44.

CHAPTER 4

1. Pablo Picasso, quoted in S. A. Nash, ed., *Picasso and the War Years, 1937–1945* (London: Thames and Hudson, 1998), 13.
2. Highmore, *Everyday Life and Cultural Theory*, 27.
3. Paul Fussell, *The Great War and Modern Memory* (Oxford: Oxford University Press, 1975), 71.
4. For narratives of the front explicitly describing the temporal dislocations I note here, see for example Aldington, Ford, Remarque, among many others.
5. Kermode, *The Sense of an Ending*, 45.
6. *Ibid.*, 46.
7. Ricoeur, *Time and Narrative*, 1:30.
8. Kermode, *The Sense of an Ending*, 116.
9. Susan Stanford Friedman, *Psyche Reborn: The Emergence of H.D.* (Bloomington, IN: Indiana University Press, 1981), 31.
10. Suzette Henke, *Shattered Subjects: Trauma and Testimony in Women's Life Writing* (New York: St Martin's Press, 2000), 45.
11. Trudi Tate, *Modernism, History and the First World War* (Manchester: Manchester University Press, 1998), 15.
12. Henke, *Shattered Subjects*, 44.
13. Susan Stanford Friedman and Rachel Blau DuPlessis, eds., *Signets: Reading H.D.* (Wisconsin: University of Wisconsin Press, 1990), 235.
14. Sigmund Freud, 'Beyond the Pleasure Principle', *The Penguin Freud Library Vol. XI*, ed. Angela Richards (Harmondsworth: Penguin, 1984), 283.
15. *Ibid.*, 336.
16. *Ibid.*, 288–9.
17. Cathy Caruth, *Trauma: Explorations in Memory* (Baltimore: The Johns Hopkins University Press, 1995), 7, 8.

18. *Ibid.*, 8.
19. *Ibid.*
20. Quoted in Mark Seltzer, *Serial Killers: Death and Life in America's Wound Culture* (New York and London: Routledge, 1998), 257.
21. Freud, 'Beyond the Pleasure Principle', 289.
22. J. Laplanche and J.-B. Pontalis, *The Language of Psycho-Analysis*, trans. Donald Nicholson-Smith (London: The Hogarth Press and the Institute of Psycho-Analysis, 1973), 78.
23. James Hafley, *The Glass Roof: Virginia Woolf as Novelist* (New York: Russell and Russell Inc., 1963), 73.
24. Friedman and DuPlessis, *Signets: Reading H.D.*, 247.
25. Henke, *Shattered Subjects*, 43.
26. *Ibid.*, 53.
27. Caruth, *Trauma*, 153.
28. *Ibid.*
29. Ricouer, *Time and Narrative*, 1:19.
30. Alan Bishop and Mark Bostridge, eds., *Letters from a Lost Generation: First World War Letters of Vera Brittain and Four Friends* (London: Little Brown, 1998), 152–3. I am grateful to Carol Acton for bringing this reference to my attention.
31. Suzanne Raitt and Trudi Tate, eds., *Women's Fiction and the Great War* (Oxford: Clarendon Press, 1997), 254.
32. Gillian Rose, *Mourning Becomes the Law* (Cambridge: Cambridge University Press, 1996), 126.
33. *Ibid.*
34. Geoffrey Bennington, *Interrupting Derrida* (London: Routledge, 2000), 129.
35. *Ibid.*, 136.
36. H.D., 'Ear-ring', *Women, Men and the Great War: An Anthology of Stories*, ed. Trudi Tate (Manchester: Manchester University Press, 1995), 96.
37. *Ibid.*
38. Bennington, *Interrupting Derrida*, 129.
39. Caruth, *Trauma*, 8.
40. Raitt and Tate, *Women's Fiction and the Great War*, 252.
41. Kermode, *The Sense of an Ending*, 23.
42. Peter Brooks, *Psychoanalysis and Storytelling* (Oxford: Blackwell, 1994), 84.
43. Kermode, *The Sense of an Ending*, 17.
44. Rose, *Mourning Becomes the Law*, 13.
45. Raitt and Tate, *Women's Fiction and the Great War*, 1.
46. Kermode, *The Sense of an Ending*, 26.
47. Gertrude Stein, *The Autobiography of Alice B Toklas* (1933; Harmondsworth: Penguin, 1966), 170.
48. Elizabeth Gregory, 'Gertrude Stein and War', Raitt and Tate, *Women's Fiction and the Great War*, 268.
49. *Ibid.*, 269.
50. *Ibid.*, 270.

51. Stein, *The Autobiography of Alice B Toklas*, 163.
52. *Ibid.*, 183.
53. Raitt and Tate, *Women's Fiction and the Great War*, 7.
54. *Ibid.*, 10.
55. Jay Winter, *Sites of Memory, Sites of Mourning* (Cambridge: Cambridge University Press, 1995), 3.
56. *Ibid.*
57. Gillian Beer, *Virginia Woolf: The Common Ground: Essays by Gillian Beer* (Edinburgh: Edinburgh University Press, 1996), 92–111.
58. Kermode, *The Sense of an Ending*, 86.
59. Tate, *Modernism, History and the First World War*, 169.
60. Laura Marcus, *Auto/biographical Discourses: Theory, Criticism, Practice* (Manchester: Manchester University Press, 1994), 2.
61. Moretti, *The Way of the World*, 33–4.

CHAPTER 5

1. Rachel Bowlby, *Feminist Destinations and Further Essays on Virginia Woolf* (Edinburgh: Edinburgh University Press, 1997), 117.
2. Bowlby does engage with issues surrounding this suggestion elsewhere in her book, through, for example, her discussion of Woolf's rewriting of life writing, the relationship between 'subjectivity and history', in the chapter from which my opening quotation is taken (Bowlby, 111), and her analysis of 'Woolf's concentration on the objects of everyday life' in her chapter on 'Things' (Bowlby, 102).
3. Hermione Lee, *Virginia Woolf* (London: Vintage, 1997), 402.
4. Beer, *Virginia Woolf: The Common Ground*, 56.
5. For a detailed description of this genesis see Jean Guiguet, *Virginia Woolf and her Works*, trans. Jean Stewart (New York: Harcourt, Brace & World, Inc., 1965), 75–95; Guiguet draws primarily on Virginia Woolf, *A Writer's Diary* (London: Hogarth Press, 1935), 101–73.
6. Beer, *Virginia Woolf: The Common Ground*, 57.
7. *Ibid.*, 13.
8. See Melba Cuddy-Keane, *Virginia Woolf, the Intellectual, and the Public Sphere* (Cambridge and New York: Cambridge University Press, 2003), 189–93 for a critique of conventional interpretations of 'Modern Fiction' as manifesto.
9. Lee, *Virginia Woolf*, 405.
10. Virginia Woolf, 'Modern Fiction', *Collected Essays*, Vol. 2 (London: The Hogarth Press, 1925), 106, 107.
11. Ann Banfield, *The Phantom Table: Woolf, Fry, Russell and the Epistemology of Modernism* (Cambridge: Cambridge University Press, 2000), 109.
12. Beer, *Virginia Woolf: The Common Ground*, 18.
13. Bowlby, *Feminist Destinations*, 243.
14. Virginia Woolf, 'A Sketch of the Past', *Moments of Being*, ed. Jeanne Schulkind (1976; Orlando: Harcourt Brace & Company, 1985), 72.

15. On the structure of supplementarity, see Derrida '. . . That Dangerous Supplement . . .', *Of Grammatology*, trans. Gayatri Chakravorty Spivak (Baltimore: Johns Hopkins University Press, 1976).
16. Woolf, 'A Sketch of the Past', *Moments of Being*, 72.
17. *Pilgrimage*, as well as *A la recherche du temps perdu*, might be seen as breaking with this restriction, rendering the whole of a life in a text the writing of which came in some senses actually to take the place of, to constitute, that life.
18. Alex Zwerdling, *Virginia Woolf and the Real World* (Berkeley, CA: University of California Press, 1986), 193.
19. Hafley, *The Glass Roof*, 98.
20. Guiguet, *Virginia Woolf and her Works*, 232.
21. Miller, *Fiction and Repetition*, 118.
22. Ricoeur, *Time and Narrative*, 2:108.
23. Susan Dick, 'Literary Realism in *Mrs Dalloway, To the Lighthouse, Orlando* and *The Waves*', Sue Roe and Susan Sellers, eds., *The Cambridge Companion to Virginia Woolf* (Cambridge: Cambridge University Press, 2000), 54.
24. Stein, *Composition as Explanation*, 12.
25. Ricoeur, *Time and Narrative*, 2:104.
26. Karen Schiff, 'Moments of Reading and Woolf's Literary Criticism', *Virginia Woolf and the Essay*, ed. Beth Carole Rosenberg and Jeanne Dubino (New York: St Martin's, 1997), 177–92, 180.
27. *Ibid.*, 185.
28. Will, *Gertrude Stein, Modernism and the Problem of Genius*, 92.
29. Woolf, 'A Sketch of the Past', *Moments of Being*, 71.
30. Miller, *Fiction and Repetition*, 118.
31. *Ibid.*, 179.
32. *Ibid.*, 180.
33. Ruddick, *Reading Gertrude Stein*, 38.
34. Miller, *Fiction and Repetition*, 2. In a further repetition, this book-losing incident has been linked by Hermione Lee to the occasion, which Woolf records in *Moments of Being*, when Woolf's half-brother George Duckworth left the second volume of his father's edition of *Middlemarch* on a train (see 'A Sketch of the Past', *Moments of Being*, 168).
35. Woolf, 'On Re-Reading Novels', *Collected Essays*, vol. 2, 126.
36. Quoted in Marcus, *Auto/biographical Discourses*, 163.
37. Hafley, *The Glass Roof*, 73.
38. Quoted in Ricoeur, *Time and Narrative*, 1:83.
39. Beer, *Virginia Woolf: The Common Ground*, 29–30.
40. Zwerdling, *Virginia Woolf and the Real World*, 12.
41. Beer, *Virginia Woolf: The Common Ground*, 82.
42. Banfield, *The Phantom Table*, 43–55.
43. Beer, *Virginia Woolf: The Common Ground*, 81.
44. Zwerdling, *Virginia Woolf and the Real World*, 11; see also Madeline Moore's description of Bernard's 'deep grounding in the mysterious reality of the quotidian', in *The Short Season Between Two Silences: The Mystical and the*

Political in the Novels of Virginia Woolf (Boston: George Allen and Unwin, 1984), 138.

45. Beer, *Virginia Woolf: The Common Ground*, 76.
46. Guiguet, *Virginia Woolf and her Works*, 295.
47. *Ibid.*, 325.
48. Quoted in Zwerdling, *Virginia Woolf and the Real World*, 268.
49. Beer, *Virginia Woolf: The Common Ground*, 3.
50. Woolf, 'The Narrow Bridge of Art', *Collected Essays*, vol. 2, 224.
51. *Ibid.*, 225.
52. *Ibid.*
53. *Ibid.*, 224.
54. Quoted in Kate Flint, 'Reading Uncommonly: Virginia Woolf and the Practice of Reading', *Yearbook of English Studies* (1996), 26, 187–98: 187.
55. Lee, *Virginia Woolf*, 402.
56. There appears to be some disagreement over the date of this essay; in Andrew McNeillie's now standard edition of Woolf's essays, it is stated that 'Reading' was 'almost certainly written in 1919' (*The Essays of Virginia Woolf*, vol. 3, ed. Andrew McNeillie [London: The Hogarth Press, 1988], 159). Jacobus seems to agree with this dating. However, in 1996, Kate Flint describes 'Reading' as a 'late essay' in 'Reading Uncommonly: Virginia Woolf and the Practice of Reading'. My preference, particularly in the light of the internal textual evidence, is to follow McNeillie.
57. Mary Jacobus, *Psychoanalysis and the Scene of Reading* (Oxford: Oxford University Press, 1999), 40.
58. Virginia Woolf, 'Reading', *The Essays of Virginia Woolf*, vol. 3, ed. Andrew McNeillie (London: The Hogarth Press, 1988), 142.
59. *Ibid.*
60. Lee, *Virginia Woolf*, 402.
61. Woolf, 'Reading', *The Essays of Virginia Woolf*, vol. 3, 148.
62. *Ibid.*, 142.
63. D. W. Winnicott, quoted in Jacobus, *Psychoanalysis and the Scene of Reading*, 4.
64. *Ibid.*, 5.
65. *Ibid.*, 41.
66. *Ibid.*, 47.
67. Woolf, 'Reading', *The Essays of Virginia Woolf*, vol. 3, 142.
68. *Ibid.*, 143–4.
69. *Ibid.*, 145.
70. *Ibid.*, 149.
71. Banfield, *The Phantom Table*, 145.
72. Woolf, 'Reading', *The Essays of Virginia Woolf*, vol. 3, 153.
73. Woolf, 'On Re-reading Novels', *The Essays of Virginia Woolf*, vol. 3, 337–8.
74. Virginia Woolf, 'How Should One Read a Book?', *The Common Reader Second Series* (London: The Hogarth Press, 1932), 259.
75. Bowlby, *Feminist Destinations*, 249.

76. Woolf, 'How Should One Read a Book?', *The Common Reader Second Series*, 260.
77. Karin Stephen, *The Misuse of Mind: A Study of Bergson's Attack on Intellectualism* (London: Kegan Paul, Trench, Trubner & Co., Ltd, 1922), 104.
78. Elizabeth Abel, *Virginia Woolf and the Fictions of Psychoanalysis* (Chicago: University of Chicago Press, 1989), 14.

AFTERWORD

1. Blanchot, *The Infinite Conversation*, 241.
2. Woolf, 'A Sketch of the Past', *Moments of Being*, 65.
3. Fine, *Marx's* Capital, 14.
4. Moretti, *The Way of the World*, 40.
5. *Ibid.*
6. *Ibid.*, 39.
7. *Ibid.*, 33–4.
8. *Ibid.*, 42.
9. James Joyce, *Ulysses* (Oxford: Oxford University Press, 1993), 204.
10. Will, *Gertrude Stein, Modernism and the Problem of Genius*, 92.
11. Highmore, *Everyday Life and Cultural Theory*, 175.
12. Virginia Woolf, 'Mr Bennett and Mrs Brown', *Collected Essays*, vol. 1 (London: The Hogarth Press, 1925), 328–30.
13. Joyce, *Ulysses*, 206.
14. Kermode, *The Sense of an Ending*, 23.
15. Pamela L. Caughie, *Virginia Woolf and Postmodernism: Literature in Quest and Question of Itself* (Urbana and Chicago: University of Illinois Press, 1991), 119.
16. *Ibid.*, 129.
17. *Ibid.*
18. Carol Greenhouse, *A Moment's Notice: Time Politics across Cultures* (Ithaca and London: Cornell University Press, 1996), 82.
19. Beer, *Virginia Woolf: The Common Ground*, 7.
20. Bell, 'The Metaphysics of Modernism', *The Cambridge Companion to Modernism*, 10.
21. Crary, *Suspensions of Perception*, 3.

Bibliography

Abel, Elizabeth, *Virginia Woolf and the Fictions of Psychoanalysis* (Chicago: University of Chicago Press, 1989).

Aldington, Richard, *Death of a Hero* (London: Chatto & Windus, 1929).

Antliff, Mark, *Inventing Bergson: Cultural Politics and the Parisian Avant-Garde* (Princeton: Princeton University Press, 1993).

Aptheker, Bettina, *Tapestries of Life: Women's Work, Women's Consciousness and the Meaning of Daily Experience* (Amherst: University of Massachusetts Press, 1989).

Arens, Karen, *Structures of Knowing: Psychologies of the Nineteenth Century* (Dordrecht: Kluwer Academic Publishers, 1989).

Armstrong, Tim, *Modernism, Technology and the Body: A Cultural Study* (Cambridge: Cambridge University Press, 1998).

Bakhtin, M. M., *The Dialogic Imagination*, trans. Caryl Emerson and Michael Holquist (Austin: University of Texas Press, 1981).

Banfield, Ann, *The Phantom Table: Woolf, Fry, Russell and the Epistemology of Modernism* (Cambridge: Cambridge University Press, 2000).

Beer, Gillian, *Virginia Woolf: The Common Ground: Essays by Gillian Beer* (Edinburgh: Edinburgh University Press, 1996).

Bell, Michael, *Primitivism* (London: Methuen, 1972).

—, 'The Metaphysics of Modernism', *The Cambridge Companion to Modernism*, ed. Michael Levenson (Cambridge: Cambridge University Press, 1999), 9–32.

Benjamin, Walter, *Illuminations*, trans. Harry Zohn, ed. Hannah Arendt (1970; London: Fontana Press, 1992).

—, *Charles Baudelaire: A Lyric Poet in the Era of High Capitalism*, trans. Harry Zohn (1973; London: Verso, 1997).

Bennington, Geoffrey, *Interrupting Derrida* (London: Routledge, 2000).

Bergson, Henri, *An Introduction to Metaphysics*, trans. T. E. Hulme (1903; Indianapolis and New York: Bobbs-Merrill, 1949).

—, *Time and Free Will: An Essay on the Immediate Data of Consciousness*, trans. F. L. Pogson (London: Swan Sonnerschein, 1910).

—, *Creative Evolution*, trans. Arthur Mitchell (London: Macmillan, 1911).

—, *Matter and Memory*, trans. Nancy Margaret Paul and W. Scott Palmer (1911; London: George Allen & Unwin, 1919).

Bishop, Alan and Mark Bostridge, eds., *Letters from a Lost Generation: First World War Letters of Vera Brittain and Four Friends* (London: Little Brown, 1998).

Blair, Sara, 'Modernism and the Politics of Culture', *The Cambridge Companion to Modernism*, ed. Michael Levenson (Cambridge: Cambridge University Press, 1999), 157–73.

Blanchot, Maurice, *The Infinite Conversation*, trans. Susan Hanson (Minneapolis: Minnesota University Press, 1993).

Bottomore, Tom, ed., *Karl Marx* (Oxford: Basil Blackwell, 1973).

Bowlby, Rachel, *Feminist Destinations and Further Essays on Virginia Woolf* (Edinburgh: Edinburgh University Press, 1997).

Breuer, Josef, 1991. 'Fräulein Anna O', *Studies on Hysteria: Pelican Freud Library Vol. III*, ed. Angela Richards (London: Penguin, 1991), 73–102.

Brewer, Anthony, *A Guide to Marx's Capital* (Cambridge: Cambridge University Press, 1984).

Bridgman, Richard, *Gertrude Stein in Pieces* (New York: Oxford University Press, 1970).

Briggs, Julia, *Virginia Woolf: An Inner Life* (London: Allen Lane, 2005).

Bronfen, Elisabeth, *Dorothy Richardson's Art of Memory: Space, Identity, Text*, trans. Victoria Appelbe (Manchester: Manchester University Press, 1999).

Brooks, Peter, *Reading for the Plot: Design and Intention in Narrative* (1984; Cambridge, MA: Harvard University Press, 1992).

—, *Psychoanalysis and Storytelling* (Oxford: Blackwell, 1994).

Bürger, Peter, *Theory of the Avant-Garde*, trans. Michael Shaw (Manchester: Manchester University Press, 1984).

Caruth, Cathy, *Trauma: Explorations in Memory* (Baltimore: The Johns Hopkins University Press, 1995).

Caughie, Pamela L., *Virginia Woolf and Postmodernism: Literature in Quest and Question of Itself* (Urbana and Chicago: University of Illinois Press, 1991).

Charney, Leo and Vanessa K. Schwartz, eds., *Cinema and the Invention of Modern Life* (Berkeley: University of California Press, 1995).

Chessman, Harriet Scott, *The Public is Invited to Dance: Representation, the Body, and Dialogue in Gertrude Stein* (Stanford: Stanford University Press, 1989).

Church, Margaret, *Time and Reality: Studies in Contemporary Fiction* (Chapel Hill: The University of North Carolina Press, 1949).

—, 'Time as an Organizing Principle in the Fiction of James Joyce', *Work in Progress: Joyce Centenary Essays*, eds. Richard F. Peterson, Alan M. Cohn and Edmund L. Epstein (Carbondale and Edwardsville: Southern Illinois University Press, 1983), 70–81.

Crary, Jonathan, *Suspensions of Perception: Attention, Spectacle, and Modern Culture* (Cambridge, MA: MIT, 1999).

Cucullu, Lois, *Expert Modernists, Matricide and Modern Culture: Woolf, Forster, Joyce* (Basingstoke: Macmillan, 2004).

Cuddy-Keane, Melba, *Virginia Woolf, the Intellectual, and the Public Sphere* (Cambridge and New York: Cambridge University Press, 2003).

De Certeau, Michel, *The Practice of Everyday Life*, trans. Steven Rendall (Berkeley: University of California Press, 1984).

DeKoven, Marianne, *A Different Language: Gertrude Stein's Experimental Writing* (Wisconsin: University of Wisconsin Press, 1983).

Deleuze, Gilles, *Bergsonism*, trans. Hugh Tomlinson and Barbara Habberjam (New York: Zone Books, 1988).

—, *Difference and Repetition*, trans. Paul Patton (London: The Athlone Press, 1994).

Derrida, Jacques, *Of Grammatology*, trans. Gayatri Chakravorty Spivak (Baltimore: Johns Hopkins University Press, 1976).

Dettmar, Kevin J. H. and Stephen Watt, eds., *Marketing Modernisms: Self-Promotion, Canonization, Rereading* (Ann Arbor: University of Michigan Press, 1996).

Dick, Susan, 'Literary Realism in *Mrs Dalloway, To the Lighthouse, Orlando* and *The Waves*', *The Cambridge Companion to Virginia Woolf*, eds. Sue Roe and Susan Sellers (Cambridge: Cambridge University Press, 2000), 50–71.

Donovan, Josephine, 'Everyday Use and Moments of Being: Toward a Nondominative Aesthetic', *Aesthetics in Feminist Perspective*, eds. Hilde Hein and Caroline Korsmeyer (Bloomington and Indianapolis: Indiana University Press, 1993), 53–67.

Doolittle, Hilda *see H.D.*

Douglass, Paul, *Bergson, Eliot and American Literature* (Lexington, KN: University Press of Kentucky, 1986).

DuPlessis, Rachel Blau, *Writing Beyond the Ending: Narrative Strategies of Twentieth Century Women Writers* (Bloomington: Indiana University Press, 1985).

—, *H.D.: The Career of that Struggle* (Bloomington: Indiana University Press, 1986).

—, *The Pink Guitar: Writing as Feminist Practice* (London: Routledge, 1990).

Eliot, T. S., *Selected Prose*, ed. Frank Kermode (London: Faber and Faber, 1975).

—, *Four Quartets* (1943; London: Faber and Faber, 1994).

Faderman, Lillian, *Surpassing the Love of Men: Romantic Friendship and Love between Women from the Renaissance to the Present* (1981; London: The Women's Press, 1991).

Fine, Ben, *Marx's Capital* (1975; London: Macmillan, 1989).

Flint, Kate, 'Virginia Woolf and the General Strike', *Essays in Criticism* (1986), 36, 319–33.

—, *The Woman Reader 1837–1914* (Oxford: Clarendon Press, 1993).

—, 'Reading Uncommonly: Virginia Woolf and the Practice of Reading', *Yearbook of English Studies* (1996), 26, 187–98.

Ford, Ford Madox, *Parade's End* (1924–28; Harmondsworth: Penguin, 1982).

Freud, Sigmund, 'Project for a Scientific Psychology', *The Standard Edition of the Complete Psychological Works Vol. I*, ed. James Strachey (London: Hogarth, 1966).

—, 'Remembering, Repeating and Working Through', *The Standard Edition of the Complete Psychological Works Vol. XII*, ed. James Strachey (London: Hogarth, 1966).

—, 'Beyond the Pleasure Principle', *The Penguin Freud Library Vol. XI*, ed. Angela Richards (Harmondsworth: Penguin, 1984).

Friedman, Susan Stanford, *Psyche Reborn: The Emergence of H.D.* (Bloomington: Indiana University Press, 1981).

—, *Penelope's Web: Gender, Modernity, H.D.'s Fiction* (Cambridge: Cambridge University Press, 1990).

Friedman, Susan Stanford and Rachel Blau DuPlessis, eds., *Signets: Reading H.D.* (Wisconsin: University of Wisconsin Press, 1990).

Fromm, Gloria, *Dorothy Richardson: A Biography* (1977; Athens and London: University of Georgia Press, 1994).

Fussell, Paul, *The Great War and Modern Memory* (Oxford: Oxford University Press, 1975).

Genette, Gérard, *Narrative Discourse*, trans. Jane E. Levin (Oxford: Basil Blackwell, 1980).

Greenhouse, Carol, *A Moment's Notice: Time Politics Across Cultures* (Ithaca and London: Cornell University Press, 1996).

Guiguet, Jean, *Virginia Woolf and her Works*, trans. Jean Stewart (New York: Harcourt, Brace & World, Inc., 1965).

H.D., *Bid Me To Live* (1960; London: Virago, 1984).

—, *Tribute to Freud* (1970; Manchester: Manchester University Press, 1985).

—, *Her* (1981; London: Virago, 1984).

—, *Notes on Thought and Vision* (San Francisco: City Lights, 1982).

—, *Asphodel* (Durham: Duke University Press, 1992).

—, *Paint It Today* (New York: New York University Press, 1992).

Hafley, James, *The Glass Roof: Virginia Woolf as Novelist* (New York: Russell and Russell Inc., 1963).

Hanscombe, Gillian E., *The Art of Life: Dorothy Richardson and the Development of Feminist Consciousness* (London: Peter Owen, 1982).

—, 'Dorothy Richardson Versus the Novvle', *Breaking the Sequence: Women's Experimental Fiction*, eds. Ellen G. Friedman and Miriam Fuchs (Princeton: Princeton University Press, 1989), 85–98.

Hawkins, Susan E., 'Sneak Previews: Gertrude Stein's Syntax in Tender Buttons', *Gertrude Stein and the Making of Literature*, eds. Shirley Neumann and Ira B. Nadel (Basingstoke: Macmillan, 1989), 119–23.

Heath, Stephen, 'Writing for Silence: Dorothy Richardson and the Novel', *Teaching the Text*, eds. Susanne Kappeler and Norman Bryson (London: Routledge and Kegan Paul, 1983).

Heidegger, Martin, *Being and Time*, trans. John Macquarrie and Edward Robinson (1967; London: Blackwell, 1988).

Henke, Suzette, *Shattered Subjects: Trauma and Testimony in Women's Life Writing* (New York: St Martin's Press, 2000).

Highmore, Ben, *Everyday Life and Cultural Theory: An Introduction* (London: Routledge, 2002).

Hobhouse, Janet, *Everybody Who Was Anybody: A Biography of Gertrude Stein* (London: Weidenfeld & Nicholson, 1975).

Holtby, Winifred, *Virginia Woolf* (London: Wishart & Co., 1932).

Isaak, Jo-Anna, 'The Revolutionary Power of a Woman's Laughter', *Gertrude Stein Advanced: An Anthology of Criticism*, ed. Richard Kostelanetz (Jefferson: McFarland & Company Inc., 1990), 24–50.

Iser, Wolfgang, *Walter Pater: The Aesthetic Moment*, trans. David Henry Wilson (Cambridge: Cambridge University Press, 1987).

Isherwood, Christopher, *A Single Man* (London: Methuen, 1964).

Jacobus, Mary, *First Things: The Maternal Imaginary in Literature, Art, and Psychoanalysis* (New York and London: Routledge, 1995).

—, *Psychoanalysis and the Scene of Reading* (Oxford: Oxford University Press, 1999).

James, Henry, *The Ambassadors* (1903; Harmondsworth: Penguin, 1986).

James, William, *Psychology: Briefer Course* (1892; New York: Macmillan, 1962).

Jameson, Fredric, *The Political Unconscious: Narrative as a Socially Symbolic Act* (London: Routledge, 1981).

Jay, Martin, *Adorno* (London: Fontana, 1984).

Joyce, James, *Ulysses* (1922; Oxford: Oxford University Press, 1993).

Kaplan, Sydney Janet, *Feminine Consciousness in the Modern British Novel* (Urbana: University of Illinois Press, 1975).

Kemp, Sandra, '"But how describe a world seen without a self?" Feminism, Fiction and Modernism', *Critical Quarterly* (1990), 32: 1, 99–118.

Kermode, Frank, *The Sense of an Ending: Studies in the Theory of Fiction* (Oxford: Oxford University Press, 1967).

Kern, Stephen, *The Culture of Time and Space 1880–1918* (1983; Cambridge, MA: Harvard University Press, 2003).

Kostelanetz, Richard, ed., *Gertrude Stein Advanced: An Anthology of Criticism* (Jefferson: McFarland & Company Inc., 1990).

Kracauer, Siegfried, *The Mass Ornament: Weimar Essays*, trans. and ed. Thomas Y. Levin (Cambridge, MA: Harvard University Press, 1995).

Kristeva, Julia, *The Kristeva Reader*, ed. Toril Moi (Oxford: Blackwell, 1986).

Kumar, Shiv K., *Bergson and the Stream of Consciousness Novel* (London and Glasgow: Blackie & Son Ltd, 1962).

Langbauer, Laurie, 'Cultural Studies and the Politics of the Everyday', *Diacritics* (1992), 22:1, 47–65.

Laplanche, J. and J.-B. Pontalis, *The Language of Psycho-Analysis*, trans. Donald Nicholson-Smith (London: The Hogarth Press and the Institute of Psycho-Analysis, 1973).

Latham, Sean, *'Am I a Snob?': Modernism and the Novel* (Ithaca: Cornell University Press, 2003).

Lee, Hermione, *Virginia Woolf* (London: Vintage, 1997).

Lefebvre, Henri, *Everyday Life in the Modern World*, trans. Sacha Rabinovitch (New Brunswick: Transaction Publishers, 1984).

—, *Critique of Everyday Life*, vol. 1, trans. John Moore (London: Verso, 1991).

Leonard, Garry, 'The History of Now: Commodity Culture and Everyday Life', *Joyce and the Subject of History*, eds. Mark A. Wollaeger, Victor Luftig and Robert Spoo (Ann Arbor: University of Michigan Press, 1996), 13–26.

Levenson, Michael, ed., *The Cambridge Companion to Modernism* (Cambridge: Cambridge University Press, 1999).

Levinas, Emmanuel, *Time and the Other* (Pittsburgh: Duquesne University Press, 1987).

Lewis, Percy Wyndham, *Time and Western Man* (London: Chatto & Windus, 1927).

Malik, Kenan, *The Meaning of Race: Race, History and Culture in Western Society* (Basingstoke: Macmillan, 1996).

Marcus, Jane, ed., *New Feminist Essays on Virginia Woolf* (London: Macmillan, 1981).

Marcus, Laura, *Auto/biographical Discourses: Theory, Criticism, Practice* (Manchester: Manchester University Press, 1994).

Marx, Karl, *Capital Voume 1*, trans. Ben Fowkes (Harmondsworth: Penguin, 1976).

Mellow, James R., *Charmed Circle: Gertrude Stein & Company* (New York: Avon Books, 1974).

Meyer, Steven, *Irresistible Dictation: Gertrude Stein and the Correlations of Writing and Science* (Stanford: Stanford University Press, 1991).

Miller, J. Hillis, *Fiction and Repetition: Seven English Novels* (Oxford: Basil Blackwell, 1982).

Moore, Madeline, *The Short Season Between Two Silences: The Mystical and the Political in the Novels of Virginia Woolf* (Boston: George Allen and Unwin, 1984).

Moretti, Franco, *The Way of the World: The Bildungsroman in European Culture*, trans. Albert Sbragia (1987; London: Verso, 2000).

Mullarkey, John, '*La Philosophie nouvelle*, or Change in philosophy', *The New Bergson* (Manchester and New York: Manchester University Press, 1999).

Nash, S. A., *Picasso and the War Years, 1937–1945* (Fine Arts Museums of San Francisco, 1998).

Neuman, Shirley and Ira B. Nadel, eds., *Gertrude Stein and the Making of Literature* (Basingstoke: Macmillan, 1998).

Nicholls, Peter, *Modernisms: A Literary Guide* (Basingstoke: Macmillan, 1995).

O'Connor, Mary, 'The Objects of Modernism: Everyday Life in Women's Magazines, Gertrude Stein, and Margaret Watkins', *American Modernism Across the Arts*, eds. Jay Bochner and Justin D. Edwards (New York: Peter Lang, 1999), 97–123.

Osborne, Peter, *The Politics of Time: Modernity and Avant-Garde* (London: Verso, 1995).

Parsons, Deborah L., *Streetwalking the Metropolis: Women, the City and Modernity* (Oxford: Oxford University Press, 2000).

Pater, Walter, *The Renaissance* (1873; Oxford: Oxford University Press, 1998).

Posnock, Ross, *The Trial of Curiosity: Henry James, William James, and the Challenge of Modernity* (Oxford: Oxford University Press, 1991).

Proust, Marcel, *Swann's Way*, trans. C. K. Scott Moncrieff (1922; Harmondsworth: Penguin, 1957).

Radford, Jean, *Dorothy Richardson* (Hemel Hempstead: Harvester Wheatsheaf, 1991).

Raitt, Suzanne, *Vita and Virginia: The Work and Friendship of V. Sackville-West and Virginia Woolf* (Oxford: Clarendon Press, 1993).

Raitt, Suzanne and Trudi Tate, eds., *Women's Fiction and the Great War* (Oxford: Clarendon Press, 1997).

Remarque, Eric Maria, *All Quiet on the Western Front*, trans. A. W. Wheen (London: G. P. Putnam's Sons, 1929).

Richardson, Dorothy, *The Quakers Past and Present* (London: Constable & Company Limited, 1914).

—, 'Comments by a Layman', *Dental Record* (1916), XXXVI, 141.

—, 'Comments by a Layman', *Dental Record* (1916), XXXVI, 356.

—, 'Comments by a Layman', *Dental Record* (1918), XXXVIII, 351.

—, *Pilgrimage*, 4 vols. (1915–67; London: Virago, 1979).

—, *Journey to Paradise: Short Stories and Autobiographical Sketches*, ed. Trudi Tate (London: Virago, 1989).

Ricoeur, Paul, *Time and Narrative*, trans. Kathleen McLaughlin and David Pellauer, 3 vols. (Chicago: University of Chicago Press, 1984–88).

Roe, Sue and Susan Sellers, eds., *The Cambridge Companion to Virginia Woolf* (Cambridge: Cambridge University Press, 2000).

Rose, Gillian, *Mourning Becomes the Law* (Cambridge: Cambridge University Press, 1996).

Rose, Shirley, 'Dorothy Richardson's Focus on Time', *English Literature in Transition* (1974), 17, 163–72.

Rosenberg, Beth Carole and Jeanne Dubino, eds., *Virginia Woolf and the Essay* (London: Macmillan, 1997).

Ruddick, Lisa, *Reading Gertrude Stein: Body, Text, Gnosis* (Ithaca and London: Cornell University Press, 1990).

Ruotolo, Lucio P., *The Interrupted Moment: A View of Virginia Woolf's Novels* (Stanford: Stanford University Press, 1986).

Schiff, Karen, 'Moments of Reading and Woolf's Literary Criticism', *Virginia Woolf and the Essay*, ed. Beth Carole Rosenberg and Jeanne Dubino (New York: St Martin's, 1997), 177–92.

Scott, Bonnie Kime, *The Gender of Modernism: A Critical Anthology* (Bloomington and Indianapolis: Indiana University Press, 1990).

Seidl, Michael, 'The Pathology of the Everyday: Uses of Madness in *Mrs Dalloway* and *Ulysses*', *Virginia Woolf: Themes and Variations*, eds. Vara Neverow-Turk and Mark Hussey (New York: Pace University Press, 1993), 52–67.

Seltzer, Mark, *Serial Killers: Death and Life in America's Wound Culture* (New York and London: Routledge, 1998).

Sheringham, Michael, 'Attending to the Everyday: Blanchot, Lefebvre, Certeau, Perec', *French Studies* (2000), 54:2, 187–99.

Shiach, Morag, 'Modernity, Labour and the Typewriter', Hugh Stevens and Caroline Howlett, eds., *Modernist Sexualities* (Manchester: Manchester University Press, 2000), 114–29.

—, *Modernism, Labour and Selfhood in British Literature and Culture, 1890–1930* (Cambridge: Cambridge University Press, 2004).

Shotter, John, *Cultural Politics of Everyday Life: Social Constructionism, Rhetoric and Knowing of the Third Kind* (Buckingham: Open University Press, 1993).

Showalter, Elaine, *The Female Malady: Woman, Madness and English Culture 1830–1980* (London: Virago, 1987).

—, *A Literature of Their Own: From Charlotte Brontë to Doris Lessing* (1977; London: Virago, 1999).

Simmel, Georg, 'The Metropolis and Mental Life', trans. Kurt H. Wolff, *Simmel on Culture*, eds. David Frisby and Mike Featherstone (London: Sage, 1997), 174–85.

Sinclair, May, 'The Novels of Dorothy Richardson', *The Little Review* (1918), 5:12, 3–11.

Sinfield, Alan, *Faultlines: Cultural Materialism and the Politics of Dissident Reading* (Oxford: Clarendon Press, 1992).

Spengler, Oswald, *The Decline of the West*, trans. Charles Francis Atkinson (New York: The Modern Library, 1962).

Stein, Gertrude, *Three Lives* (1909; London: Penguin, 1990).

—, *Tender Buttons* (1914; New York: Dover Publications Inc., 1997).

—, *Geography and Plays* (1922; New York: Something Else Press, 1968).

—, *Composition as Explanation* (London: Hogarth Press, 1926).

—, *The Autobiography of Alice B Toklas* (1933; Harmondsworth: Penguin, 1966).

—, *Narration: Four Lectures*, ed. Thornton Wilder (1935; Chicago: University of Chicago Press, 1969).

—, *Wars I Have Seen* (1945; New York: Random House, 1994).

—, *Painted Lace and Other Pieces 1914–1937* (New Haven: Yale University Press, 1955).

Stephen, Karin, *The Misuse of Mind: A Study of Bergson's Attack on Intellectualism* (London: Kegan Paul, Trench, Trubner & Co., Ltd, 1922).

Stevens, Hugh and Caroline Howlett, eds., *Modernist Sexualities* (Manchester: Manchester University Press, 2000).

Stonebridge, Lyndsey, *The Destructive Element: British Psychoanalysis and Modernism* (Basingstoke: Macmillan, 1998).

Tate, Trudi, ed., *Women, Men and the Great War: An Anthology of Stories* (Manchester: Manchester University Press, 1995).

—, *Modernism, History and the First World War* (Manchester: Manchester University Press, 1998).

Tichi, Cecelia, *Shifting Gears: Technology, Literature, Culture in Modernist America* (Chapel Hill and London: University of North Carolina Press, 1987).

Tratner, Michael, *Modernism and Mass Politics: Joyce, Woolf, Eliot, Yeats* (Stanford: Stanford University Press, 1995).

Tylee, Claire, *The Great War and Women's Consciousness: Images of Militarism and Womanhood in Women's Writing 1914–64* (Basingstoke: Macmillan, 1990).

Underhill, Evelyn, *Mysticism* (1911; London: Methuen, 1960).

Watts, Carol, *Dorothy Richardson* (Plymouth: Northcote House, 1995).

Weber, Max, *The Protestant Ethic and the Spirit of Capitalism*, trans. Talcott Parsons (1904–05; London and New York: Routledge, 2001).

West, Rebecca, *The Return of the Soldier* (1918; London: Virago, 1980).

Will, Barbara, *Gertrude Stein, Modernism and the Problem of Genius* (Edinburgh: Edinburgh University Press, 2000).

Willis, Susan, *A Primer for Daily Life* (London and New York: Routledge, 1991).

Winning, Joanne, *The Pilgrimage of Dorothy Richardson* (Wisconsin: University of Wisconsin Press, 2000).

Winter, Jay, *Sites of Memory, Sites of Mourning* (Cambridge: Cambridge University Press, 1995).

Woolf, Virginia, *Collected Essays*, vol. 1 (London: Hogarth Press, 1925).

—, *Collected Essays*, vol. 2 (London: Hogarth Press, 1925).

—, *The Common Reader Second Series* (London: Hogarth Press, 1932).

—, *A Writer's Diary* (London: Hogarth Press, 1935).

—, *A Room of One's Own* (1928; Harmondsworth: Penguin, 1945).

—, *Moments of Being*, ed. Jeanne Schulkind (1976; Orlando: Harcourt Brace & Company, 1985).

—, *The Complete Shorter Fiction*, ed. Susan Dick (London: Triad Grafton Books, 1987).

—, *The Essays of Virginia Woolf*, vol. 3, ed. Andrew McNeillie (London: The Hogarth Press, 1988).

—, *Between the Acts* (1941; Harmondsworth: Penguin, 1992).

—, *Mrs Dalloway* (1925; Harmondsworth: Penguin, 1992).

—, *To the Lighthouse* (1927; Harmondsworth: Penguin, 1992).

—, *The Waves* (1931; Harmondsworth: Penguin, 1992).

—, *A Woman's Essays*, ed. Rachel Bowlby (Harmondsworth: Penguin, 1992).

—, *Orlando* (1928; Harmondsworth: Penguin, 1993).

Zwerdling, Alex, *Virginia Woolf and the Real World* (Berkeley: University of California Press, 1986).

Index

Lightning Source UK Ltd.
Milton Keynes UK
UKOW02f2345141016

285286UK00001B/336/P